Speaking in Subtitles

For Ivy and Csilla

Speaking in Subtitles

Revaluing Screen Translation

Tessa Dwyer

EDINBURGH
University Press

Edinburgh University Press is one of the leading university presses in the UK. We publish academic books and journals in our selected subject areas across the humanities and social sciences, combining cutting-edge scholarship with high editorial and production values to produce academic works of lasting importance. For more information visit our website: edinburghuniversitypress.com

© Tessa Dwyer, 2017, 2018

Edinburgh University Press Ltd
The Tun – Holyrood Road
12 (2f) Jackson's Entry
Edinburgh EH8 8PJ

First published in hardback by Edinburgh University Press 2017

Typeset in Monotype Ehrhardt by
Servis Filmsetting Ltd, Stockport, Cheshire,
and printed and bound in Great Britain by
CPI Group (UK) Ltd, Croydon CR0 4YY

A CIP record for this book is available from the British Library

ISBN 978 1 4744 1094 6 (hardback)
ISBN 978 1 4744 4099 8 (paperback)
ISBN 978 1 4744 1095 3 (webready PDF)
ISBN 978 1 4744 1096 0 (epub)

The right of Tessa Dwyer to be identified as author of this work has been asserted in accordance with the Copyright, Designs and Patents Act 1988 and the Copyright and Related Rights Regulations 2003 (SI No. 2498).

Contents

Figures

Acknowledgements

Thanks to family and friends for all their support over the years, and especially to Rhian and my mother Joan for providing invaluable assistance and proofing. Thanks also to colleagues and mentors Mehmet Mehmet, Angela Ndalianis, Ramon Lobato and Con Verevis, and to Gillian Leslie and the team at Edinburgh University Press. Additional thanks to the School of Media, Film and Journalism at Monash University for a grant that helped with final publication preparations.

Portions of Chapters 5 and 6 were published previously in 'Fansub Dreaming on Viki: "Don't Just Watch But Help When You Are Free"', *The Translator* 18 (2) (2012): 217–43. Reprinted by permission of the Publisher (Taylor & Francis Ltd, http://www.tandfonline.com).

Introduction

When *Holy Motors* (2012) was awarded the 2013 Los Angeles Film Critics Association Award for Best Foreign-Language Film, director Leos Carax didn't attend the ceremony. Instead, he sent an acceptance speech in the form of a short film around a minute in length. I love this short piece, but my love of it has nothing to do with its image montage or, for that matter, with Carax's films – none of which I had seen when I first viewed it. It's the voice that draws me in, and the words oozing over the visuals, dripping with a viscosity thicker than the blood that appears flowing through streets. Carax's accented English imposes itself upon this film and the award it nominally accepts, constructing a self-reflexive basis for critique. His voice-over begins with an introduction: 'So, I'm Leos Carax, director of foreign-language films.' Immediately, the audience

Figure I.1 Subtitled frame from Leos Carax's acceptance speech video for the 2013 LA Film Critics Association Awards.

feels a rug being pulled from under it. Sure, Carax is a foreign-language film director: he's just been awarded a prize to say so. And yet, isn't this statement also nonsensical? Ultimately, what *is* a foreign-language film director? Someone who makes films in languages he or she doesn't speak? Which languages are foreign languages? Why, when and for whom? Carax continues: 'Foreign-language films are made all over the world ... except in America', and ends with the declaration, 'cinema *is* a foreign language'. I wholeheartedly agree, and in this book I set out to unpack the intimate relationship that cinema and related screen media enjoy with foreignness and language difference.

Today, the most widely viewed films across the globe are produced in English. Reports produced by the UNESCO Institute for Statistics based on theatrical film data gathered from countries around the world demonstrate the 'clear predominance of the English language and consequently a lack of linguistic diversity' (Albornoz 2016: 31). As Charles Acland (2012) summarises, English 'is the dominant language of origin for the most visible and available films viewed by most countries'. According to these reports, the market dominance of English and Hollywood has only increased in recent years. In 2013, all of the global top twenty films were English-language productions whereas in 2012 one was shot in French (Albornoz 2016) and in 2009, 20 per cent were *not* English-language films (Acland 2012). At the same time, native English speakers constitute less than 5 per cent of the world population, and this figure is currently decreasing (Lewis et al. 2016; Graddol 1997).[1] These grossly uneven statistics demonstrate incontrovertibly that a major proportion of screen media today is experienced either in a foreign language or in translation. Consequently, language difference and transfer must be acknowledged as central, rather than peripheral, to contemporary screen media and their analysis. Operating in tandem with other factors affecting distribution, translation plays a major role in determining what films or programmes are seen, where and when, and how they are framed and understood.

Despite this centrality, translation is routinely devalued and ignored within screen culture, particularly within Anglophone contexts. Media makers and distributors regularly sideline translation requirements, affording them minimal care and funds. Despite the ability of DVD technology to record up to 32 separate language tracks, for instance, distributors often provide inadequate translation options, at times presenting hearing audiences with subtitles prepared for deaf and hard-of-hearing viewers (O'Sullivan 2011: 202).[2] Within screen scholarship, translation is frequently conceived in the negative, as a type of 'bad object'[3] that destabilises the potent myth that film speaks a universal language that transcends linguistic and cultural difference, existing somehow *beyond* translation.[4] Consequently, Screen Studies tends to consider language in metaphoric rather than literal terms, with theories of film grammar and film semiotics affording little space for thinking about actual language politics and pragmatics.[5] To date, Screen Studies has produced only a handful of edited collections addressing questions of translation, and fewer monographs.[6] Even within the discipline of Translation Studies, the audiovisual constitutes a marginal, albeit growing, area of research in a field dominated by literary models (see Pérez-González and Susam-Sarajeva 2012: 157).[7] As a result, much work remains to be done in elucidating the machinations of this crucial cog in global media flow.

Speaking in Subtitles addresses this gap in critical knowledge, challenging screen translation's systemic neglect and arguing it is high time that operations of dubbing and subtitling are taken seriously. Its central aim is to *revalue screen translation*. This involves, firstly, rethinking its value for screen culture broadly and, secondly, unscrambling screen translation's internal value politics through analysis of specific dubbing and subtitling practices. This twofold approach is integrated through a focus on screen translation error and excess. It is in moments of dysfunction and irregularity, I argue, that screen translation's politics of value are brought most effectively into play, enabling and inviting *re*valuation of this critical component of transnational screen culture. Focusing on screen translation error and excess, this book institutes a three-part programme of revaluation. It proposes, firstly, that error and failure are fundamental, rather than anomalous, to screen translation practices. Secondly, it examines errant, improper instances of dubbing and subtitling, and how they exemplify emerging, participatory modes of cultural engagement. Lastly, it frames translation itself as a re-evaluative process that is integral to the ongoing evolution and vitality of screen culture.

Rather than striving to avoid or overcome translation's 'bad object' status within screen culture and theory, this book confronts it directly, examining how and why it occurs, its internal lines of discord and excess productivity. I draw attention to the multiple, competing ways in which dubbing and subtitling are devalued and dismissed, and I ponder how errant or improper practices challenge the dominance of quality considerations within screen translation discourse. Specifically, I examine four areas of screen translation that lie beyond the parameters of professional, 'quality' practice and are consequently identified as 'improper.' These four areas of practice relate to amateurism, parody, censorship and media piracy. Non-professional, errant modes of screen translation are becoming increasingly paradigmatic of the current translation environment, as it becomes less controlled and more communal in response to new digital technologies and the decentralising impulses of globalisation (Tymoczko 2005: 1088–9). In detailing these trends, I consider how 'improper' practices shift the terms of screen translation politics and discourse.

Introducing Errancy

The term 'value politics' directs attention towards complex factors involved in attributing worth (or worthlessness) to translation. Translations are typically judged good or bad in relation to originals, yet they are also evaluated via myriad socio-political agendas, assumptions and associations that often remain unacknowledged. Such factors merge language constraints with industry convention and national identity politics. Chapter 1 provides an introductory overview of such value politics, which I continue to unpack in following chapters. In Chapter 4, for instance, I explore how state-directed media censorship can affect the value attributed to professional subtitling operations. Value is a nebulous and problematic concept, as much translation scholarship acknowledges. In a special issue of *The Translator* focused on 'Bourdieu and the Sociology of Translation and Interpreting', editor Moira Inghilleri (2005: 125) notes for instance how 'interest in Bourdieu's work is part of a shift within translation studies away from a predominant concern with translated textual products and toward a view of translating and interpreting as social, cultural and political acts intrinsically connected to local and global relations of power and control'.

Within Translation Studies, interest in Pierre Bourdieu is linked to descriptive and polysystems approaches, the theories of Theo Hermans, Gideon Toury, Andre Lefevre, Susan Bassnett and Maria Tymoczko, and to a variety of interdisciplinary 'cultural turns'. These scholars and scholarship shifts address the complexity of factors that contribute to notions of translation value (aesthetic, economic, educational, social) as well as translator agency and process. Yet, despite the lessons of post-structuralism, translation and screen scholars often revert to rather uncomplicated notions of 'quality'. Despite complex theorisation around the limitations, pitfalls and instability of 'quality' criteria – owing to cultural specificities, institutionalisation or intellectual bias, for instance – 'quality' is regularly referred to in a presumptive manner, as something shared and unvarying. Despite past unpacking within Translation Studies, concepts of quality are too often couched in common-sense frameworks where they find refuge from revisionist rethinking. This is because quality is a useful concept and also a powerful one.

It is not my intention to argue that 'quality' be removed from consideration, but rather to re-evaluate this concept by elucidating connections between abstraction and practice. Notions of quality play a logical role in any type of translation assessment, yet remain radically unstable. Every practising translator holds subjective ideas about what constitutes 'quality' translation, and these ideas constantly shift and evolve. While many language service providers establish clearly prescribed quality standards and guidelines, 'in practice', concepts of quality defy such regulatory restriction. When notions of 'quality' are actualised in translation practice, they are put to the test and transformed ever so slightly each time. Hence, I argue, quality remains an open variable rather than a closed constant. Here I pose a link between straightforward pragmatics and the conceptual complexities of post-structuralist thought.

To develop this link, I have found the writings of Gilles Deleuze and Félix Guattari particularly useful, especially the central actual/virtual distinction set out in Deleuze's *Cinema 1* (1986 [1983]) and *Cinema 2* (1989 [1985]). While the philosophical particulars of Deleuze and Guattari are beyond the scope of this book, they provide a scaffold for some of its theoretical traversals. Echoed in many related philosophical and deconstructionist projects, Deleuze's actual/virtual divide engages with thought processes *in general* and the way they connect with the world. Gap and difference are foundational to any process of connection, and, hence, this relation between thought and expression, the virtual and the actual, is based upon differences in kind rather than degree. For Deleuze, the actual–virtual relationship is central to the interconnection between thought and the world, abstraction and materiality. This is a vital relationship and one that both Deleuze and Guattari approach with renewed vigour. For Deleuze (1989 [1985]: 46), the actual and the virtual 'differ in nature, and yet "run after each other", refer to each other, reflect each other, without it being possible to say which is first, and tend ultimately to become confused by slipping into the same point of indiscernibility'. In becoming actualised, the virtual is transformed and radically altered, explains Deleuze (1991 [1966]: 97), as 'it is difference that is primary in the process of actualisation' and 'differentiation is always the actualisation of a virtuality that persists across its actual divergent lines' (95). Although Fredric Jameson (1997: 412) voices a temptation to 'take sides' between the virtual and the actual, Deleuze does not entertain such an evaluative, comparative approach. Rather, he insists that each informs the other and although qualitatively distinct they are nonetheless ultimately inseparable. Together they form a circuit, a 'crystalline structure' (Deleuze 1989 [1985]: 69). This relation is one of ongoing translation and transformation.

Deleuze's notion of the crystalline nature of actual–virtual relations proves particularly useful for interrogating translation's 'double bind' between the specific and the universal, the concrete and the conceptual (Derrida 1979: 79; 94). As Derrida eloquently explores, translation articulates and brings to the fore underlying points of actual/virtual overlap within all language, expression, communication and modes of being. Translation expresses this overlap in an extremely economical fashion, functioning itself like a crystalline form that is constantly in flux, intercultural and in–between. Every word of a translation is both actual and virtual, in that each word refers or speaks to two languages at once – one actual (the target language) and the other virtual (the source language). At the same time, as Derrida (1979: 98) expounds, each translated word is also an interpretation or a choice that 'arrests' meaning, settling upon certain significations and closing-off others – disambiguating by diverging from the virtual, coexistent meanings of the source word. As it closes off certain pluralities of meaning, it also opens new ones, setting its source in motion. Hence, translation activates actual-virtual relations at every turn.

Concepts of translation value, I argue, need to proactively embrace their virtuality. Rather, too often, discussions of translation quality and worth gloss over the knotty path from abstraction to actualisation – knots that are dwelt upon in detail by both Derrida and Deleuze. Too often, this path is presented as unproblematic and self-evident; a presumption prevails that concepts of quality can simply be grafted on to sites of practice. It is here that this book seeks to intervene, arguing that the virtual abstraction within concepts of quality and value needs to be acknowledged and nurtured, rather than pinned down. When conceptualisation of translation quality is able to recognise or admit its open virtuality and instability, it is not invalidated, I argue, but strengthened, proving elastic and resilient. This book rallies against prescriptive theories that seek to control what counts as good or bad practice *in general* – which is akin perhaps to instituting a regulatory 'guidelines and standards' approach. Due to their straightforward simplicity and identity-forming role, 'good' and 'bad' are useful, buoyant concepts that are here to stay. I advocate preserving their internal lines of virtual possibility only in order to keep them open and engaged with translation practice.

So, why promote 'errancy' as a critical concept over 'quality'? Because, quality is so familiar and engrained, it is not easily dislodged. Notions of quality are so over-determined I argue, it is difficult to return this concept to a state of openness. The concept of errancy, on the other hand, and its critical significance for translation theory and practice, are unfamiliar and unsettling. In this way, the concept of errancy is performative, and not simply descriptive. It activates a process of reflection or re-conceptualisation by forcing a question as to where the value of translation lies. I do not introduce this concept in order to advocate for 'bad', error-prone translation, although I do question how and why errors occur, and seek to illuminate the contexts and contingencies that affect error-prone practices. I also contend that error needs to be thought about broadly, and extrapolated upon to enable a critical fashioning of 'errancy'. Errancy as concept embraces the potential for error (for risk, uncertainty, compromise, contamination and inauthenticity) that I argue inhabits all translation.

Translation always entails risk, sometimes known and at other times, uncalculated. In its day-to-day operations, translation risks all these elements and more, and judges the risk worth taking – for the sake of increased or enhanced access and circulation, new connections, revitalisation and at times, politicisation, empowerment and re-evaluation. Translation cannot help but risk niceties in its attempts to mediate between non-equivalent cultures, values, languages and communities. Translation is also inherently de-authorising and uncontrollable, as demonstrated by the complex challenges it continues to pose for copyright conventions and intellectual property law (see Hemmungs Wirtén 2011; Braxton 2014). As practice and profession, translation is necessarily subject to the compromising contingencies that attend actualisation. Translation is also a skill that has been practised for centuries by amateurs and non-professionals who today include students, netizens, fans and children who act as language brokers for immigrant parents or peers (see Antonini 2010). As Ignacio Garcia (2010) notes, the crowdsourcing made possible via online networking (discussed in Chapter 6) has greatly extended the scope of this 'mass amateurisation'.

The concept of errancy offers a bridge between the abstractions of translation theory, the concrete and complex contingencies of practice and diverse fields of 'improper' translation activity. Errancy thinks through the relation between theory and practice. It engages with professional, commercial, amateur *and* resistant modes of screen translation, and their overlap in practices like paid crowdsourcing, for instance (see Garcia 2015). It also draws attention to the ways in which cultural worth and value are constructed, consumed and performed. Errancy as a critical concept is inherently re-evaluative and it rehearses the 'negative' dynamics that characterise much deconstructionist thought, which has long espoused the value and productivity of translation's inevitable failure and undoing of the 'original' (see de Man 1986: 84). Consider, for instance, Walter Benjamin's seminal essay 'The Task of the Translator' (1968 [1923]) in which the 'task [*Aufgabe*]' of the title also translates as 'defeat' (de Man 1986: 80).

Benjamin's essay provides the foundation for much deconstructionist interest in translation, which I have found invaluable for thinking about 'error screens'. Following Benjamin, Derrida (1985a: 171) insists on translation's 'necessity *as* impossibility', and Paul de Man (1986: 84) terms it a form of 'disarticulation'. Also influenced by deconstruction theory, Antoine Berman (2000 [1985]: 288) identifies twelve 'deforming tenden-cies' of translation, illustrated via practical examples, while Lawrence Venuti (1995: 43) examines the translator's invisibility and marginality within Western society as a whole, since at least the seventeenth century onwards. What is different about the approach adopted in the present book is, firstly, the application of 'negative analytics' (Berman 2000 [1985]: 286) to screen translation in particular and, secondly, the endeav-our to bring theories of translation in line with actual modes, methods and sites of practice – not by concentrating on isolated examples, as Berman does, but by mapping whole areas of practice – such as fansubbing and censorship – and thereby linking textual analysis to materially grounded, *con*textual considerations.

While many translation scholars criticise deconstruction for its retreat into theoretical abstraction and linguistic play at the expense of 'empirical-functionist' considerations (Ertel 2011), I focus on its usefulness for recon-sidering the relationship *between* theory and practice.[8] Moreover, I argue that the deconstructive notion of translation failure is particularly pertinent to screen translation and its over-determined association with the nega-tive. In contrast to the singular modality of literary and textual translation, where new tends to supplant old, screen translation always involves their meeting. Within the multimodality of the audiovisual, subtitles superim-pose themselves over the 'original' image track, altering its appearance in the process through the introduction of a new graphic register: the textual. With dubbing, new sounds replace old, yet moving lips on screen continue to mouth absent, source dialogue. These dubbed voices erase the sound yet not the image of the source speech. With voice-over, on the other hand, translation coexists with *both* source images and sounds, as source voices tend to remain faintly audible beneath the spoken translation.

Overall, the multimodality of screen media compels 'original' and translation to face off against one another, forcing their comparison.[9] Coexisting with the 'original', screen translation is felt as disjuncture when lips become out-of-sync with their supposed voices, or when sub-titles do not match the length of an utterance. Moreover, screen media's visual and the aural modes each transmit both verbal and non-verbal signs, while subtitling and dubbing largely focus on verbal signification only. Consequently, screen translation displays an exaggerated form of dysfunction that requires productive rethinking. The over-determined errors and excesses of screen translation signal the inevitable, necessary failure of translation processes *in general* while also relating to the specific constraints of screen media production and reception.

Speaking in Translation

A further key area of theory orienting this discussion is transnational screen discourse. Like translation, the discourse of transnationalism engages with screen media via its varied movements across national, cultural and linguistic borders.[10] As its etymology suggests, *trans*national screen scholarship examines screen media as *in-between*, as traversal. In this way, the transnational exhibits an investment in transitory groundings, remaining attuned to both the local and the global. The difference of the transnational (as opposed to the 'international', the 'supranational' and the 'global') is precisely its ability to interject grounding and diversity into conceptions of the global.[11] Whereas the term 'global' threatens to eclipse the national, 'transnationalism' acknowledges the continuing relevance of nations and national boundaries, enabling a more complex, embedded sense of how globalisation proceeds and manifests. As Acland (2003: 36–7) proposes, detailed analyses of located, 'transnational publics' are needed to adequately 'identify and dissect the forces and implications of globalizing culture'. Transnationalism aids in specifying the nature of 'this globalization that we have agreed is occurring' (32).

Ultimately, the detailed analyses of dubbing and subtitling politics presented in this book demonstrate translation's strategic, double role within screen culture – how it both *grounds* and *mobilises* screen culture. Clearly, translation enables screen media to move, facilitating the crossing of national, cultural and linguistic borders. Such global, transnational movement is integral to historic and contemporary media forms, having characterised the medium of film, for instance, since its emergence during the late nineteenth century.[12] However, cross-cultural media distribution and circulation constitute only one of the major ways in which translation broadly affects screen culture. The other relates not to movement but to stasis. Paradoxically, translation also halts or suspends media flows, momentarily grounding them within concrete localities and contexts. Subtitling and dubbing provide a tangible trace of the specific linguistic, cultural and geopolitical routes that media travels, crystallising global media flows in petrified form.[13] Both processes – stop and flow – are vital components of screen culture and both are illuminated and facilitated by screen translation. Moreover, improperness and dysfunction accrue, I contend, in this internal disjunction between grounding and groundlessness.

The examples of screen translation discussed in this book are primarily drawn from film and television, largely bypassing video gaming and amateur media channels. Nevertheless, the term 'screen' acknowledges how today film and television are regularly experienced and mediated across diverse interfaces —on mobile phones, personal computers, i-pods and i-pads. As Henry Jenkins (2006a: 3) observes, screen culture today is characterised by convergence, whereby content circulates 'across different media systems, competing media economies, and national borders'. My focus on film and television at the expense of other screen media is foremost pragmatic, seeking to somewhat narrow the field of investigation. Additionally, as Toby Miller (2010: 139–40) discusses, film and television often provide the impetus for alternative media forms (such as anime music videos). As discussion of fansubbing indicates, film and television can no longer afford to neglect their current economic, political and technological enmeshment within a broad media spectrum. Although fansubbing has historically prioritised television over other media, for instance, it is currently penetrating commercial film translation practice (see Caffrey 2009; Díaz Cintas 2005). The term 'screen' is broad enough to accommodate both film and television while also gesturing towards points of contact with a range of other media. Media convergence and dissemination also complicate notions of the 'original', and throughout this book this term appears in quotation marks in order to emphasise its contested nature. While this word has practical applications that make it difficult to avoid, I propose that it is conceptually problematic and unstable, being complicated, for instance, by the existence of Directors' Cuts, alternative versions, reception contexts, and, of course, translation.

Although this book's title prioritises subtitling, its focus extends to encompass dubbing and to a lesser extent, some voice–over and captioning.[14] This primary focus upon subtitling and dubbing reflects the fact that these two techniques are presently the dominant industry modes, while also setting investigative limits for my project as a whole. While acknowledging that subtitling and dubbing do not represent the sum of screen translation activities, I also use these terms in their broadest sense to refer to numerous non–dominant methods. Sometimes used in the live reporting of sports events and other news items, voice–over is often referred to as a form of dubbing (see Franco et al. 2010: 31), while closed-captioning is identified as an intralingual or same-language mode of subtitling (Gambier 2003: 174). Hence, I utilise 'subtitling' and 'dubbing' as umbrella categories that include numerous variants. Although constituting subsets of the broader categories 'titling' and 'revoicing,' the terms 'subtitling' and 'dubbing' hold greater purchase within screen discourse and remain sufficiently broad to cover most screen translation types. In this book, I use these terms in their broadest sense, to cover a wide range of titling and re/voicing practices.

Methodology and Structure

Speaking in Subtitles examines contemporary issues, practices and pragmatics in screen translation and covers recent historical and contemporary phenomena from a range of cultures and contexts. It does not focus on one particular instance or method of screen translation or on any particular language or languages. Neither does it restrict itself to a particular place or time. Rather, its structure reflects the in-between non-space or 'noplace' (Sallis 2002: xii) of translation,[15] weaving its way between continents, eras and genres to rest at temporary, arbitrary locations. Reflecting its interdisciplinary, interstitial subject matter, this book utilises a diversity of methods ranging from close textual readings to empirical mapping, archival research and meta-critical analysis.

The book is structured in two parts, each comprising three chapters. The first section considers 1960s and 1970s developments when Translation Studies coalesced into a discipline and the translation industry experienced increasing institutionalisation and standardisation. It canvasses the attitudes and approaches to translation that emerged from that period and how they continue to exert influence today. It also examines how screen translation is affected by national specificities, audience types and cultural hierarchies. The second section explores current areas of screen translation practice that lie beyond professional or 'quality' parameters and can consequently be termed 'improper' or 'errant'. These include emergent participatory practices like fansubbing and crowdsourcing, as well as more familiar forms of media piracy and censorship. Digital dissemination, online networking and streaming are explored in order to assess how new technologies are changing screen translation and global screen industries alike. Within these sections connections are traced between current and past practices by emphasising residual and ongoing strains of dysfunction and excess. By following lines of 'errancy' rather than fidelity, this monograph highlights elements of screen translation that are regularly overlooked. Whether informal, error-prone or excessive, improper practices bring into relief the linguistic power dynamics that structure global screenscapes.

Chapter 1 provides an overview of screen translation attitudes and approaches, read through the polarising issue of 'subtitles versus dubbing'. Dominating the little attention paid to translation within Anglophone Screen Studies, and shaping much research within Translation Studies, the sub/dub war encapsulates the entangled prejudices and value politics that beset this field. Despite seeking to determine which technique produces the best result, sub/dub debates reveal a reductive, combative logic that feeds dismissal and devaluation. Hence, the sub/dub war both *reflects* and *effects* screen translation dysfunction.

Chapter 2 puts to the test attitudes and assumptions canvassed in Chapter 1 via the case study of New York's short-lived Invisible Cinema, established by Anthology Film Archives during the early 1970s. Judging both subtitling and dubbing impure and inauthentic, the Invisible Cinema drew attention nevertheless to the re-evaluative role that translation plays within global screen culture by keeping 'originals' in circulation and contention. Borrowing from deconstruction theory, this chapter recasts translation flaws and failures as central and necessary for screen culture as a whole. Discussion extends to Anthology's present-day operations and the continuing legacy of its idiosyncratic screening practices.

Chapter 3 offers a segue between the book's two parts, examining how dubbing is deployed as a self-reflexive mode of *mis*translation in the film *Can Dialectics Break Bricks?* (1973). Engaging extensively with the notion of abusive translation developed by Derrida (2007 [1978]) and updated by Abé Mark Nornes (1999; 2007), I argue that errant forms of screen translation evade theoretical containment and indicate a path for revaluation grounded by practice.

Introducing the book's second section focused on areas of errant screen translation practice, Chapter 4 examines censorship and media piracy, where 'quality' norms tend to be overshadowed by politics of control and resistance. Censorship and piracy deploy subtitling and dubbing to radically different ends, intersecting with errancy in both unregulated and over-regulated contexts. Focusing on pragmatics, this chapter discusses both professional and informal translation, and draws attention to non-Western, non-English-speaking contexts as sites of geopolitical tension.

Chapter 5 focuses on the emergent, 'participatory' translation activity of fansubbing ('fan subtitling'), examining its origins within anime subculture and ongoing evolution. It approaches fansubbing as an informal practice and subset of media piracy, with its own ethical standards and rules of conduct, that highlights the growing significance of translation as a mode of cultural participation responsive to the intensifying multilingualism of global media and technology. Fans are discussed as 'lead users' of new technologies who trial functionality and uncover emergent uses, demands and desires – exemplifying the increasingly active and unruly ways in which people consume and engage with media today.

The book's final chapter offers a case study of global TV site Viki (www.viki.com) that provides subtitles in hundreds of languages for screen media from around the world. Here, fansubbing methods and fan repurposing of technology are adopted in a corporate context, underscoring the commerce/community tensions that characterise 'participatory culture' (Jenkins 2006a). The example of Viki also pinpoints the critical role played by language and multilingual publics within the evolving dynamics of convergence.

Although language and translation have been systemically overlooked within Screen Studies, they are set to become major areas of interest as online technologies dramatically alter the global mediascape, affecting modes of access and availability, redirecting content flows and challenging copyright and intellectual property regulations. The concrete translation practices explored within this book identify language diversity as a major trajectory within digital and online modes of media engagement. Paying attention to improper sites of subtitling and dubbing provides a crucial key, I argue, to revaluing translation's role within screen culture broadly – translation irregularities articulate the necessary risks involved in both mobilising and grounding transnational screen culture. Translation errancy brings to the surface shifting politics of value, while keeping screen culture active and alive. As Carax intones, 'cinema *is* a foreign language, a language created for those who need to travel to the other side of life'.

Notes

1. According to Ethnologue (Lewis et al. 2016), English is currently spoken as a first language by 339 million. Over a decade earlier, this figure was estimated at 375 million (Graddol 1997: 10). According to the United Nations (2015), the world population reached 7.3 billion in 2015. Ethnologue places English in third position globally, behind Spanish at 427 million speakers and Chinese at 1,302 million speakers, with Chinese Mandarin alone at 897 million.
2. Seeing 'disregard for the specificities of audiovisual translation' as 'fairly typical for North American DVD producers', Carol O'Sullivan (2011: 200–2) reports that the Lion's Gate Region One DVD of *Haute Tension / High Tension* (2003) included only hard-of-hearing subtitles, as also occurred

with *Passion of the Christ* (2004). In such cases, hearing audiences receive redundant descriptions of music and sound effects as well as expository subtitles at points where no dialogue occurs.

3. On typical 'good' and 'bad' objects within Film Studies, see Toby Miller (2010: 138). Miller's aim to consider cultural texts as 'unstable entities that change their very composition as they move across time and space' (154) is significantly aided, I propose, by an examination of screen translation.

4. On the idea of film as universal language, see Miriam Hansen (1985; 1991) and Mattias Frey (2010).

5. Abé Mark Nornes (2007: 18), Carol O'Sullivan (2011: 4; 204n3) and Ginette Vincendeau (2011: 341–2) make a similar point. For a comprehensive account of film semiology, see Robert Stam et al. (1992).

6. Apart from special issues of screen journals and magazines including *Cinephile* (2012), *Spectator* (2010), *Cinemascope* (2005), *Cinema et Cié* (2003) and *Schnitt* (2001; 2003), edited Screen Studies collections that specifically address interlingual translation include Mamula and Patti (2016), Distelmeyer (2006) and Egoyan and Balfour (2004). English-language monographs include Nornes (2007) and Ferrari (2010), as well as historical studies such as Wahl (2016), Jarvinen (2012) and Rossholm (2005). Perspectives from Translation Studies and Linguistics include Dror Abend-David (2014), O'Sullivan (2011), Berger and Komori (2010) and Cronin (2009).

7. Audiovisual Translation (AVT) began to crystallise as a veritable sub-field of Translation Studies (TS) only in the late 1980s and early 1990s, despite the appearance of occasional journal issues on the subject since the 1960s and Istvan Fodor's *On Dubbing* (1976). In a seminal article on the emergence of AVT studies, Dirk Delabastita (1990: 99) noted the marginal status of AVT in relation to literary translation, referring to it as an 'almost completely neglected' field within TS. For a discussion of terms relevant to AVT (alternatively referred to as 'screen translation' and 'multimedia translation') see Yves Gambier (2003).

8. Jonathan Rée (1994: 42) points out that, within English-speaking contexts, post-structuralist philosophy 'has been evaluated as much in terms of its language (delicious or unpalatable according to taste) as of what it tries to say'. He relates this focus on language to the fact that much of this theory has been imported into English from French, leading him to suggest that philosophy as a whole 'is a creature of translations'.

9. For Christine Adamou and Simone Knox (2011: 9), the 'co-presence of two texts' within both subtitling and dubbing produces an 'inherent (intertextual) richness' that is further complicated by casting and vocal performance (in the case of dubbing) and the 'feedback-effect' of subtitling, creating moments of 'reflexive slippage' (15). On multimodal analyses of screen translation, see Delabastita (1990: 109), Aline Ramael (2001), Christopher Taylor (2003), Ali Hajmohammadi (2004), Yves Gambier (2006), Carol O'Sullivan and Caterina Jeffcote (2013) and Luis Pérez González (2014; 2007).

10. On screen transnationalism, see in particular, edited collections by Lúcia Nagib et al. (2012), Natasa Durovicová and Kathleen Newman (2010) and Elizabeth Ezra and Terry Rowden (2006). See also Mari Pajala (2014), Paul Julian Smith (2012), Ginette Vincendeau (2011), Tim Bergfelder (2005), Acland (2003) and Ella Shohat and Robert Stam (1996).
11. On differences between these overlapping terms, see Will Higbee and Song Hwee Lim (2010), Mette Hjort (2010) and Bergfelder (2005).
12. On the contestable origins of cinema, see André Gaudreault (2012) and Thomas Elsaesser (2012). On early film transnationalism, see Andrew Higson (2010) and Torey Liepa (2008).
13. In the Philippines, for instance, the Malay and Bahasa Indonesian subtitles of many pirated films signal their geographic point of arrival via the island of Mindanao, whereas those with 'Chinese-flavoured' English subtitles come via Hong Kong or Singapore (Baumgärtel 2006a: 389), as discussed in Chapter 4.
14. For a summation of different AVT types from 'double dubbing' to 'surtitling,' see Gambier (2003: 172–8). Audio description for blind or visually impaired audiences and TV closed-captioning for deaf and hard-of-hearing audiences are two further techniques that sit outside narrow understandings of subtitling and dubbing.
15. In his preface to *On Translation*, John Sallis (2002: xii) proposes that translation demarcates a 'noplace, nowhere' typology. Also relevant here is Michel Chion's (2009 [2003]: 87) notion of 'stateless cinema'.

Part 1

Devaluation and Deconstruction

CHAPTER 1

Sub/Dub Wars:
Attitudes to Screen Translation

It is not often that the topic of screen translation makes headlines. It did so on 7 August 1960, when *The New York Times* published a Sunday column by chief film critic Bosley Crowther captioned 'Subtitles Must Go!', which 'raised eyebrows – and as it developed, blood pressures – from coast to coast' (Scheuer 1960). So began the eponymous sub/dub war, which raged in *The New York Times* and a host of like publications until Crowther's retirement in 1966. In many respects, Crowther's defence of dubbing was unusual, yet it was also symptomatic. For although Crowther's anti-subtitling stance was provocatively atypical, bucking the enduring trend within Anglophone film appreciation to associate subtitles with authenticity, his tone was not. Lambasting subtitles rather than championing dubbing, Crowther's headline signals the negativity that pervades attitudes towards translation within Anglo-American film culture. Additionally, his inclination to pit subtitling and dubbing against one another is entirely characteristic of Anglophone screen culture attitudes towards translation – which are still dominated today by this single, polarising issue.

This chapter posits the ongoing sub/dub debate as a succinct expression of the messy value politics that surround screen translation. Initially exploring how current screen culture perspectives are informed by the 1960s *New York Times* debate, it then proceeds to unpack attitudes to translation by plotting them in relation to concrete examples of subtitling and dubbing *in practice*. This analysis notes how sub/dub debates within screen discourse privilege mode over execution, in contradistinction to Translation Studies. It also considers how Translation Studies reconfigures the sub/dub split in relation to national boundaries, and, in doing so, exposes and contextualises the Anglo-American parameters of Crowther's 1960s sub/dub war. This cross-disciplinary overview of attitudes and approaches traces the prescriptive tone that typically accompanies value negotiations and quality assessments within screen translation discourse, providing a solid basis for the project of *re*valuation that occupies the remainder of this book.

1960s Polemics

In his initial call to arms, Crowther expressed his 'strong conviction' that 'the convention of English subtitles on foreign-language films should be – or must be – abandoned when those films are shown in the US market and replaced by the use of dubbed English dialogue' (1960a). Describing subtitles as inadequate, 'wrong', 'thoroughly inartistic' and 'obsolete', he states: 'it is foolish to hobble expression with an old device that was mainly contrived as a convenience to save the cost of dubbing foreign-language films when they had limited appeal'. Those who do not understand the original dialogue, he argued, 'have to spend a lot of precious time reading instead of looking at what is going on' making it 'rough on the eyesight to have to keep darting the eyes back and forth from the images to the subtitles' (Crowther 1960a). Welcoming how 'the American market is crying out for more and varied films and more international distributors are seeking wider scope for their films', Crowther identified dubbing as an effective means of bringing foreign films to the masses, liberating them from exclusively 'showing in "art" theatres', and tabling them instead for general release (1960b). 'More Americans would see foreign pictures if they were effectively dubbed,' he writes, adding that such increased exposure would enable foreign cultures and ideas to broaden and enrich American society.

Identifying himself as a 'former purist in the matter of original dialogue', Crowther's provocative anti-subtitling stance constituted a 'public volte-face' (Nornes 2007: 12) and caused much controversy amongst art house, foreign-language film viewers.[1] Notably, he exposed the hypocrisy and illusory assumptions underlying the association between art house sensibilities and subtitling. Describing as 'snobbish' the notion 'that foreign-language films (some of which have even been dubbed in their own language!) are linguistically inviolable', Crowther unearthed a chink in the authenticity of European art cinema where, as Mark Betz (2009: 69) explains, 'national language at the level of the sound track and ... national character in the person of the director combine to form an almost inviolable bond – a bond that is broken ... only by the travesty of the dubbed print'. By identifying dubbing as a mainstay of much European *auteur* production, Crowther essentially deconstructed the very notion of the 'original' by discrediting its linguistic purity or authenticity. By underscoring the tenuousness of *auteurist* ideals and their remove from the transnational realities of film production, he destabilised the 'high/low tenor of American art film culture in the 1960s' (Betz 2009: 49).

In response to the explosive outcry following his denouncement of subtitling, Crowther named films outright where, 'quite simply, the original dialogue is dubbed' (1960b). His first example is *La dolce vita* (1960). On watching this film in Rome in its 'original' language, Crowther was 'shocked to discover … that the Italian dialogue and the lip movements sometimes did not match at all'. He then explains that this is a common phenomenon in Italian films known for their use of post-synchronised sound.[2] Recognising the power of translation as nation-building device, Mussolini decreed in 1929 that all foreign films screened in Italy were to be dubbed into Italian, thereby reducing foreign exposure and influence (Betz 2009: 90).[3] At this point, revoicing also became mandatory for domestic productions, which were dubbed into a standardised, official form of Tuscan Italian. 'When Mussolini took power in 1922,' explains Ruth Ben-Ghiat (1997: 439), 'almost 30 per cent of Italians communicated exclusively in one of the dialects'. By dubbing all domestic productions into 'official' Italian, a form of linguistic unification was achieved in a country riddled by regional divisions and intra-national dialects.

The Italian film industry's dependence upon dubbing (see Fleeger 2016) produced some unanticipated results. As Betz (2009: 68) notes, along with Peter Lev (1993), Italy's post-synchronisation rule helped shape the flourishing international art film movement of the 1950s and 1960s, as shooting without sound facilitated the characteristic use of international polyglot casts. Along with Italian lead Marcello Mastroianni, *La dolce vita* boasts the former Miss Sweden, Anita Ekberg, and a number of French actors, most notably Anouk Aimée. For Michel Chion (1999 [1982]: 86), Fellini's polyglot casts produce a veritable 'poly-voice'. 'The freedom allotted in Italy for the synching of voices is already enormous,' he states, 'but Fellini in particular breaks all records with his voices that hang on the bodies of actors only in the loosest and freest sense, in space as well as in time' (Chion 1999 [1982]: 85).

Betz's exploration of tensions residing within the polyglot sound track of co-produced European art films reproduces and extends many of Crowther's arguments. On watching a number of Antonioni films from the early 1960s, Betz notes that the Italian dialogue coming from the mouths of French and English stars is typically out-of-sync, dubbed by uncredited Italian voice actors (2009: 55–6). 'In fact,' he notes, 'the sync is frequently off at times for even the Italian actors', leading him to conclude that there 'is no "original" sound track to speak of for any of these films:

they are always already dubbed in any release print one can see and hear'
(56). These comments echo Crowther (1966), who states:

> it is simply naive to assume that there are such things as original, pristine dialogue
> recordings, except in the rarest instances. So many films now made in Europe are
> being made with multi-lingual casts or are being shot 'wild' (to save expenses) and
> having the dialogue recorded later.

Crowther (1966) reports that, despite being shot in a mix of French,
Italian and German, for instance, *Le meurtrier / Enough Rope* (1963)
was shown in New York's Little Carnegie Theatre in a French-language
version. 'No doubt, many people thought they were hearing the pristine
dialogue duly translated by subtitles,' he teases. He also points out that
Claude Chabrol's *Le scandale / The Scandal* (1967)[4] was 'shot in two
separate and distinct versions, English and French', resembling Multiple-
Language Version (MLV) filmmaking of the early sound era when films
were shot simultaneously in numerous language versions – typically with
different casts using the same sets – in order to eliminate the need for
either subtitling or dubbing.[5] After revealing that Fellini once told him
he preferred the German dubbing of *La dolce vita* to the Italian version,[6]
Crowther (1966) concludes:

> We'll probably go on receiving in most of our first-run New York theatres the so-
> called 'original' versions of foreign-language films. But don't think that you'll be
> seeing (or hearing) a non-dubbed film. It will simply be a question of which dubbed
> version you will be seeing.

For Crowther (1965), many history films and films set in foreign locations, by their nature, repudiate ideas of linguistic authenticity. In relation
to *He Who Must Die* (1958), for instance, a modern-day Jesus allegory set
in Crete, he states:

> The nicety of language fidelity is not open to criticism in this case because the film,
> in its original version, was spoken not in Greek but in French. So it is just as reason-
> able and convincing to hear it spoken in English.

In this way, Crowther argued that dubbed and otherwise 'inauthentic'
sound tracks were central to the industry though often unnoticed and
invisible, even to film purists and cognoscenti. As Thomas Rowe (1960:
117) observes, 'audience consciousness of lip synchronization is confined
to films in its own language. Even film critics are blithely indifferent to
the fact that most of the foreign films shown in original version with
subtitles are egregiously out of synch by American standards, although

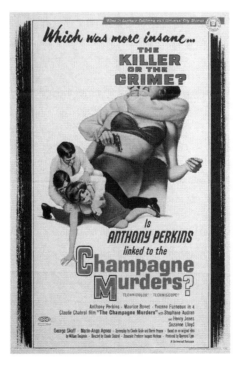

Figures 1.1 and 1.2 Publicity posters for *Le scandale* (1967) and *The Champagne Murders* (aka *The Scandal*) (1967). © Universal.

their criticism invariably notes such defects in the dubbed version.' Demonstrating how dubbing and post-synchronisation are embedded in the very technology of sound filmmaking, Crowther presents a particularly challenging re-evaluation of interlingual translation that to date remains largely unprocessed and unacknowledged within Screen Studies.[7] Part of the reason for this neglect surely relates to the inherently deconstructive implications of Crowther's renegade stance. These views had little long-term impact on the distribution or viewing of foreign films in the US, demonstrating just how entrenched is the association between subtitling and foreign-language art cinema.

According to Betz (2009: 50), subtitling ultimately won the war. Although Crowther's impassioned defence of dubbing drew attention to the value politics affecting screen translation, exposing as unstable any notion of language authenticity, Betz proposes that the 1960s sub/dub debate resulted in the 'common knowledge' that subtitling is superior to dubbing, at least within Anglophone contexts. To illustrate this point, he refers to David Bordwell and Kristen Thompson's seminal text *Film Art: An Introduction* (2004 [1979]: 388), which asserts matter-of-factly, 'most people who study films prefer subtitles' as 'dubbing simply destroys part of the film' (Betz 2009: 50–1). When such assumptions are treated as received wisdom, they tend to be insufficiently analysed. In part, it is the sub/dub split itself that enables such attitudes to proceed unchallenged. In contrast, Crowther advocated for the wide distribution and easy comprehension of foreign-language films via dubbing, positing access as the primary value of screen translation, not authenticity. He also reversed established sub/dub dynamics, *re*valuing dubbing by *de*valuing and de-authenticating subtitling. Consequently, his destabilisation of screen translation attitudes remains subject to the sub/dub split, and these duelling dynamics remain part of his legacy today.

Approaching screen translation in terms of dualities engenders comparative evaluations and simplistic, black-and-white approaches that tend to bypass subtleties and entangled politics. It also produces an overriding dynamic of devaluation that facilitates screen translation's sidelining. Consequently, screen translation has been mainly relegated to the personal asides of critics and reviewers like Crowther, and has tended to elicit emotional, dramatic responses. In 1945, Jorge Luis Borges denounced dubbing as a 'malignant artifice' that produces 'monsters' (2004: 118) while Marcel Martin (quoted in Lu 2009: 161) referred to dubbing as an 'evil expression of art' in his *Le langage cinématographique* (1955). French filmmakers Jean-Marie Straub and Danièle Huillet (1985: 150) later claimed that dubbing and post-synchronisation made audiences 'deaf and insensitive'. These extremist attitudes may have contributed to translation's neglect and trivialisation within Screen Studies 'proper,' while enabling prejudices to fester and become entrenched.

Moreover, the corrosive, ongoing war between subtitling and dubbing imbues even relative wins with a sense of fault and failure. While ostensibly the sub/dub debate concerns a search for quality, seeking to discern which method produces the best result, it invests in the negative nevertheless, always positioning either subtitling or dubbing as 'bad'. Paradoxically, it is this very division itself that assures negative determinations. As Abé Mark Nornes (2007: 15) notes, in many ways it is the sub versus dub mentality that is the problem, and it is this rigid, factional logic that his *Cinema Babel* aims to confound. Unlike Nornes, however, I am not in any hurry to move beyond this warring dynamic, preferring instead to linger awhile, contemplating how its varied contours and contradictions provide a succinct expression of the entangled prejudices and predispositions that surround screen translation. In this task, I have found the contributions of Crowther, Betz and Nornes invaluable for the way they unpack and rethink the underlying assumptions of contemporary attitudes and practices. In revisiting arguments first posed by Crowther and extending their theoretical scope, this chapter dismantles such sub/dub logic by bringing to light its underlying contradictions and complexities.

Some fifty years after Crowther, Betz's exploration of film soundscapes as sites of contestation and transformation steeped in ideological import makes an important contribution to Screen Studies that, like Crowther, elucidates how subtitles have come to function as 'markers of authentic nationhood' in many Anglo-American contexts, despite the fact that they can operate to efface rather than preserve 'the marks of national differences' (2009: 89). Betz points out, for instance, how subtitling is a far more global industry than dubbing, which conversely depends on local actors and sound studios, and often bolsters local filmmaking through the provision of technical equipment, technical expertise and actors (90–1).[8] Hence, in relation to European co-productions with polyglot casts, Betz (85–8) suggests that the desire on the part of Anglo-American art film audiences to watch subtitled rather than dubbed prints is nothing short of fetishistic – a point he illustrates in relation to *Il gattopardo / The Leopard* (1963). In this film, American lead Burt Lancaster delivered his lines in English during the shoot and later did his own English-language dubbing (85). Hence, he argues that this English-language dub is particularly 'authentic' or 'original'. Nonetheless, US art house audiences prefer to watch it with subtitles. Betz reports that 'Anglo-American viewers invariably opt for dubbed-in-Italian, subtitled-in-English versions as the more authentic ones, the more artistic ones, the ones truer to the intentions of their auteurs' (85). He continues:

> In such cases, to demand a unilingual Italian sound track is to erase the linguistic polyvocality that registers the political economy of art filmmaking in that country from the 1950s through the 1970s. As the films were predominantly shot without sound, there is no 'original' sound track to fret about. Yet art film viewers invariably prefer to listen to the dialogue dubbed into Italian and watch an image track with not one but two added idiosyncrasies – subtitles, of course, but also the major characters' lips out of synch with the language quite evidently not emerging from their body. (Betz 2009: 87)

Like Crowther, Betz exposes how unquestioned allegiance to the authenticity of subtitling can, paradoxically, result in doubly mediated, exaggeratedly *in*authentic experiences.

Split Practices

Finding forceful expression in the 1960s *New York Times* polemic, screen culture's sub versus dub mentality can be understood as a 'macro'-approach that reduces the issue of translation to one central divide. In this way, it largely bypasses the minutiae of practice. Rather than examining how levels of expertise or textual approach (such as 'free' or 'faithful') might produce differing results, it instead interrogates how the different technical parameters of subtitling and dubbing affect screen content and experiences. This approach prioritises mode over and above execution. Consequently, how well or badly subtitling or dubbing has been rendered does not feature as a prominent part of the sub/dub war. This is not to suggest that Crowther or his contemporaries did not care about matters of quality. They did. They argued however that the choice of mode necessarily affects quality before or beyond levels of expertise. While the manner in which subtitles are executed can reduce or accentuate their effects, detractors argue it will not eradicate distractions and distortions understood to constitute part of their very make-up. Similarly, the fact that dubbing leaves no telltale trace of 'original' dialogue (see Nornes 2007: 336–7) is understood by detractors as symptomatic of an *essential* duplicity and inauthenticity. Thus, even instances of 'quality' subtitling and dubbing do not tend to quell complaints in sub versus dub discussions.

New Republic critic Stanley Kauffmann (1960: 27) made this clear by prefacing his contribution to the debate with the proviso that he was comparing 'good dubbing with good subtitling; no one on either side defends bad work'. Likewise, Crowther's advocacy of dubbing considers its potential for excellence and he states, 'bad examples ... should not prejudice the case':

> With further recourse to dubbing and more experience in the field, our laboratories should be able to give us virtually flawless vocal replicas. Eventually it would be intelligent for foreign directors to anticipate the projection of their films in the American market with dubbed English dialogue. Perhaps, with many multi-lingual actors, they themselves could direct the English voices to be used. (1960a)

In contrast, Translation Studies approaches tend to exhibit 'micro'-preoccupations, sometimes examining issues of execution to the exclusion of context.[9] Certainly, this is a generalisation, yet it remains a useful means of characterising trends that dominate this field. In part the micro-focus of Translation Studies results from its 'social-scientific or practice-oriented' tendencies (Nornes 2007: 17). Additionally, distinctions between domestication/foreignisation, freedom/fidelity and equivalence/function tend to be considered in relation to literary-derived, dialogue-focused appraisals of film and television, whereas in screen discourse these issues are debated in relation to a broader set of considerations including the viewing experience, film aesthetics and the multimodal (see Wehn 2001: 70-1).[10] Translation Studies' micro focus extends to sub/dub comparisons, often resulting in detailed, data-driven research that strives to achieve a degree of scientific impartiality (see Delabastita 1990: 98; Ramière 2010: 103). Hence Screen and Translation Studies approaches can seem worlds apart. However, when Translation Studies addresses national preferences – when entire communities or countries choose one mode of screen translation over and above another – the sub/dub split assumes new proportions. Rarely surfacing within Anglophone screen discourse on translation, issues of national context tend to invert micro/macro tendencies. These national geopolitics present an enlarged frame of reference for thinking about screen translation, testing the limitations of Anglo-American research and reception contexts by bringing a more international perspective into focus.

As the sub/dub split feeds off the notion that these two translation methods function in an oppositional manner, analysis of the underlying technical and semiotic distinctions constitutes a preliminary step in unpacking attitudes, assumptions and approaches. Translation scholar Dirk Delabastita (1990: 102) proposes two means of distinguishing between these techniques. Identifying dubbing as *aural* and subtitling as *visual*, he also proposes that dubbing *substitutes* whereas subtitling *adds*. Notably, the substitution produced through dubbing mostly involves *subtraction*, removing sounds/voices before replacing them. In contrast, subtitling supplements, introducing new lines of text that overlay the image or sit beneath on a black bar or matte (as with letterboxing). With voice-over, these dynamics shift. Like subtitling, voice-over tends to involve addition rather than subtraction with untranslated and translated speech co-existing, one on top of the other. Usually lagging behind by a few seconds, the translating voice tends to speak over the 'original,' which remains faintly audible beneath (see Franco et al. 2010: 43).

Most screen culture critiques of subtitling revolve around the identification of three main problems: (1) distortion or misrepresentation, (2) disruption and (3) elitism. While the charge of distortion concerns the subtitle's effect on the source film, disruption arguments are made in relation to both film aesthetics and film audiences, whereas claims of elitism mainly concern audiences and processes of reception. All these criticisms follow from the fact that subtitles necessarily involve the introduction of a new graphic register. The addition of text is understood to distort the visual purity of the image and misrepresent the fullness or subtlety of its sounds while requiring audiences to break modes of identification and suture in order to *read* rather than watch and listen. For this reason, subtitles are often interpreted as elitist – they disrupt cinematic illusion, leading to 'considerable loss of pleasure' and alienating large sectors of the audience, not least those unable to read (Ascheid 1997: 34). Additionally, as dubbing adapter Mario Paolinelli (quoted in Castellano 2005) notes, when audiences read subtitles, they spend a considerable amount of time looking at the bottom of the screen and hence, tend to miss around half of a film's visuals. This loss is further compounded by the unavoidable degree of condensation required by subtitles as, according to veteran subtitler Herman Weinberg (1948: 51), actors 'especially French and Italian, speak faster than one can read a translation of what they say'. In fact, Translation Studies research has consistently shown that subtitling results in the loss of around 20 per cent to 50 per cent of a film's dialogue.[11] Lastly, technical difficulties continue to plague this device, as when subtitles merge into white backgrounds.

In *Lost in Translation* (2003), Bob Harris shoots a Japanese whisky commercial aided by an interpreter, Ms Kawasaki, who turns out to be particularly ineffectual, repeatedly transforming the director's lengthy instructions into brief, nonsensical English statements. Without any knowledge of the Japanese language, Bob's queries ('That's all he said?') and his ironic acting style go unheard and un-noted. This scene plays on the particularly common frustration experienced by viewers of subtitled films when, for instance, a lengthy speech might be translated by a monosyllabic 'yes' or 'no', or left untranslated altogether. In this scene,

Figure 1.3 Disappearing subtitles in *Ringu / The Ring* (1998). © Basara Pictures.

the interpreter stands in for the reductive subtitle and Bob's exasperation exemplifies the phenomenon referenced in the film's title. As critics like Crowther point out, this effect is more pronounced in relation to subtitles than dubbing. The fact that subtitles *add* text rather than *substituting* sounds enables the preservation of 'original' dialogue, which is supplemented rather than erased. Supplementation, however, poses its own pitfalls: the 'original' and the translation *coexist*, inviting a process of comparison that inevitably exposes points of disparity between the two. As Nornes (2007: 262) writes, 'both the original and the translation are simultaneously available, as if they were *en face*'.[12] For translation scholar Henrik Gottlieb (1994: 102), this factor marks subtitling as an '*overt* form of translation', in contrast to dubbing, which he describes as 'covert'.

Many viewers identify with Bob's frustration. When audiences observe jarring differences between the length of an utterance and its translation, their viewing experience is considerably disrupted. Such observations do not necessarily require knowledge of a foreign language, as Bob demonstrates. Moreover, although 'quality' subtitling may be able to somewhat minimise the disjunction between 'original' and 'copy', critics counter that subtitles are by nature reductive, resulting in an unavoidable degree of mismatch or non-equivalence. This point is confirmed by Translation Studies research and professional subtitlers who readily admit that, in transforming spoken dialogue into written form, subtitles are utterly dependant upon the 'art' of condensation (see Mailhac 2000: 130). As Weinberg (1985: 10) reminisces, 'the whole point of subtitling is to have as

Figure 1.4 Bob and his interpreter mis/communicate in *Lost in Translation* (2003).
© Focus Features.

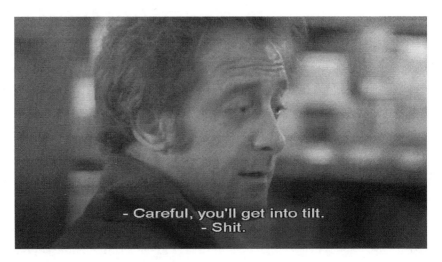

Figure 1.5 In *Friday Night* (2002), conversation that is inaudible is rendered clearly (and hence amplified) in the English subtitles. © Arena Films.

few words on the screen as possible'. No matter how skilled the subtitler, a degree of selection, condensation and thus reinterpretation will always be necessary. The reductive nature of subtitling is exaggerated by censorship cuts (see Weinberg 1948) and can also be affected by syntactic or stylistic differences between languages (see Béhar quoted in Rosenberg 2007). For subtitler Sionann O'Neill (O'Neill and McMahon 2011), when translating between French and more succinct English, 'less is more'.

Figure 1.6 In *Cleo from 5 to 7* (1962), a radio broadcast is subtitled on the Criterion Collection DVD release. In an earlier English version discussed by Shohat and Stam (1985), these background sounds went untranslated. © Ciné Tamaris.

Reduction and condensation are only some of the ways in which subtitles can distort a film's meaning. Just as subtitles can be cryptically monosyllabic, they can, at times, become over-articulate. Director Claire Denis (2004: 74–5) describes one such experience that occurred during the subtitling of her film *Vendredi soir* / *Friday Night* (2002) for a scene in which a character looks from her car into a café, watching the people inside. The dialogue of the characters in the café is barely audible, yet it is rendered clearly (and thus amplified) in the English-language subtitles (74–5). Denis (75) reports that the subtitler refused her suggestion to 'print them with one letter missing or one word missing' and that she still regrets this decision.[13] Ella Shohat and Robert Stam (1985: 47) note that subtitles can also distort as a result of their vococentric focus, prioritising spoken dialogue over other forms of language communication and neglecting elements such as signage, text, radio and television broadcasts, song lyrics and more abstract noise including background conversations. In *Cléo de 5 à 7* / *Cleo from 5 to 7* (1962), radio allusions to the war in Algeria went untranslated in one English version that, according to Shohat and Stam (1985: 47–8), was consequently depoliticised. In such cases, the film's 'original' soundtrack is preserved, yet it is far from unaffected by subtitles.

One area of aural complexity regularly silenced by subtitles is language difference or multilingualism.[14] Subtitles tend to function as a levelling agent in films that contain subtle displays of linguistic diversity. Although the subtitles employed in the festival screenings of *Linda Linda*

Linda (2005) differentiated between instances of Japanese and Korean dialogue through the use of parentheses, the DVD release distributed by Viz Pictures provides stock-standard English subtitles that effectively mask the narrative significance of scenes featuring language difference.[15] Language levelling or flattening can be even more pronounced in dubbing (Rowe 1960: 119).[16] *Lost in Translation* is again instructive on this point.[17] The limitations of dubbing are instantly revealed when one tries to imagine this film in a dubbed version: the character of the interpreter being rendered redundant if the film universe is made to fit a monolingual frame. Notably, *Lost in Translation* references Godard's *Contempt*, a film that contains French, German, Italian and English dialogue all negotiated via the interpreter Francesca Vanini.[18] According to Lev (1993: 86), Godard created Vanini's character solely in order to make the film impossible to dub. Against Godard's wishes, co-producer Carlo Ponti released the film in an Italian dubbed (and edited) version, conforming to the country's strong dubbing tradition (Betz 2009: 79). In protest, Godard removed his name from this version (302n52).

For those who oppose dubbing, inauthenticity appears built into the very fabric of this technique. Dubbing or sound-mixing processes are predicated on the fact that film images and sounds are produced, recorded and stored separately, thereby creating the potential for modification and manipulation. When the 'original' language is entirely removed from a film, critics argue, so too are credibility and accountability. This charge

We always meet at the incinerator.

Figure 1.7 In *Linda Linda Linda* (2005), Makihara struggles to declare his love to Korean exchange student Son by speaking her language. The fact that he is speaking Korean in this scene is not registered in the subtitles on the Viz Pictures DVD release.
© Bitters End.

of inauthenticity is not one of many arguments mounted against dubbing but, rather, an all–encompassing complaint that delves to the heart of the technique's basis in processes of replacement, erasure and substitution.[19] No matter how competent or faithful the translation approach, critics of dubbing claim that the very technique itself is duplicitous. By substituting rather than supplementing, it can essentially pass as 'original'. Hence, Gottlieb (1994: 102) terms dubbing 'covert', while Antje Aschied (1997: 35) observes that 'this *new text constitutes the original* for most spectators'.[20]

Conversely, the additive, supplementary nature of subtitles is often seen to lend them accountability and transparency, with binliguls able to play 'spot–the–difference' between translated and 'original' versions (see Ramière 2010: 102; Grillo and Kawin 1981: 26). Moreover, it is not only language experts who are able to note discontinuities, as noted in relation to *Lost in Translation*. As subtitles don't stand in for the 'original', they announce their own complicity in processes of mediation, essentially making the fact of translation visible. Instantly recognisable as a post-production device, subtitles tend to remain external from the story world being depicted (see Pedersen 2011: 8).[21] In this way, they are inherently self–reflexive and anti–illusionary (see Ascheid 1997: 34–5), functioning as graphic inscription of the translation process and declaring their mediating, interpretative role. For Ascheid, subtitling 'foregrounds the translation process by visibly underlining one text with another, hence creating a *double text*' (34).

According to Michael Watt (2000), the honest, upfront nature of subtitling even enables the use of footnotes or parentheses to express the complexities of *double entendre*, word play, jokes and sarcasm. Watt celebrates the fact that 'subtitles confess their true nature as a tool to aid understanding', applauding them for respectful treatment of both the audience and the film. For Watt, dubbing infantilises and grossly underestimates the audience, whereas subtitles acknowledge and respect the realities of language difference. Referring to Stam's work on cinematic intertextuality, Ascheid (1997: 34) notes the particular ' "dialogism" present in the subtitled film, which opens up its linguistic devices for open acknowledgement', resulting 'in the perception of "difference" rather than the confirmation of "sameness" and identity'. By accepting and even amplifying linguistic complexity, the anti–illusionary nature of subtitles is consciousness–raising. According to this logic, subtitles bring audiences closer to a meaningful engagement with the foreign.

Competing translations of the seminal, experimental French-language film *La jetée* (1962) help to illustrate this point. In 2000, Warner Home Video released this film on a compilation DVD *Short 2: Dreams*. This

and that this moment he had been
granted to watch as a child,

Figure 1.8 Subtitles in *La jetée* (1962). © Argos Films.

version replaced the previous English subtitles with a new English dub. With a few notable exceptions, the Amazon product reviews that followed express disappointment and dissatisfaction with Warner's decision to dub. Reviewers argued that the dub lacked the 'stark and ominous' tone of the French narration, altering the film's mood while severing its ties to place, 'taking it not simply out of France but out of the era in which it was filmed'. These comments reiterate the oft-heard claim that subtitling is more authentic than dubbing, as it preserves foreign-language, source *sound*. By supplementing rather than erasing the aural index of foreignness, subtitles are understood to respect the 'original', enabling a full appreciation of actor performances as expressed through the quality and intonation of the voice.[22] Moreover, reviewers of the dubbed *La jetée* note that the music and special effects are 'mixed far lower' in this version, reducing the dramatic effect of the final scene in particular. They propose that, by enabling audiences to both watch *and hear* foreign language media, subtitles preserve 'original' anchorings in specific bodies, places and times.

One online reviewer responded quite differently, however, arguing that dubbing is particularly appropriate for this type of 'artsy, still-photograph movie-short', enabling the audience to 'truly experience ... all of the film at once' rather than being required to continually read lines of text at the bottom of the image thereby 'most likely miss[ing] some of the (at times) rapidly changing still-pictures as the film progresses'. This viewpoint deploys a decidedly different notion of authenticity to that promoted by subtitle enthusiasts, measured in relation to the cinematic *experience* rather than the source text. Dubbing is understood to respect the cinematic mode, facilitating the 'suspension of disbelief' so critical to filmic processes of identification and illusion, enabling unreflexive absorption in cinematic spectacle. Ascheid (1997: 35) states: 'the initial attempt of the film original to disguise its own construction and mask itself through the "impression of reality" in the cinema is maintained for most audiences through the dubbing effort'. From this perspective, dubbing is seen as 'properly' cinematic, not requiring any modal transposition (from speech to text, for example). Instead of turning film into 'a kind of high-class comic book with sound effects' (Canby 1983), dubbing is unimodal and hence closer to literary translation in that it replaces same with same (see Ascheid 1997: 35). As Pierre-François Caillé (quoted in Whitman-Linsen 1992: 55; her translation) states, 'cinema is a factory of illusions. Dubbing attempts to give the illusion of an illusion.'

The English dubbing of *Wo hu cang long / Crouching Tiger, Hidden Dragon* (2000) available on the Sony Pictures 2001 DVD presents a case in point. Overseen by director Lee and executive producer/co-screenwriter James Schamus, this highly acclaimed English dubbing was done by the film's bilingual stars Chow Yun-Fat and Michelle Yeoh amongst others (Nornes 2007: 14; Schamus 2000). In this, it seems to realise the 'heights' of dubbing envisioned by Crowther, remaining faithful to the film's 'original' voices in terms of accent, tone, tenor, pitch and body type – all identified as strategic considerations in the dubbing process (Whitman-Linsen 1992: 19). In Chinese-language markets, however, the film did not do particularly well (Ross 2001; Kim 2006; Klein 2004: 36), a fact that Sheldon Lu (2007) partly blames on the Cantonese accents of its lead stars, which led to 'dialectic implausibility' for this *wuxia pian* period film.[23] In fact, as Christina Klein (2004, 36) notes, of the film's 'four main actors, only Zhang Ziyi spoke fluent Mandarin, Chang Chen spoke with a Taiwanese accent while Chow Yun-Fat and Michelle Yeoh, having been raised in Cantonese- and English-speaking households respectively, delivered their lines phonetically'. Evidently, the language intrigues of this film are complicated by the demands of transnational stardom and co-production, which present considerable challenges to notions of linguistic 'originality' and 'authenticity'.

Crouching Tiger, Hidden Dragon was subtitled on its initial theatrical release in the US, and enjoyed unprecedented box office success for a foreign-language film (Rich 2004: 167).[24] Significantly, this subtitled release was accompanied by a dialogue-free trailer that essentially hid the fact it was a Chinese-language film (158). Dialogue-free trailers for subtitled, foreign-language films began to appear in the mid-1980s and 1990s (see Rich 2004). Ruby B. Rich comments, 'the no-foreign-tongue trailer became a point of entry that Miramax adopted, sanctioned, and would virtually put on steroids for the remainder of the decade, all in the effort to increase the number of bodies (and dollars) for its foreign language films' (159). According to Orion, this somewhat deceptive strategy was necessary in order to forge inroads into the US market, which Rich describes in terms of 'monolingualism and cinematic illiteracy ... prone to global illiteracy' (164).

While Crowther objected to subtitles on the grounds that they ghettoise films within the art circuit, with *Crouching Tiger, Hidden Dragon* the distributors reasoned that, despite its populist address, dubbing might alienate the key demographic for foreign-language film viewing in the US. The results exceeded expectations, with the film 'crossing-over' to audience sectors that typically do not attend subtitled films. However, for Carol O'Sullivan (2011: 105-6), the success of the film's theatrical English-subtitled release needs to be considered in relation to the fact that, although shot in Mandarin, its script was actually written in English by James Schamus (2000) before going through multiple translations back and forth between English and Mandarin. O'Sullivan (2011: 106–9; 119) relates this fact to a growing trend towards the use of partial subtitling (and even pseudo-subtitling) as a means of accruing cultural prestige, thereby highlighting the constructed nature of subtitling's supposed authenticity.[25] Partially subtitled films are those in which some, but not all, dialogue is subtitled. As O'Sullivan (107) explores, the most successful partially subtitled films tend to include subtitles for only one-quarter to a third of a film's dialogue. Pseudo-subtitling describes the process of dialogue development that occurred in *Crouching*, where the script was first written in English, translated into Mandarin and then re-translated back into English subtitles (Schamus 2000). In this case, 'the "source dialogue" of such subtitled speech is in fact the "target dialogue" of the translation' (119). Pseudo-subtitling can also refer to the subtitling of artificial languages, such as the Elvish of the *Lord of the Rings* trilogy (2001–3).

Interestingly, the Miramax English dubbing of *Siu lam juk kau / Shaolin Soccer* (2001) pays tribute to the sloppy dubbing processes characteristic of 1970s Hong Kong action films (see Chute 1988: 34), while also marking and preserving differences in accent between Stephen Chow's lead character and that of Mui played by Wei Zhao. Dubbing himself, Chow's Cantonese accent contrasts with Mui's Mandarin accent dubbed by Bai Ling (Nornes 2007: 224). The unusual effect is 'parodic by design' according to Nornes. 'A brilliant example of abusive dubbing,' he states,

'*Shaolin Soccer* provides a foreignising translation deeply engaged with the sensibility of the creators of the film and its audiences' (224). Notably, however, Brian Hu (2006) interprets Miramax's English dub in a different light, labelling it a form of de-Sinification that was accompanied by re-editing, re-titling and the digital removal of all Chinese script from the film's visuals.[26] Whether one sides with Nornes or Hu on the 'quality' of *Shoalin*'s English dub, this language transfer strategy was not well received by US or Canadian audiences (Pinsker 2005), confirming resistance to dubbing on the part of Anglophone foreign-film viewers.[27]

As Delabastita (1990: 105n2) notes, each count against either subtitling or dubbing can be countered by an inverse claim or evaluation approaching the matter from a different angle. Virgil Grillo and Bruce Kawin (1981: 27–9) are extreme in this regard, suggesting that illegible subtitles (caused by white text on white backgrounds) invoke heightened interest in viewers, creating an 'intense connection' and a form of 'double-consciousness'. More convincingly, Delabastita notes the striking similarity of arguments used to denigrate either subtitling *or* dubbing. Both, for instance, are claimed to destroy an element of 'originality' conceived in terms of either visual or aural purity. Additionally, most arguments in defence can alternate as grounds for attack. Dubbing, for instance, is claimed to be more accessible than subtitling, and hence democratic. However, this mass appeal also fuels charges of commercialism and domestication. A mutually exclusive logic seems to underpin 'for' and 'against' arguments indicating that it is clearly unproductive to attempt any weighing up of pros against cons. As the ongoing nature of this sub versus dub debate demonstrates, such an approach only leads to an extended stalemate or critical impasse. Arguments circle endlessly around varying notions of quality and authenticity fashioned in relation to an impossible ideal of non-translation. Each side of this debate relies upon divergent notions of authenticity, authorship, equivalence, fidelity and originality. Furthermore, they presuppose specific national, class and ethnic contexts, as I go on to explore. In this way, when analysed in detail, the mode-focused, 'macro' nature of the sub/dub split within screen discourse points to the radical instability of the values being debated. In contrast, Translation Studies research into screen translation often hails from countries or regions where either subtitling or dubbing dominates. Within such contexts, there is much scope for exposing the cultural assumptions that underlie authenticity claims.

In challenging art cinema's predilection for subtitling over dubbing, Betz (2009: 48) makes an important aside relating to the issue of nationality, noting that this 'aesthetic distinction' is confined to Anglo-American contexts. In other parts of the world, he notes, sub/dub preferences are not based on aesthetic considerations but depend instead on a country's 'size, wealth or tradition'. In the Nordic states, for example, he describes how 'low-genre films are distributed and exhibited, cheek-by-jowl with art films, in subtitled versions' (48). Indeed, the significance of geography or nationality within screen translation divisions cannot be overstated, and Anglo-American sub/dub politics are largely denatured by consideration of screen translation in other parts of the world. Betz's point is informed by a key strain of Translation Studies research that examines national preferences, identifying certain countries as belonging to either subtitling or dubbing 'camps'. Emerging during the 1960s and 1970s, the 'two camps' theory was cemented in the late 1980s and early 1990s by a spate of qualitative research largely focused on Europe, commissioned by industry bodies such as the European Institute for Media.[28]

In the 1970s, Hans Vöge (1977: 121–4) deferred to national considerations specifically in order to challenge the subjective tenor of pro-dubbing arguments put forth by Caillé and Edmond Cary in a 1960 special issue of translation journal *Babel*.[29] He suggested that Caillé and Cary's defence of dubbing stemmed from their French nationality and consequent cultural habituation to this technique ('the audience is unaccustomed to foreign sounds *because it never hears any*') as France predominantly dubs foreign-language media imports (124). Following Vöge, Translation Studies contributions to the sub/dub debate tended to be less subjective in tone, moving either towards relativised, contextual approaches examining national differences or conversely, towards empirical, data-driven micro-analyses. Both such contributions differ considerably from screen discourse approaches examined above, displacing preoccupations with technical, modal constraints with a focus on national and/or execution issues. In this way, Translation Studies research exposes a range of issues largely overlooked within screen culture's circuitous sub versus dub dynamics.

National Differences

Within Translation Studies, the major European *dubbing* countries are collectively referred to as FIGS, incorporating France, Italy, Germany and Spain. As Gottlieb (1997: 310) explains, 'in the 1930s dubbing became the preferred mode of film translation in the world's big market speech communities'. Throughout Europe and beyond, other countries that predominantly dub foreign-language films often share languages with the FIGS grouping. Austria, for instance, though a relatively small country with upwards of 8.5 million inhabitants, nevertheless belongs to the German-speaking community (over 76 million) and consequently constitutes a dubbing nation (see Lewis et al. 2016). According to Richard Kilborn (1989: 430), 'the larger the language-audience the more likely it is that dubbing can be entertained as a commercial proposition'. Western European *subtitling* countries, on the other hand, include Belgium, Cyprus, Denmark, Finland, Greece, Luxembourg, the Netherlands, Norway, Portugal and Sweden (Luyken et al. 1991: 31; Koolstra et al. 2002: 326; de Linde and Kay 1999: 1). Georg-Michael Luyken et al. (1991: 32) describe subtitling as a cheaper method of screen translation that is typically preferred by smaller (often less wealthy) nations with small language markets. In 1998, Thomas Blomberg of Subtitling International UK claimed the cost of subtitling a hundred films was equivalent to dubbing one (Korman and Seguin 1998: 10). A more conservative estimate is given by Jan-Emil Tveit (2008: 94) that dubbing costs on average around five to ten times as much as subtitling, while Luyken et al. (1991: 105-6) note that costs vary considerably from country to country.

Various theories are put forth within Translation Studies to explain national screen translation preferences. The three most significant factors tend to be a country's economic wealth, the size of its language community and the 'health' of its national film industry based on import/export ratios. Luyken et al. (1991: 32) propose that the size of the language community coupled with its percentage of media imports dictates the choice of method. They conclude that large language communities (in excess of 20 million households) importing under 30 per cent of their film and television content tend to dub, while smaller language communities in countries with a higher percentage of imports tend to subtitle (Luyken et al. 1991: 32, see also Díaz Cintas 1999: 36). Poorer, developing countries with high illiteracy levels complicate the picture. In such situations, a mixture of dubbing and subtitling prevails in an attempt to keep costs at a minimum while ensuring that successful films remain accessible to mass audiences (Luyken et al. 1991: 32).

Theories explaining national preferences make sense up to a point, yet ultimately prove unable to account for the numerous idiosyncrasies that emerge within national attitudes and practices, even within Europe. Many of the former Eastern European countries, for example, directly contradict conclusions based on other European territories. According to Josephine Dries (1994–5: 36), within the so-called 'Eastern bloc', 'where one would expect countries to choose subtitling, being a cheaper, less complex and faster way of language conversion, dubbing is given preference'. Analysing data in relation to television and cinema translation, Dries categorises the Czech Republic, Slovakia, Bulgaria and Hungary as dubbing countries while noting that 'neither of these four countries have a dominant language or a vast audience which, when compared with the Western situation, would "justify" this' (36). Conversely, although one of the largest of the former Eastern European countries, with over 19 million inhabitants, Romania subtitles 90–100 per cent of its television and cinema imports.[30] Within these territories, other anomalies surface: Hungary subtitles 60 per cent of its cinema imports, yet dubs 80 per cent of its foreign-language TV, and, while Poland subtitles all cinema imports, voice-over is used for foreign-language TV (36).[31]

Martine Danan (1991: 606) also contests the notion that national dubbing or subtitling preferences are primarily dependent on economics. She contends that 'the cultural and linguistic identity of a nation' is a major determining factor along with its historical and political contingencies (606). Danan points out that, during the early sound film era in the 1930s, Italy, Germany and Spain were all fascist countries that deployed dubbing as a tool for unification and nation building (611). These countries 'all insisted on having one standardised national language for the sake of national unity, and forbade minority groups to speak their own dialects or languages' (612). In such contexts, Danan (612) argues, dubbing becomes 'an assertion of the supremacy of the national language and its unchallenged political, economic and cultural power'. Whereas subtitles underline foreignness, she claims that dubbing suppresses it, and testifies to a 'dominant nationalistic system'. For Danan, translation preferences reveal 'how a country perceives itself in relation to others' (613).

While country size, wealth and politics certainly impact upon screen translation choices, such explanations can oversimplify matters. Even within the FIGS territories, translation preferences are by no means stable, uncontested or uncomplicated. In Spain, for instance, the dubbing label obscures the linguistic diversity of the region. Here, film and television productions are sometimes dubbed in up to five versions: in Basque, Catalan, Galician, Spanish/Castellaño and Valencian (Zabalbeascoa et al. 2001: 102). While Spanish is spoken by over 400 million worldwide, Catalan is spoken by only around 9 million (Lewis et al. 2016). Nevertheless, Catalonia remains a dubbing region and hence, as Gottlieb (2004: 83) notes, it breaks the rule that 'Western European speech communities with less than 25 million speakers' tend to adopt subtitling over dubbing. Additionally, while dubbing was mandatory in Spain until 1967, the number of commercially released subtitled films has steadily increased over recent decades (see Sokoli 2011: 138–9, and Zabalbeascoa et al. 2001: 105), a trend also commented upon by Jorge Díaz Cintas (2003: 196–9) who notes that many Hollywood films are now available in Spain in either a subtitled or a dubbed version (see also Sokoli 2011: 138-9). According to Jeffrey D. Himpele (2009: 365), in Bolivia Spanish-dubbed films have also now often been replaced by subtitled films, although 'many people in the immigrant and popular classes ... read very little of the subtitles'.

Cees M. Koolstra et al. (2002: 349) note how aesthetic, genre and audience factors significantly affect sub/dub choices, even in countries such as Germany that are typically associated with just one method.[32] Distinctions between television and cinema also come into play. In France, Koolstra et al. (350) report that, although almost all foreign-language television is dubbed, 'about half of the movies are ... subtitled'. In addition, they note, 'younger viewers – in subtitling as well as dubbing countries – seem to be developing a preference for subtitling'. This swing is also reported by director of subtitling at Paris-based LVT Claude Dupey (quoted in Halligan 2000). Shifts are also developing within subtitling countries (see Díaz Cintas 2003: 197). In 2000, for instance, the Mexican Supreme Court declared the mandatory subtitling of films unconstitutional (excluding children's and educational films), following a suit by United International Pictures (UIP), Buena Vista/Columbia TriStar and 20th Century Fox (Tegel 2000: 16). These three US Majors claimed the subtitling statute 'discriminated against the estimated 20 million illiterate Mexicans' (16).[33]

Despite the various complexities that complicate the 'two camps' theory, it nevertheless lends the sub/dub debate a crucial geo-specific inflection, qualifying and diversifying its rehearsal within screen culture through the introduction of a much-needed transnational perspective. Polemical 'for' and 'against' arguments are typically restricted to English-speaking territories such as Australia, Canada, Ireland, the UK and the United States, where mainstream audiences have little exposure to foreign-language media and translation. As Luyken et al. (1991: 32) point out, these territories belong to 'the large Anglophone audiovisual market and are neither classical "subtitling" nor "dubbing" countries, but use these Language Transfer mechanisms as needed and in a mixed manner'. Within this context, the screen translation mix tends to be influenced by genre or audience distinctions and inevitably involves what Nornes (2007: 12) refers to as a 'class dimension'. Surveying British audience attitudes, Kilborn (1989: 432) concludes, 'the more "upmarket" you are, the more likely it is you will express a preference for subtitling'. As Nornes (2007: 12) offers, in Anglophone countries foreign-language film audiences are restricted in size and tend to be 'elite and well educated'. Clearly, Nornes is referring to foreign-language 'art' film audiences, rather than those for foreign exploitation or 'body genre' films, which tend to be dubbed (see Dwyer 2014). This literate and dedicated foreign 'art' film demographic has proved itself willing to endure the additional effort required by subtitles.[34]

The situation in countries that import the majority of their screen content from foreign-language sources is vastly different as translation affects *mainstream* viewing practices. In Belgium, for instance, Philippe Meers (2004: 165–7) notes that local audiences consider American English the film language *par excellence* and tend to attach notions of otherness to domestic productions, considered conspicuously national and geographically bound in comparison to the fluid, transnational 'core' symbolised by US screen culture. A similar effect is noted by Díaz Cintas (2004: 25) in relation to Spain, where translated US films 'occupy a primary position and the Spanish films a secondary position'. As Kilborn (1993: 649) points out, such factors dramatically affect a culture's willingness to engage with foreign-language media by influencing the 'general esteem in which foreign languages and cultures are held'. Hence, Kilborn distinguishes Britain's 'characteristically insular mind-set' from the 'more enlightened attitudes' that prevail in 'many European countries'.

Evaluating Execution

Typically, Translation Studies has sought to distance itself from 'subjective judgments' through a focus on 'objective criteria' and empirical studies (Mailhac 2000: 129). Often, this type of research echoes the contrastive dynamics that characterise screen discourse debates, comparing specific instances of subtitling and dubbing to each other or to 'originals', in order to assess losses (Ramière 2010: 103–4). This approach tends to mix macro and micro issues, taking execution factors into consideration alongside modal, technical constraints while sometimes extending to national considerations. In two insightful articles on the sub/dub debate, Richard Kilborn (1989; 1993) considers a range of modal, national and empirical factors, surveying British and European broadcasting policy on foreign-language programming. Koolstra et al. (2002: 347) note that, even when not addressed directly, national factors can influence mode-based approaches behind-the-scenes. Notably, much Translation Studies scholarship on screen translation hails from Europe, and dubbing supporters are often (although not always) based in FIGS countries. As Koolstra et al. comment, 'the effect of habituation' surfaces in analytic approach as much as viewing practices (see also Vöge 1977).

In spite of the perils of habituation and national conditioning, execution-based, data-driven contributions to the sub/dub debate are useful for dismantling cultural assumptions by putting them to the test (see Koolstra et al. 2002). The supposed authenticity of subtitling, for instance, is challenged by Jean-Pierre Mailhac's (2000) detailed textual analysis of the English subtitling and dubbing of *Gazon maudit / French Twist* (1995). Mailhac's research reveals that subtitling weakened the film's 'colloquial, slangy and strong language' in 46 cases, compared to 27 cases in which dubbing did the same (144). These findings lead him to conclude that a 'film can actually suffer a great deal more in a subtitled version than it would in a sympathetically dubbed version' (151). Hence, his modal preference for dubbing is based upon empirical evaluation of execution factors. He contends that subtitling *per se* is unable to adequately represent linguistic diversity and fast speech. Mailhac also argues that subtitling is less likely to retain the 'original' tone and force of much dialogue (especially vulgarisms and colloquialisms) and that it regularly elides representations of cultural and linguistic diversity.

Mailhac's findings echo those of Thomas Herbst (1997) and Miguel Mera (1999), both based in FIGS countries, who claim that subtitles frequently reduce 'original' dialogue by around 50 per cent and are hence *less* respectful and *less* faithful than dubbing. According to Mera (1999: 83), dubbing actually lends itself to 'more accurate translations' than subtitling because it does not require this same degree of condensation. Comparing the Spanish dubbed version of *Braveheart* (1995) to its 'original' English version, Mera finds little semantic variation (84). He concludes that dubbing as a technique tends to preserve more of the 'original' dialogue than subtitling and consequently, offers a more textually faithful mode of translation. Moreover, Mera challenges the dominant tendency to view subtitling as additive (see Delabastita 1990: 102), proposing, instead, that it is subtitling not dubbing that *subtracts* (78) by removing large portions of a film's dialogue. Contrary to dubbing, moreover, he points out that, with subtitling, no substitution occurs to fill in the blanks left in subtitling's wake. According to Mera's data, in the English subtitling of *El angel exterminador / The Exterminating Angel* (1962), 'almost half of the "literal" dialogue is lost' (77). While subtitle subtractions may appear minor on a line-by-line basis, Mera argues that the cumulative effect is dramatic (78). In this way, his findings directly oppose the common perception that dubbing erases where subtitling preserves (see Bordwell and Thompson 2004: 388).

Curiously, despite his findings, Mera (1999: 83) concludes that subtitling is better suited to 'truth genres' such as news reportage and documentaries, and that dubbing is most suited to entertainment and action films. Hence, he advocates for subtitling in instances when fidelity and authenticity are at a premium, despite demonstrating that it is less textually faithful than dubbing. This contradictory argument also rehearses another common tendency within translation scholarship to supposedly 'resolve' the sub/dub dilemma by advocating for a case-by-case approach. Kilborn (1993), Díaz Cintas (1999), Mera (1999), Koolstra et al. (2002), Tveit (2008) and Paola Guardini (1998) all suggest that the choice between subtitling and dubbing should be made on a case-by-case basis, depending on what type of media content is being translated, for what purpose, and with which audiences in mind. For these scholars, the case-by-case approach is more impartial and objective than blanket forms of judgement based on mode alone. In practice, however, this approach is rarely less evaluative, prejudiced or prescriptive than others.

Guardini (1998: 91) advocates for subtitling as a better method of translation for 'genres in which the source language expression is vital, such as drama'. Subtitling better suits such genres, she argues, because it 'respects the source target text by not erasing any element of it', whereas dubbing institutes a destructive splitting between the 'original' visuals and the translated sounds (110). For Tveit (2008: 95–6) also, genre needs to be taken into account, as does the target audience. He proposes that, in most cases, subtitling is superior to dubbing, except in relation to media aimed at small children, documentaries narrated by off-screen voices and fast-paced content that is dialogue-heavy (95–6). Kilborn (1993: 657), on the other hand, advocates for a flexible mixing of subtitling and dubbing modes 'within a single programme if necessary', as do Koolstra et al. (2002: 349), while Díaz Cintas (1999: 38) maintains, optimistically, that different subtitled and dubbing options should *both* be made available for viewing publics to choose between.

Case-by-case, hybrid and conjunctive approaches to Audiovisual Translation (AVT) often purport to 'resolve' the sub/dub split. Díaz Cintas (1999: 38) claims that the combination of subtitling *and* dubbing effectively ends any dilemma. However, far from avoiding reductionist evaluations or resolving split dynamics, such an approach often reintroduces into Translation Studies the kinds of value judgements and subjective arguments that characterised some 1960s and 1970s approaches. Mera (1999: 38), Tveit (2008: 95) and Guardini (1998: 110), for example, all suggest that subtitling is, ultimately, more authentic than dubbing, reverting to a type of generalist, mode-based evaluation common within screen culture attitudes. Consequently, they all maintain that subtitling is best suited to certain genres and formats over others. However, while Mera argues that subtitles are best suited to news, documentary and 'art' films, Tveit and Guardini disagree. For Tveit (2008: 95), documentaries are better served by dubbing, while Guardini (1998: 91) advocates primarily for the subtitling of dramas, claiming that in this genre, 'source language expression is vital'. The lack of cohesion between these case-by-case conclusions forcefully indicates how differently values of authenticity are interpreted and applied. Ultimately, these case-by-case approaches are based in value judgements indistinguishable from those of more 'emotionally loaded "dubbing vs. subtitling" discussions' (see Gottlieb 2004: 86).

The contradiction at the heart of Mera's (1999) position is particularly interesting. Despite his findings that subtitling is less faithful and less accurate than dubbing due to the unavoidable degree of condensation it requires, Mera proposes nevertheless that 'news and documentary programs would generally be more credible if they were subtitled', as would 'art' films 'aimed at the intellectual minority'. His paradoxical position that subtitles are *less* faithful yet, at the same time, *perceived as being more* faithful and hence credible, exposes how values of authenticity are less related to fact than fiction. Sitting uncomfortably alongside his empirical discrediting of subtitling, Mera's ultimate validation of this technique (for 'serious', credible content) begins to resemble an imported value that doesn't quite ring true. In this regard, I position Mera's approach as indicative of broad trans/national shifts currently affecting screen translation practices, as subtitling gains ground in traditional dubbing territories across the globe, as I go on to explain.

According to Fionnuala Halligan (2000: 12), 'the US majors are gradually trying to change European habits and periodically blanket subtitle the entire region'. Admittedly, within a global context, subtitling's advance remains minimal, considering that dubbing is preferred by the world's two leading language communities (in terms of native speakers): Chinese and Spanish (Lewis et al. 2016). Nevertheless, changes in national AVT preferences have been reported by a number of scholars including Kilborn (1993), Koolstra et al. (2002), Díaz Cintas (2003), Tveit (2008) and Pedersen (2011). One major factor affecting swings towards subtitling is the continuing growth of English as a second language, which proceeds hand in hand with decreases in the percentages of native English speakers (Graddol 2006: 60–3). As Gottlieb (2004: 85) pithily summarises the situation, 'English has established itself as a second language – a brother tongue rather than mother tongue – to the educated masses of the modern world'.

As increasing numbers of younger generations display a partial knowledge of English, the subtitling of English-language media becomes a more practical option as partial knowledge of English mitigates losses resulting from subtitle condensation (Gottlieb 2004: 85; Adamou and Knox 2011: 10). Additionally, subtitles can aid language acquisition and therefore appeal to language learners (Gottlieb 2004: 88; Tveit 2008: 93). Clearly, screen translation practices and preferences are thoroughly entangled in the emerging language politics of the global era. Gottlieb (2004: 83–4) explains that, along with the global adoption of English as a second language, Anglophone cultural values and tastes are also being transferred. The notion that subtitles are authentic, that they preserve rather than destroy the foreign, and, consequently, that they are best suited to art films, along with other 'serious' genres, has now migrated to many parts of the world. Gottlieb refers to this as a 'semi-conscious linking of art movies and subtitles' (84).

Notably, as subtitling is becoming increasingly prominent within traditional dubbing territories, this method is also experiencing unprecedented levels of popularity on multiplex screens, having become 'all but an unmarked norm' within mainstream UK and US screen media (O'Sullivan 2011: 109). According to O'Sullivan, the prevalence of subtitles within Anglophone screen culture has now reached 'epidemic' proportions, signalling increasing global awareness of linguistic diversity and multiculturalism (107–9). As the British Council reports, global communications media (such as news reportage and the Internet) are becoming increasingly multilingual and diverse, as languages such as Chinese, Spanish and Arabic begin to challenge the traditional dominance of English as a global *lingua franca* (Graddol 2006: 45–7). For O'Sullivan (2011: 130–2), however, the increasing presence of subtitles on mainstream Anglophone screens does not necessarily entail a greater openness to foreign languages and cultures. Rather, she draws attention to the way in which the specific types of subtitling being privileged (which she refers to as 'pre-subtitling') might actually 'close down ... active listening to foreign-language dialogue' (130) and perpetuate linguistic stereotyping (132).

As O'Sullivan (2011: 116) explains, the current popularity of subtitles on Anglophone screens is largely confined to forms of pre-subtitling, where subtitles are envisioned from an early stage as integral to the narrative or diegesis. In such cases, subtitles indicate the presence of language difference in the story or screen world being depicted, rather than at the point of distribution (as with 'post-subtitling'). Hence, the increase of subtitles at the multiplex does not indicate any increase in the number of foreign-language films being shown. Rather, it demonstrates an increase in the representation of heterolingual or multilingual *themes* within mainstream English-language productions. For O'Sullivan, this change registers foremost the increasing *prestige* of subtitles, which exceeds their practical use-value. Typical forms of pre-subtitling include 'partial subtitling' and 'pseudo-subtitling', which, according to O'Sullivan (200), 'build on audiences' thirst for authenticity combined with a perceived greater tolerance for partially subtitled films, or at least for subtitling as a decorative device'. For O'Sullivan, the differences between pre- and post-subtitling are crucial and deeply political. Specifically, pre-subtitling practices tend to eliminate the losses and reductions that are, to a degree, inevitable within post-subtitling, as the scripts on which they are based are generally written in the target language of the translation (119–20).

O'Sullivan's analysis of pre- and post-subtitling highlights the authenticating role that subtitles increasingly play on Anglophone screens, confirming and cementing this traditional Anglophone association. She points out how subtitling is deployed primarily to add *value* rather than *function* to screen productions. Partial subtitles do this in a particularly economic way, enabling Anglophone viewers to 'have it both ways': to enjoy the authenticating status of subtitles without having to actually spend much time reading and processing them. Ultimately, this Anglophone, mainstream 'sea change in linguistic representation' only affirms the complications and centrality of screen translation's value politics. It also provides insight into Mera's case-by-case approach and the implication within his argument that the *perception* of accuracy is more important than its achievement. This conclusion betrays his investment in subtitling not as an authentic, 'quality' practice but, rather, as a *sign* of authenticity – a view that is currently being projected on mainstream, multiplex screens around the world. As subtitling gains in popularity across traditional dubbing regions, more and more cultures invest in this Anglophone value system, repeating unchallenged the association between subtitling and authenticity.

Battling On

In many ways, screen translation constitutes a battlefield, with war continuing to rage between its two dominant modes: subtitling and dubbing. This battle is at once historic and current, figurative and practical. It is also culturally specific. In the past, screen culture sub/dub debates have been most vocal in Western, English-speaking contexts where neither method is entrenched. Over the last couple of decades however, this situation has changed, as screen translation preferences have become more fluid and mixed, even in countries recognised as subtitling and dubbing strongholds (Dìaz Cintas 2003: 196; O'Sullivan 2011: 198–200). Globalising impulses add to the complexities of ongoing sub/dub splits, as Anglo-based associations between subtitling and authenticity spread to other parts of the world (Gottlieb 2004: 83–4). In this chapter, I have argued that the sub/dub mindset needs to be examined in depth, and attention paid to its fracturing effects as it factionalises screen culture and divides nations. The Translation Studies approach to this debate provides a useful degree of contextualisation, bringing both national and execution issues into frame.

Despite its ostensible search for quality, the sub/dub debate functions to cement translation's negative dynamics, enforcing acts of devaluation and resulting in unproductive impasse. As Dìaz Cintas (2003: 201) offers, the 'debate on the relative advantages of dubbing versus subtitling has been the subject of excessive academic interest but has not made any significant contribution to progress in the field'. Continuing to dominate current attitudes and approaches to screen translation, this divisive split demonstrates the significance of limitation, dysfunction and excess within screen translation discourse and practice. As O'Sullivan demonstrates, elements of loss and dysfunction (such as delay) are inbuilt within processes of translation and it is unrealistic to expect either subtitling or dubbing to overcome such obstacles. Such expectations result in excessive performances of pseudo-translation that doubly remove audiences from authentic experiences of the foreign.

Notes

1. Notably, certain foreign-language films and television programmes *were* being dubbed and receiving wide circulation: namely, 'low cultural' content such as Hong Kong martial arts films, spaghetti westerns, Japanese animation and exploitation films – or art films repackaged as exploitation, a fate that met *Les yeux sans visage / Eyes without a Face* (1959) which debuted in the US in 1962 as *The Horror Chamber of Doctor Faustus*, playing in a 'dubbed, mangled version' on a double bill with US–Japanese co-production *The Manster* (1959) (Hawkins 2000).
2. Thomas Rowe (1960: 117): 'Most Italian pictures are so indifferently post-synched in the original version that any relationship between what the actors are saying and what their lips are doing sometimes appears little more than sheer coincidence.'
3. Additionally, Italy's dubbing mandate reflected that in 1931, 21.6 per cent of the population was illiterate (Guardini 1998: 93).
4. In the US, the film was also known as *The Champagne Murders*.
5. On Multiple Language Versions (MLVs), see Ginette Vincendeau (1988), Natasa Durovicová (1992), Joseph Garncarz (1999), Chris Wahl (2007; 2016), Lisa Jarvinen (2012), Tessa Dwyer (2005; 2016b) and Andrew Higson (2010).
6. In 1968, Fellini was one of five Italian directors (including De Sica and

Leone) who defended dubbing as a means of cinematic expression (see Guardini 1998: 94). These directors joined a lively debate that had been raging within the Italian film community for numerous decades, at least since Antonioni's article 'Vita impossibile del signor Clark Costa' appeared in 1940 (see Sisto 2010: 87). In 1967, Antonioni was amongst fourteen filmmakers who presented a manifesto at the Amalfi *Filmcritica* conference against the 'post-synchronisation of Italian films' and the 'dubbing and translation of foreign films' (quoted in Geoffrey Nowell-Smith 1968: 145).

7. For exceptions, see Betz (2009: 50), Abé Mark Nornes (2007: 10–16), Kerry Seagrave (2004: 144–7) and Fausto Pauluzzi (1983).

8. Hamid Naficy (2006) reports, for instance, how Iran's dubbing industry helped foster local productions.

9. Clara Cerón's (2001) research into subtitle punctuation constitutes an extreme instance of such micro-preoccupation.

10. For exceptions, see Luis Pérez González (2007), Patrick Chaume Varela (1997) and Patrick Zabalbeascoa (1997).

11. See Henrik Gottlieb (2004: 86), Cees M. Koolstra et al. (2002: 328) and Miguel Mera (1999: 77). Herman Weinberg (1948) explains how his job entailed firstly deciding which dialogue to translate ('usually at least 85 per cent') before beginning 'the job of boiling lines of a foreign tongue down into bits of English', after which the subtitles were submitted to censors and industry regulators, usually resulting in further cuts.

12. Similar temporal disjuncture can surface within dubbing when lip movements become out-of-sync. See Lori Myers (1973), István Fodor (1976, 21), Rowe (1960, 117). On lip-sync and digital morphing technologies see Wehn 2001: 70.

13. A similar effect occured in the English subtitles for Godard's *Sauve la vie (qui peut) / Slow Motion* (1980), rendering 'readable what was barely audible, even for native French speakers, in the original' (Shohat and Stam 1985: 47n23).

14. On multilingualism in screen translation, see Berger and Komori (2010).

15. At the 2006 Melbourne International Film Festival, *Linda Linda Linda* was screened in a subtitled version that differentiated between Korean and Japanese language through the use of parentheses. On the loss of regional accents in subtitling and the use of italics to indicate foreign dialogue, see Jean-Pierre Mailhac (2000).

16. On representing language diversity in dubbing, see Lu Danjun (2009), Mailhac (2000), John Sanderson (2010), Patrick Zabalbeasco and Montse Corrius (2012) and Patrick Zabalbeasco and Elena Voellmer (2014).

17. On filmic representations of interpreters, see Carol O'Sullivan (2011: 3).

18. See Dwyer (2005) and Wendy Haslem (2004). On the thematic of translation in *Contempt*, see Joanna Paul (2008).

19. On dubbing within sound engineering, see Elizabeth Weis (1995) and Sandra Pauletto (2012).

20. As Antje Aschied (1997: 35) notes (citing Barbara Godard), both dubbing and literary translation are unimodal and substitutive, which facilitates the 'elimination of self-reflexive elements'.

21. A major exception is when subtitles become 'a source of play', as in films such as *Wakiki Wabbit* (1943), *Man on Fire* (2004), *Austin Powers: Goldmember* (2002) and *The Imposters* (1998), where subtitles enter the diegetic space of the narrative (see O'Sullivan 2011, 160–5). At times, even post-production subtitles are treated in a playful, creative fashion, as with *Film Socialisme* (2010) (see Bréan 2011) and the theatrical Anglophone release of *Nochnoi dozor / Night Watch* (2004) (see Kofoed 2011).

22. On screen voice and authenticity, see Mary Ann Doane (1980; 1985).

23. Steve Ross (2001) reports that *Crouching* had a mixed reception in Asia, doing well in Singapore and Taiwan, but not in Korea, Japan, Hong Kong and Mainland China.

24. According to Beth Pinsker (2005), the film made more than $128 million, adding that 'most subtitled films even most independent films never crack $1 million'. Rich (2004: 167) reports slightly higher takings. On Ang Lee's decision to use Mandarin rather than Cantonese, see Christina Klein (2004).

25. O'Sullivan (2011: 116) makes an important distinction between pre-subtitling ('where subtitling is envisioned from early in production') and 'conventional post-subtitling at the point of distribution'. Both 'partial subtitling' and 'pseudo-subtitling' are common types of pre-subtitling that arise from narrative representations of language difference.

26. Brian Hu (2006) notes that 'under pressure from fans, the title was changed back and the English dub was scrapped in favour of English subtitles'. See John Williams (2009) on historical techniques of foreign text removal and 'dissolve translation'.

27. According to Pinsker (2005), Miramax released 'a dubbed version in Canada and a subtitled one in the United States a few months later. The Canadian experiment worked out so poorly that it may just be the English-language industry's last attempt at dubbing and the US release made only $500,000.'

28. For research commissioned by the European Institute for the Media, see Roland Hindmarsh and Georg-Michael Luyken (1986), Georg-Michael Luyken et al. (1991) and Josephine Dries (1994–5).

29. On 1960s/1970s Translation Studies research into sub/dub questions, see Jorge Díaz Cintas (1999: 35).

30. On Romanian screen translation (official and informal), see also Tessa Dwyer and Ioana Uricaru (2009).

31. In Poland, voice-over actors often become *bona fide* stars, attracting large followings. Tomasz Knapik is one of the most famous Polish voice-over stars; his voice instantly recognisable to viewers throughout the country (Wagstyl 2006).

32. Thomas Herbst (1996, 103) notes that, in Germany, 'the *arte* channel has

become a valuable and notable exception' to the dubbing rule. See also Miika Blinn (2008).

33. Notably, Mexican TV broadcasting is dubbed. See Simeon Tegel (2000).

34. In subtitling regions, audiences quickly adapt to subtitle processing, with no additional cognitive effort required, as distinct from Anglophone contexts where they are largely unaccustomed to this device. See Dirk Delabastita (1990), Keith Rayner (1998), Cees M. Koolstra et al. (2002), Gottlieb (2004) and Marie-Josée Bisson et al. (2014).

CHAPTER 2

Vanishing Subtitles:
The Invisible Cinema (1970–4)

Opening on 1 December 1970 to launch the foundation of New York's Anthology Film Archives, the Invisible Cinema was utterly unique in its design, programme and philosophy. In a review for *Vogue* magazine, Barbara Rose (1971: 70) described its seating bank as nothing short of 'revolutionary'. Meanwhile, Anthology declared it the 'first true Cinema', positioning it as the centrepiece of its 'film museum exclusively devoted to the *film as an art*' (Sitney 1975: vi–viii). The cinema featured ritualised, cyclic screenings of a handpicked selection of 'essential' viewing comprising 'monuments of cinematic art' (v). Within this reverential space,

Figure 2.1 Launch of the Invisible Cinema with (left to right) Paul Morrissey, Michel Auder and Andy Warhol. Photograph by Gretchen Berg. © Gretchen Berg and Anthology Film Archives.

anything considered extraneous to a formalist avant-garde appreciation of 'pure' cinema was eradicated or, at the least, minimised as far as possible to the point of invisibility – whence its name. Such impurities ranged from banter between audience members to commercialism of any kind (hence, largely excluding narrative cinema) to the violations of dubbing and subtitling. The Invisible Cinema's blanket rejection of screen translation methods exceeds the binary logic of the sub versus dub debate canvassed in Chapter 1. Moreover, the rationale behind this rejection appears far removed from Bosley Crowther's anti-subtitle campaign of the previous decade. Rather than making foreign-language films accessible for a mass public, Anthology's uncompromising insistence upon untranslated foreign 'originals' seems almost engineered to alienate and exclude a general audience. In an interview with Stanley Eichelbaum (1971), Anthology's Jonas Mekas conceded that the Invisible Cinema's no-subtitles policy had met with some complaints, retorting: 'but we're not concerned with the audience. We're interested in film.' By banning both dubbing and subtitling Anthology instituted a strict division between production and reception, clearly prioritising the former over the later. Admittedly, the Invisible Cinema obsessed over the act of reception, even attempting to foster a suitable 'posture' for film contemplation (Sitney 1975: viii). However, this focus on reception was solely concerned with reducing its impact on the film itself as hallowed object, curtailing the contamination of film 'art' via extra-filmic elements such as the audience. In a nutshell, the act, context and agent of reception were to be made 'invisible' in order to ensure the untainted purity of film. Annette Michelson (1998: 5) notes that even the historically accurate practice of providing musical accompaniment for silent films was strictly forbidden at the Invisible Cinema, 'on the grounds that such accompaniment – including that of specially or originally commissioned scores – had been primarily the response to the demands of exhibitors, and not necessarily structurally intrinsic to the author's filmic project'.

Providing a colourful conclusion to the sub/dub debates of the preceding decade, the Invisible Cinema's public denouncement of screen translation *as a whole* produces a moment of crystallisation, making it possible to see – almost in petrified form – a number of converging interests, attitudes, prejudices and practices. The crystal that is formed in this unique cultural-historical moment points foremost to the productive, transformative power of translation – to its socio-cultural impact beyond the linguistic, communicative realm. This chapter examines the Invisible Cinema and its extremist, zero-translation screenings in order to demonstrate how Anglo-American film culture (whether alternative or mainstream) deploys the inevitable flaws of dubbing and subtitling to excuse and defend widespread disengagement from language difference and translation in general. It proceeds by first detailing the disappearing act that the Invisible Cinema performed on screen translation, along with the various effects this disappearance wrought on foreign-language films and their reception. It then proceeds to consider how Anthology utilised issues of translation to define and cement its own aesthetic and ideological position. Ultimately, despite its strategy of differentiation, striking similarities emerge between the Invisible Cinema's radical rejection of translation and less severe instances of mainstream resistance.

Throughout this discussion, notions of failure continually surface. Motivated by the supposed inadequacies of both dubbing and subtitling, Anthology's no-translation screening policy was largely scrapped following the Invisible Cinema's demise in 1974, remaining in relic form only. Today, foreign-language films included in Anthology's Essential Cinema repertory tend to be screened both with and without subtitles. Audiences can pick and choose which format they prefer. Outside the Essential Cinema collection however, foreign-language films are screened with English subtitles. In part, the end of the Invisible Cinema and the unique vision for which it stood signals the gap separating ideas from their realisation. To its credit, Anthology proactively set out to bridge this gap, seeking to produce a new mode of 'practical criticism' (Sitney 1975: vi). Conceived as the embodiment or physical manifestation of Anthology's critical position, the Invisible Cinema constituted an integral part of this plan. It was here that formalist film avant-garde concepts could be put to practical effect. Yet, processes of actualisation necessarily involve transformation and re-routing. While the Invisible Cinema's ban on screen translation presented a forceful statement in support of its purist vision, when put to the test this policy failed on numerous fronts, frustrating audience members and compromising Anthology's corollary aim to raise the visibility and impact of experimental film, growing audiences via the availability of regular, affordable screenings (see Alfaro 2012b: 45–6).[1]

Ironically, the Invisible Cinema's denunciation of both dubbing and subtitling had a reverse-effect. Instead of demonstrating the *in*essential nature of translation for film, this radical, zero-tolerance policy ultimately demonstrated the ongoing indispensability of translation to this first global, mass medium. If anything, the Invisible Cinema threw the spotlight *on to* translation not away from it, while its anti-subtitling stance proved short-lived and unsustainable. Although translation-free screenings do persist at Anthology, preserved in fossilised form as an optional mode of viewing some Essential Cinema films only, subtitles have wreaked their revenge, becoming a mainstay of its feature programming. Hence, the Invisible Cinema's failed legacy is that today translation remains the critical factor in distinguishing 'essential' from 'non-essential', regular programming.

Disappearing Act

Setting out to redefine 'the essentials of the film experience' (Sitney 1975: vi), the Invisible Cinema constituted a ninety-seat screening space designed by Austrian experimental filmmaker Peter Kubelka, also a founding member of Anthology and part of its selection committee. As its name suggests, the Invisible Cinema sought to 'practically not be there'. According to Kubelka (1974: 32), 'an ideal cinema should not at all be felt'. Rather, all feeling or sensation should occur in response to the film and all attention be devoted exclusively to the screen. Anthology's manifesto declared that the 'viewer should not have any sense of the presence of walls or the size of the auditorium. He should have only the white screen, isolated in darkness as his guide to scale and distance' (Sitney 1971: vii). To this end, the Invisible Cinema sought to stage its own disappearance through a range of technical and interior design innovations that aimed to direct all attention 'on the filmic image and sound, without distractions' (vii). 'In a cinema', states Kubelka (1974: 32), 'one shouldn't be aware of the architectural space, so that the film can completely dictate the sensation of space'.

To achieve this ideal of non-presence, the Invisible Cinema took standard blackening procedures to the extreme. Seats, ceilings and walls were all lined in black velvet, the floor in black carpet and 'doors and everything else were painted black' (Kubelka 1974: 32). On the *Cinema Treasures* website, cinemagoer Gerald A. DeLuca (2004) recalls the 'all-black, side-partitioned seating', which for Stan Brakhage (quoted in Sitney 2005: 108) created an effect of 'drifting in a black space, a black box, and black ahead of you, nothing visible except the screen'. Inside, a strong white lamp directed audiences towards this unadorned, illuminated screen. Kubelka clarifies that the 'cinema had ... no curtains in front of the screen, as, unlike most film spaces, it was not conceived as an imitation of theatre' (32). All architectural features were removed apart from some large cast-iron columns that proved too solid for the sledgehammer (Sitney 2005: 35), as well as exit signs above the doors that Kubelka (35) felt compromised the overall design. Finally, by far the most controversial and emblematic aspect of the Invisible Cinema was its seating bank. Steeply raked to ensure unencumbered sight lines, seating rows comprised

Figure 2.2 The Invisible Cinema's emblematic seating pods. Photograph by Michael Chikiris. © unknown.

head-height side partitions that encased viewers in a wooden surround. As Rose (1971) reports, these 'unique viewing facilities ... caused as much controversy as the highly selective group of works assembled as a kind of canon of pure film art'.

The Invisible Cinema's partitioned seating pods sought to shield audience members from their neighbours, both visually and aurally, in order to heighten concentration on the film. For Kubelka (1974: 34), this seating arrangement fostered the creation of a 'sympathetic community' in which one was aware of others yet not disturbed by them. 'Isolated visually,' notes Michelson (1998: 5), 'the viewer could establish minimal tactile contact with her neighbor's hand, but aurally, one was well insulated, with structure and materials inhibiting conversation and effectively muffling all sound from sources other than that of the screen'. Complementing its ritualised, program of Essential Cinema, this seating design was based on the principle that 'one responds to the anticipation of art with a different posture than to the expectation of an entertainment' (Sitney 1975: viii). *Vogue* art critic Rose (1971) expressed her approval: 'I find the viewing situation at Anthology the best I have ever experienced ... The concentration permitted by such a seating arrangement lends a particular degree of both intensity and abstraction to the film experience that the self-conscious works shown at Anthology appear to demand.'[2]

In addition to subduing unwelcome noises from other audience members, the seating pods were designed to amplify sounds emitted from the centre of the screen, mimicking hearing devices used during World War II resembling 'big ears' (Kubelka 1974: 32). The wooden encasings 'concentrated the sound coming in directly from the screen and subdued sounds coming from other directions in the room, thereby creating a maximum of silence within which the sound from the film would be undiluted'. For Kubelka (qtd in Thompson 1970), the 'isolated seat, like a handcupped ear, simply directs and connects the spectator to the screen, ruling out interferences'. Evidently, Anthology recognised both image *and sound* as essential components of film art. The absorbent coverings used throughout the interior also served an acoustic purpose by enhancing sound insulation, while state-of-the-art equipment included 'remote control of focus and sound so that the manager ... [could] ... ensure optimal quality from his seat in the house' (Sitney 1975: viii) which was equipped with a direct telephone link to the projection booth (Sitney 2005: 35).

As part and parcel of its commitment to purity, this 'best conditions' (Sitney 1975: vi) cinema refused to screen films that were either dubbed or subtitled, denouncing translated prints as 'defaced' copies (viii):

> One of the essential principles put forward by Anthology Film Archives is the presentation of film in *absolutely* original versions, without dubbing or subtitles. Synopses will be provided for the audience when necessary. At first a few films will be shown in their titled versions, but these will be replaced as soon as arrangements can be made for the undefaced copies. It is possible to see the subtitled prints of many of the films in our collection in the commercial theatres throughout the country. But where else can one see the film exactly as the author made it? There is a sacrifice involved in the substitution of the purity of the image for the sense of the words, but it is a necessary one.

Evidently, dubbing and subtitling were understood by Anthology as strictly post-production devices, completely inessential to the primary process of filmmaking. Considered extraneous to the essence of film and destructive of its visual and/or aural purity, they were no more welcomed in the theatre than the sound of crunching popcorn. As Mekas put it, subtitles 'destroy the rhythm and form of a film' (qtd in Eichelbaum 1971: 140). Although in many ways a spectacle in its own right, the unique design of the Invisible Cinema – at once both minimal and hyperbolic – ostensibly sought to eliminate anything that might distract and thus detract from the film as the filmmaker intended it to be shown. Since 'the author works for the eye and the ear of the beholder,' states Kubelka (1974: 32), 'it is evident that no other visual or acoustic signals, other than those planned by the film's author, should reach the beholder'. Dubbing and subtitling techniques were seen as a concession to the desire of the audience over and above that of the filmmaker. In contradistinction, Anthology declared itself a museum to film art and deified the name of the author-*auteur* above all else, operating much like a temple of worship (Michelson 1998: 5).

Despite this strict ruling against dubbing and subtitling, translation of a sort persisted at the Invisible Cinema nevertheless. Translations of foreign-language dialogue and/or inter-titling were prepared in-house as typed, print synopses. Reminiscent of silent film days when synopses might be posted in the cinema lobby in lieu of a lecturer or narrator (Bowser 1990: 19), this practice sought to effect a form of 'invisible' translation, banishing it from the visual and acoustic terrain of screenings and relegating it instead to the extra-filmic space of the page. Evidently, print synopses were seen to offer means of translation that did not compete or otherwise interfere with the audio-visual domain of film itself, as the printed pages would have surely been illegible in the dramatically darkened conditions of the cinema. In effect, Anthology's synopses sought to render subtitles as invisible as the cinema's blackened co-ordinates, shifting them from the illuminated space of the screen to the dim obscurity of the page.

As many of the foreign-language films screened at the Invisible Cinema belonged to the silent era, synopses often constituted translated transcripts of film inter-titles. A number of these transcripts remain on file at Anthology, including one prepared for Dziga Vertov's *Shagai, Soviet! / Stride, Soviet!* (1926), signed by Matt Sliwowski (n.d.), that announces itself a 'translation of the titles as they appear in the film'. In the 'Translator's Note', Sliwowski stresses the effort he has taken 'to retain the original graphic design and word order to the maximum'. Fidelity to the source material is obviously a primary concern, as one would expect from a translation prepared under the auspices of Anthology. Sliwowski goes to great lengths to preserve the visual poetry of the inter-titles by retaining elements of layout and capitalisation. In this regard, the transcript faithfully captures the way in which the film's inter-titles underscore the graphic and aural materiality of language, experimenting with textual composition while introducing tonal difference via the mix of uppercase and lowercase letters. Sliwowski also retains Russian-language syntax where possible and uses parentheses to indicate words added 'to make the English translation more clear'. Caption 13, for instance, reads: 'and [when] the steam HEATING operates'.

At several points, Sliwowski (n.d.) adds a brace bracket [}] by hand to indicate 'captions which come in a series without any image in between'.

The need for such a strategy and accompanying notation results from the qualitative difference that exists between the multimodality of the audio-visual and the singular, static entity of the page. Had the translations appeared on screen in the form of subtitles or intertitles, this cumbersome textual device would not have been necessary. At one point in the film, a pile of books is being burned. Part of a book title is obscured and Sliwowski indicates this omission by inserting a question mark in parentheses: '(?...) of the Old Testament'. This use of brackets and symbols repeatedly exposes the means of production, interrupting the translation's flow and highlighting the translator's agency. By preserving the original word order, the English titles are made to sound unfamiliar, as in captions 22 ('somewhere / a horse fallen / from hunger') and 23 ('somewhere / dies a camel / covered with / snow'). While some concessions are made to the norms of the target language, these are clearly marked so that any alteration to the 'original' can be identified. Clearly, this transcript aims towards a literal, word-for-word fidelity to its source, and seeks to provide an experience of foreignness over and above familiarity. The alienating effect of foreign word order combined with highlighting of the translator's mediating role disrupts the text's overall fluency. The reader is continually reminded of the very fact of translation. In this way, although making translation 'vanish' during film screenings, the Invisible Cinema foregrounded it within these in-house synopses. Sliwowski's careful, foreignising translation provides a key for decoding Anthology's mixed approach to foreign-language films and film viewing.

Sound/Side Effects

While the exaggerated darkness inside the Invisible Cinema prevented patrons from reading synopses during screenings, nevertheless Anthology committee member Ken Kelman identifies 'rattling papers' as a characteristic sound within the screening space (Sitney 2005: 34). By making it a matter of policy to issue audiences with typed translation transcripts, an unintended rustling noise resulted. The materiality of these translation transcripts is noted in a *New York Times* review by Howard Thompson (1970), who comments on the 'predominantly young, casually clad and near capacity' audience that the cinema attracted for Aleksandr Dovzhenko's first sound film *Ivan* (1932): '[c]lutching a synopsis and credits they tested the unconventional-looking seats a bit tentatively'. Kelman goes so far as to suggest that rather than subduing the extraneous sounds of rustling papers, the unique design of the cinema actually 'made it worse' as 'noises bounced around a little' (quoted in Sitney 2005: 34). It seems that the act

of removing translation from the screen to ensure the absolute 'originality'
of the cinema's images and sounds produced an unintentional side/sound
effect, with rattling papers compromising Kubelka's (1974: 32) ideal
'maximum of silence'. As one impurity is traded for another, we glimpse
the distance separating concept and realisation.

Even in visual terms alone, the Invisible Cinema did not quite live up
to its name. Complaining about the shininess of the black seat hoods,
Kelman (quoted in Sitney 2005: 34) states: 'That was a little distracting
because right in front of me was this shine that didn't exactly reflect the
movement of the screen. Anything more or less at eye level, you're going
to see, and so the Invisible Cinema was not invisible.' Moreover, Sitney
recalls how the seating pods 'generated a great deal of heat' and seemed
to escape the reach of the air-conditioner, creating a 'soporific problem'
referred to by Kelman as 'the dozing off phenomenon' (109). Brazilian
experimental filmmaker Hélio Oiticia also noted this effect. Describing
the Invisible Cinema as 'a horrible place', Oiticia (quoted in Small 2008:
86n16) writes in 1971:

> the place is completely black, one sits in a way in which you can only see the screen,
> as the chairs have 'ears', with [flaps], so that you are isolated from your neighbor;
> i feel the worst claustrophobia; it seems as if everything has stopped, and i don't
> understand how this could be the best way to see films (it makes you go to sleep).

In addition to introducing acoustic and visual impurities and hinder-
ing airflow, both the design and philosophy of the Invisible Cinema
disappointed in yet other ways. Another anticipated effect of transferring
translation from the screen to the page was a consequent lack of comprehension. 'There is a sacrifice involved,' announced Anthology, '... in the
substitution of the purity of the image for the sense of the words, but it
is a necessary one' (Sitney 1975: viii). Anthology seems here to concede
that, despite its specially prepared synopses, the language of foreign films
would, to a degree, be lost. As Mekas conceded (quoted in Eichelbaum
1971: 140), the sacrifice was not welcomed by many in the audience.
Indeed, *New York Times* film critic Vincent Canby (1970: 38) argued that
Anthology's anti-subtitle stance stifled the sensual possibilities of film
while disrespecting the work of seminal theorists and filmmakers such as
Bazin and Godard who 'fought to elevate the importance of movie sound
(by which, I think, they must also mean sense) to that of the image'.

For Canby (1970: 38), the Invisible Cinema's austere translation policy
reflected its general tone of aesthetic militancy and effectively foreclosed
the 'potential sensual experience' of film. Declaring its no-translation
stance of 'debatable value', he proposed that it perpetuated the 'esthetic

[*sic*] domination' of the image over sound. By publicly sacrificing the 'sense' of foreign words, language is reduced to a surface sound-effect. Presented as yet another aesthetic *object*, foreign language is appreciated for its material qualities alone – its grain, pitch, tone, timbre and texture, rather than its meaning or functionality. Despite recognising sound as an essential component of film art (as reflected in its high-end sound technology and idiosyncratic seating design), the Invisible Cinema did not accord language the same respect. Rather, in emphasising materiality over and above meaning, sense was forsaken for surface.

Through the Cracks

Reporting on the Invisible Cinema for the *New York Times*, Canby (1970: 38) writes: 'All films, whenever possible, will be shown in their original versions, meaning, in the case of foreign films, with their original soundtracks and without subtitles'. Here, Canby collapses the Invisible Cinema's translation-free screening policy into one all-encompassing issue: subtitling. To a degree, this response is quite valid. For Canby, dubbing simply did not fit the profile of the 'serious' (Sitney 1975: ix), devotional audience coveted by Anthology. Nevertheless, Canby's response both cuts to the heart of the matter *and* misses the mark. Certainly, it correctly surmises that Anthology's blanket rejection of film translation actually played out in relation to subtitles alone. In reality, it was subtitles, and, by extension, art cinema conventions and mores, that were being contested. In neglecting to mention dubbing at all, Canby suggests that this translation practice was beneath consideration, understood as so antithetical to Anthology's mission as to be largely irrelevant. However, Canby fails to note that in becoming doubly invisible in this way, dubbing might potentially slip through the cracks. Indeed, I contend that it is precisely in relation to dubbing that some of the preconceptions upon which Anthology's translation policy was based become unstuck.

Films that typically utilise dubbing in their very construction – such as musicals – have certainly been included in Anthology's programme after the Invisible Cinema's demise, and it is not inconceivable to imagine that a European co-production – dubbed in its 'original' version – could have made its way into the Essential Cinema collection.[3] Including a film like Rossellini's *La prise de pouvoir par Louis XIV / The Rise to Power of Louis XIV* (1966) at least complicates the collection's claim to linguistic purity and authenticity. Made at a point when Rossellini declared himself a veritable dubbing enthusiast, *La prise* contains a polyglot cast and crew, registering the multilingual hybridity of European filmmaking at the time. Moreover, the film was made for television, commissioned by the Office de Radiodiffusion Télévision Français (ORTF) (Norman 1974: 11), and consequently courted a mass audience. In fact, for the US market, Rosssellini specifically preferred that his late-career history films like *La prise* be broadcast dubbed on television (see Betz 2009: 298n7). Evidently, Rossellini never *intended* that 'the sense of the words' in his films be sacrificed for the 'purity of the image' (Sitney 1975: viii). Hence, in screening *La prise* untranslated altogether, the Invisible Cinema actually undermined Anthology's stated objective 'to respect the filmmaker as an artist and show the film as it was intended to be shown' (Mekas quoted in Eichelbaum 1971: 140).

Concurring with Canby, I agree that the target of Anthology's no-translation screening policy was in fact quite singularly focused: it was subtitling that was being rejected, and, along with it, the attitudes and demands of the international art cinema movement. However, rather than opposing this method outright, the Invisible Cinema simply attempted to hide it from view. Dialogue titling persisted, but in a space removed from the filmic. Here, a destabilising ambiguity emerges. Despite ostensibly transcending the dualistic sub/dub logic and proposing an alternative, archaic form of print translation in its wake, the Invisible Cinema's screening policy ultimately extends many of the arguments fleshed out by *pro*-subtitle advocates, admittedly stretching them to breaking point. In this way, the Invisible Cinema's anti-translation measures demonstrate the circular and self-defeating nature of debates that typically surround film translation practices. Unlike dubbing, it is argued, subtitling enables the 'original' film to remain intact, thus preserving its integrity. While some critics concede it is not optimal to obscure a portion of the screen with this added textual supplement, they argue that such a level of interference is minimal in comparison to dubbing and hence, sufferable (see, for example, Canby 1983; Kauffmann 1960; Bordwell and Thompson 2004: 388). Anthology agreed with this argument up to a point. The 'original' film was to be respected and to remain intact. In contradistinction however, Anthology viewed the interference of subtitles as major and *in*sufferable. In this way, Anthology's Invisible Cinema can be seen to take pro-subtitling arguments regarding authenticity and purity to their logical conclusion. Ironically, this results in a particularly mixed, ambiguous message: pro-subtitling arguments redouble, folding back upon themselves to expose their ultimate unsustainability, mutating into a denunciation of subtitling itself.

On the Map

According to Noam Elcott (2008: 18), Anthology's founding mission was 'to promote American avant-garde film and its European predecessors'. Many foreign-language filmmakers are represented in the collection (including Bresson, Buñuel, Clair, Cocteau, Dovzhenko, Duchamp, Eisenstein, Feuillade, the Lumières, Rossellini and Ozu amongst others), thereby forcing the issue of translation. Indeed, Anthology recognised the issues raised by translation as central to its project, identifying translation as a convenient means of consolidating and concretising its philosophical and artistic position. In choosing to publicly reject both subtitling and dubbing, Anthology implicitly recognised the crucial role that translation plays in culture work, mediating experiences of the foreign, conditioning modes of reception and defining different genres of *audiences* in addition to *films*. In this way, the Invisible Cinema's translation policy brought to light issues generally ignored or trivialised within screen discourse and culture. Moreover, the extremity of its translation policy attracted attention, coming to function as a kind of position statement differentiating this fledgling organisation from venues like The Carnegie and Joseph Papp's Little Theatre also seeking to stake a claim for 'the art of film' (Sitney 1975: vi).[4]

By prioritising the topic of translation, Anthology utilised this commonly overlooked issue to mark itself on the map, attracting attention by the extremity of its position and its trend-bucking nature: it was precisely the association between European art cinema and *subtitling* that Anthology set out to attack. In declining to mention dubbing at all, therefore, Canby correctly identified subtitling as the true target of Anthology's no-translation policy and, along with it, the predisposition and predilections of the art house circuit. It was this largely narrative-based, international art cinema from which Anthology sought to distance itself, denouncing its commercialism and lack of purity:

> the art of cinema surfaces primarily when it divests itself of commercial norms. The narrative commercial films included in our collection represent radical exceptions, cases where art has emerged despite the conditions of production and popular expectation. (Sitney 1975: x)

If Anthology aimed foremost to redefine the very notion of film art as primarily non-narrative, formalist and avant-garde, then subtitling – the hitherto darling of foreign-language art cinema – had to be taken to task. The Invisible Cinema's no-subtitles stance one-upped the elitist aura of art cinema, proving its more serious, formal and pious credentials whilst promising a level of purity and authenticity normally unattainable. So much more than simply a movie theatre or film club, Anthology established itself as a *museum* dedicated to 'furthering serious film viewing' (Sitney 1975: ix–xi).

On staff at the *New York Times* during Crowther's reign, Canby would have been well aware of Crowther's position on the topic of film translation. In fact, it does not seem unlikely that Canby's very interest in Anthology could have been piqued by its unusual foregrounding of screen translation. It is also likely that the founders of Anthology, for their part, would have been aware of the *New York Times* sub/dub debate. As Fausto Pauluzzi (1983: 131) notes, this debate 'soon became a source of reference to those who habitually saw and discussed foreign films'. In reaction to Crowther's maverick pro-dubbing position, numerous critics rallied together in defence of the subtitle's artistic credentials, restating and reinvigorating the prevailing wisdom that subtitles present a more authentic and less deleterious form of film translation than dubbing. When the Invisible Cinema opened and Anthology issued its manifesto, it deliberately and provocatively challenged this logic. In this way, its puritan, no-translation screening policy functioned as a kind of position statement, no less significant than its canon of Essential Cinema and its controversial seating pods.

Ultimately, the Invisible Cinema's rejection of screen translation *in total* ends up prioritising it as an issue, inadvertently serving to highlight its role in defining viewing experiences and social hierarchies, and in cultural gate-keeping. In this way, the Invisible Cinema's experimental screening regulations testify to the performative, productive power of translation and its capacity to produce 'a new utterance whose primary purpose is an independent statement about or reference to the subject matter itself' (Tymoczko 2009: 404). Apart from its utilitarian, interlingual function, subtitling (and dubbing) was intolerable for Anthology because of the manner in which it inevitably draws attention to the mutable conditions of film reception and, by extension, the contingencies of film production. In this way, subtitling and dubbing directly contravened Anthology's conception of film as an ahistorical and transcendental, aesthetic artefact. As Sitney (1975: v) explains, matters of historical context were considered inessential and subordinate to 'formal properties'. Moreover, the subtitle's embeddedness within art house cinemagoing signals its particularly active role in meaning-making processes – how subtitling itself can create a set of assumptions regarding both films and their audiences. While the Invisible Cinema's opposition to both subtitling and dubbing distinguished it from the broader art cinema movement, at the same time it nevertheless exaggerated the art house desire for foreign authenticity and originality. In this sense, the Invisible Cinema opposed the prioritised translation method of the art house circuit while paradoxically reaffirming its underlying philosophy, fighting its means rather than its ends. While Crowther challenged the art house desire for linguistic authenticity, declaring it illusionistic and fetishising, the Invisible Cinema merely asserted that such desires were ill served by the subtitle.

Out of Sync

Michelson (1998: 10–12) interprets Anthology's idiosyncratic selection, screening and seating practices as 'perverse acts of sacralization of the fetish', which she describes as 'oppositional' and 'transgressive'. Elcott (2008) disagrees. Quoting Kubelka who claims that the Invisible Cinema was a 'normal cinema... as normal as a camera or a projector' (1974: 35), Elcott (2008: 20) takes this idea further, suggesting that it was in fact a 'classical cinema', one that 'shored up the conditions of reception taken more or less for granted since the 1920s and now threatened by multimedia and expanded cinema ... and by the increasingly dominant televisual distribution of movies'. Consequently, for Elcott (19) the Invisible Cinema as an institution was markedly incongruent with its own exhibition programme and Anthology's avant-garde vision.[5] Elcott (21–2) views the avant-garde films that constituted the mainstay of the Essential Cinema collection as experimental and radically self-reflexive, while he sees the Invisible Cinema's 'disappearing' design as continuing the illusionary project of classical narrative cinema in which the viewer is absorbed within a totalising filmic universe and transported away from the realities of film exhibition and reception. For Elcott, the fetishistic nature of the Invisible Cinema blocked its avant-garde potential.

According to Jean-Louis Baudry (1974–5 [1970]: 40), whose 'Ideological Effects of the Basic Cinematographic Apparatus' is attributed with launching Apparatus Theory, traditional cinema viewing is based on the model of the camera obscura, which reiterates the 'perspective construction of the Renaissance'. Kubelka's (1974: 35) conception of the Invisible Cinema as a 'machine for viewing' recalls Baudry's commentary on cinema 'as an ideological machine' where 'the darkened room and the screen bordered with black like a letter of condolences already present privileged conditions of effectiveness – no exchange, no circulation, no communication with any outside' (1974–5 [1970]: 44). He continues, 'projection and reflection take place in a closed space and those who remain there, whether they know it or not (but they do not), find themselves chained, captured, or captivated'

(44). For Baudry, cinema's ideological effects resulted as much through identification with the camera (the apparatus) as with the world or characters portrayed on screen, leading him to declare, 'the forms of narrative adopted, the "contents" of the image, are of little importance so long as an identification remains possible' (46). In striving to make itself disappear, the Invisible Cinema recalls Baudry's postulation that 'concealment of the technical base will also bring about an inevitable ideological effect' (41).

While many of the experimental films included in Anthology's collection consciously partake in 'the revealing of the mechanism, that is of the inscription of the film work' (Baudry 1974–5 [1970]: 46), exposing the means of production and highlighting the materiality of the filmic medium, the Invisible Cinema itself perpetuated traditional viewing conditions, and hence produced the 'transcendental subject' (43) that Baudry argues is 'necessary to the dominant ideology' (46). While a film like Brakhage's *Blue Moses* (1963), for instance, reveals a preoccupation with the 'pure' materiality of film-as-film, the Invisible Cinema's design encouraged absorbed contemplation via a process of self-effacement. Indeed, for Elcott (2008: 19), 'the Invisible Cinema was conceived and implemented as a buffer against the televisualization of movies, not as an extension of an avant-garde project'. He deems it classical, reactionary and out-of-sync with the experimental nature of its screening programme (19–21).

On the other hand, Eric de Bruyn (2004) identifies retrograde elements as systemic to the entire nature of the formalist film avant-garde. Although the Invisible Cinema fostered a formalist preoccupation with the filmic, for de Bruyn (2004: 166) this interest in the apparatus went only so far. Its 'literal function' he suggests was downplayed in favour of its 'transcendent quality'. Here, de Bruyn takes to task the visible/invisible dynamic deliberately invoked by Anthology's radical cinema, suggesting that the 'apparatus of projection was made invisible to make the medium itself wholly apparent'. Elcott (2008: 21) echoes this sentiment, stating that this was 'an invisible cinema for the exhibition of visible film'.

In contrast to Elcott, neither de Bruyn nor Michelson identifies any incongruity between Anthology's critical position and the Invisible Cinema. While Michelson (1998: 10) refers to the sacralising and fetishistic nature of Anthology's museological mode of cinephilia, the Invisible Cinema only confirms and concretises this 'perversity'. Similarly, for de Bruyn, the films being screened at the Invisible Cinema were not at odds with their surroundings. Rather, the classically illusionist, transcendental leanings of the Invisible Cinema demonstrate the limitations of Anthology's brand of avant-gardism. For de Bruyn (2008: 165),

Anthology limited itself to a restricted notion of the cinema as a single-screen, single-source entity and hence achieved only a limited sense of political consciousness or critique. In contrast, the more materialist strain of the formalist avant-garde represented by Expanded Cinema exponents such as Stan VanDerBeek, Malcolm Le Grice and Oiticia sought to step outside the film frame, engaging with conditions of reception and making the audience a part of the work.

Taking formalism to a point of 'extreme "purism" or "essentialism"', for Wollen (1975: 172), the artisanal American avant-garde movement (mostly centred around New York), 'ironically ... ended up sharing many preoccupations in common with its worst enemies.' The 'anti-illusionist, anti-realist film,' for instance, repeats the commitment to ontology and essence driving advocates of cinematic realism like Bazin (Wollen 1975: 172). Hand in hand with its overt essentialism and fetishisation of quality, the Invisible Cinema massaged Anthology's elitist tendencies. Although affordable, this 'temple for the ritual celebration of cinema as an artistic practice' (Michelson 1998: 5) was designed for a limited and devoted crowd – those able to withstand the alienating experience of subtitle-free screenings and isolationist seating. In this way, the Invisible Cinema limited the scope of Anthology's vision. Ultimately, its concrete manifestation of Anthology's critical overhaul proved too rigid and prescriptive, resulting in a crumbling effect that culminated in the cinema's abrupt demise three years after its construction (Sitney 2005: 112–13).

Dream's End

In 1974, the experiment of the Invisible Cinema came to a resounding end. Anthology's patron, filmmaker Jerome Hill, died of cancer, and funding from his estate was withdrawn. Anthology was forced to relocate to premises in Soho where it remained until 1979 when its present home was purchased – a refurbished courthouse on Second Avenue in the East Village. With the move to Soho, the question of reconstructing the Invisible Cinema was raised yet, according to Sitney (2005: 112), Mekas never seriously contemplated reconstruction. 'Dreams are very difficult to repeat,' he states, 'and that was a dream' (quoted in Sitney: 113). Although de Bruyn's (2008: 165) dismissal of the Invisible Cinema as a 'financial fiasco' does not seem entirely fair (as its admission price of US$1 – equivalent to around $6 today – suggests that it was never envisioned as financially self-sustaining), without the patronage of Hill the experiment seemed to become untenable. Disappointed, Kubelka (1974: 35) clung to the hope that the Invisible Cinema's time was yet to come, seeing it as a 'model for the future'. Eventually, over a decade later, it was resurrected as 'Das Unsichtbare Kino' at the Austrian Film Museum, Vienna, in 1989 and remains in operation today.

With the Invisible Cinema's demise, Anthology's translation policy was revised. Along with most other independent screening venues declaring allegiance to cinematic 'art', Anthology submitted to the ruling logic of the subtitle. Foreign-language films that do not form part of the Essential Cinema collection are today screened in their 'original' language versions *with subtitles*. Additionally, many Essential Cinema screenings are also accompanied by subtitles. In May 2016, for instance, Jia Zhangke's *Still Life* (2006) was screened in Mandarin with English subtitles, while three Jean Cocteau films included in the Essential Cinema collection were also screened with subtitles. Unsurprisingly, dubbed prints do not appear in the programme, unless perhaps their presence remains 'invisible'. Anthology's decision to amend its anti-translation (or anti-*subtitling*) stance following the Invisible Cinema's closure suggests the compromised nature of its effort to disrupt the association between subtitling, art and authenticity. Unlike Crowther, Anthology's opposition to the subtitle did not seek to expose the underlying fetishism and essentialism of pro-subtitling arguments or to debunk any perceived elitism. Neither did it offer a sustainable alternative. Rather, the 'sacrifice involved in the substitution of the purity of the image for the sense of the words' (Sitney 1975: viii) created an ongoing point of tension between Anthology's early vision and that of foreign-language filmmakers and foreign film audiences. Failure thus inhabits both the means and the message of Anthology's zero-translation policy. Although the Invisible Cinema strategically set out to distinguish itself from other alternative cinemas by declaring both dubbing and subtitling banned, the shortcomings of these translation devices were re-evaluated following its own eventual demise.

Non-translation

Another way to frame the Invisible Cinema's rejection of screen translation is to see it as one iteration of an idea recurrent throughout screen history, which John Sallis unpacks in relation to Western philosophical thought: the 'dream of nontranslation' (2002: 1). In declaring that foreign-language films were to be viewed without screen translation of any sort, the Invisible Cinema insisted that the medium of film transcends translation, existing somehow *beyond* it. Interestingly, the idea that film *is*, should *be*, or might in the future *become*, a medium that exists beyond translation unites screen culture across continents and eras, and relates directly to its global aspirations.[6] The Invisible Cinema's translation-free screenings rehearse this dream or myth of film-as-universal language. Since the silent era, this myth has played an instrumental role in shaping film discourse and culture, despite the myriad modes of translation that accompanied film from its inception.[7] During the silent era, film's ability to communicate across national and linguistic boundaries was repeatedly framed in relation to the biblical Tower of Babel story, as Miriam Hansen (1991: 76–7) has productively explored.[8] Hansen declares that the 'myth of a visual language overcoming divisions of nationality, culture, and class, already a topos in the discourse on photography, accompanied the cinema from the Lumiéres' first screening through the 1920s' (78). The notion of universality was enthusiastically adopted by the US industry to explain its appeal to diverse immigrant and illiterate audiences and used as a marketing device to facilitate foreign expansion (Hansen 1991: 78). Even after the wide-scale adoption of sound in the late 1920s, some still clung to this ideal of non-translation, advocating for Esperanto to become the official *lingua franca* of talkies (Rossholm 2006: 53; Quaresima 2006: 20).

For Sallis (2002: 1), the recurrent, unshakeable 'dream of nontranslation' does not *efface* the importance of translation but rather *affirms* it. Without translation there can be no possibility of its transcendence. Noting how ideas of non-translation often collapse into forms of utopian idealism or colonising mastery, Sallis (4) argues that this dream persists 'against mounting odds' precisely because, without it, translation cannot occur. The dream endures because it is conditional to translation itself. For Sallis, non-translation and untranslatability are necessary, foundational aspects of all translation. At the Invisible Cinema, Anthology sought to realise its dream of non-translation via radical screening protocols. Here, the 'purity' of film art was cultivated, largely conceived as an expression of form over content. Consequently, words were sacrificed in favour of images, and foreign film viewers were left adrift in a sea of indecipherable words. In concretising this dream, however, Anthology inevitably compromised its vision and reduced its force. Translated synopses were produced that contaminated screenings nevertheless due to the audible obdurateness (rustling) of the printed page. Audience members complained. The filmmaker's intended effect was sacrificed and, enduringly, the issue of translation was prioritised, not minimised. Publicly denouncing dubbing and subtitling in its manifesto, the Invisible Cinema raised the visibility of these mundane techniques and underlined the significance of translation as a whole by using it to differentiate itself from other independent and experimental screening spaces, cement its formalist agenda and, finally, disturb audience members' expectations, making them sit up (quite literally, in seating pods) and take notice.

Today, translation continues to trouble Anthology's critical position, long after the Invisible Cinema's demise, bifurcating its screening programme. Translation synopses are provided for *some* Essential Cinema screenings. Yet, most foreign-language films in the Essential Cinema collection are now accompanied by English subtitles, and English subtitles feature regularly throughout the rest of the programme. In 2016, for instance, Essential Cinema screenings included Cocteau's *Orpheus* (1954) in French with English subtitles and Vertov's *Three Songs about Lenin* (1934) in Russian with no subtitles and an available English synopsis. Hence, the early ban against both subtitling and dubbing is inconsistently practised. Translation synopses remain in limited form as a relic of an earlier era and a signifying characteristic of the Essential Cinema collection and its 'purist' aesthetic. Issues of translation not only differentiate some 'essential' films from others but also serve to quarantine the Essential Collection from the rest of the Anthology programme.

According to Mekas, the dream of non-translation embodied by the Invisible Cinema never finally converted into the practical (see Sitney 2005: 41). Rather, it was a compromised, failed venture. For Derrida, translation is also inherently flawed, and this structural failure becomes a central concern of deconstruction. Indeed, translation is at the crux of Derrida's (1984: 123) search via deconstruction 'for the "other" and the "other of language"', as it challenges Western metaphysics' 'ideal of perfect self-presence, of the immediate possession of meaning' (115). In *The Ear of the Other*, he states that translation represents the 'thesis of philosophy' and that the 'philosophical operation, if it has an originality and specificity, defines itself as a project of translation' (1985b: 119–20). Here, he echoes Walter Benjamin (1968 [1923]: 77) who states, 'the language of truth ... whose divination and description is the only perfection a philosopher can hope for, is concealed in concentrated fashion in translations'. Derrida (1985b: 125) goes on to assert, 'every contract must be a translation contract. There is no contract possible, no social contract possible without a translation contract, bringing with it ... paradox.' Ultimately, he is interested in the limit of philosophy as translation, the points where philosophy 'finds itself defeated' – finds that it 'cannot master a word meaning two things at the same time and which therefore cannot be translated without an essential loss' (120). Deconstruction for Derrida exists at this limit point between translation and untranslatability, transmissibility and the irreducibly specific (1979: 93).

Derrida describes translation as an arbitrary form of arrest or suspension [*arrêt*] that by putting something 'in other words' does not paralyse so much as set in motion (1979: 114–15). The process of translation can never 'put the same thing into other words,' he writes, or 'clarify an ambiguous expression' (75). Rather, it 'amasses the powers of indecision and adds to the foregoing utterance its capacity for skidding'. In choosing a word, phrase or signified to replace another, the translator necessarily curtails the free play of signification set in motion by words, yet, at the same time, she starts new words on new significatory trajectories via her selection. Translation necessarily involves actualisation. Hence, 'meaning' in its pure virtuality or open possibility is made concrete: every decision the translator makes is an interpretation whereby meaning is captured, frozen, seized. For Derrida, the loss or failure that inhabits all translation results from this necessary concretising and arresting of open 'polysemia' and 'dissemination' (1979: 91). Such loss is nevertheless vital and productive. As Deleuze (1991 [1966]: 103) offers, 'differentiation is never a negation but a creation, and that difference is never negative but essentially positive and creative.'

Following Benjamin, Derrida (1985b) proposes that translation expresses the virtual kinship amongst languages. Consequently, translation is not concerned with representing or communicating any 'original'. Rather, it exceeds the 'original' by intimating a purely virtual point of contact that exists *between* 'original' and translation. Benjamin (1968 [1923]: 79–80) describes this point of contact or kinship as 'pure language' [*reine Sprache*]. Glossing Benjamin, Derrida (1985b: 124) states that translation expresses 'that there is language, that language is of language, and that there is a plurality of languages which have that kinship with each other coming from their being languages'. The 'impossible' aim of translation is to reconstitute a whole 'in such a way that the whole ... will be greater than the original itself and, of course, than the translation itself' (123). As Paul de Man (1986: 82) notes, the 'pure', linguistic kinship that Benjamin invokes suggests that translation is 'a relation from language to language, not a relation to an extralinguistic meaning'. In this way, it is metalinguistic and hence, inherently theoretical or philosophical (82). This metalinguistic kinship equates to a type of virtual unity found within actual, specific differences, suggesting that languages are unified precisely by their incommensurable differences from one another.

For Derrida, Benjamin's concept of 'pure language' constitutes an ideal that cannot be rendered concrete. As Edwin Genztler (2002: 200) notes, the 'translator, unlike the deconstructionist, must stop the fertile and enjoyable play of the signifier between literary systems and take a stand'. For Derrida (1985b: 123), actual translations are predestined to fail in their aim to render concrete virtual potentialities of meaning. Nevertheless, this failure is itself significant and productive. Moreover, as failure is a conditional component of all translation, it does not preclude success. Although 'translation never succeeds in the pure and absolute sense of the term', for Derrida, a 'good' translation succeeds in 'promising success' by providing a 'presentiment' of the 'possible reconciliation among languages' (123). Translation acts as a meeting point between languages: rendered or actual language registers the virtual imprint of another. Kinship is expressed in this relationship *between* languages, and, additionally, in the incommensurability between the actual and the virtual.

Concrete Impurity

In relation to the Invisible Cinema, how does Derrida's re-evaluation of translation as failure challenge Anthology's denouncement of screen translation as a form of 'defacement'? Alternatively, do dubbing and subtitling challenge Derrida's own qualitative distinctions between 'good' and 'bad' translations? As detailed in Chapter 1, anti-subtitle advocates argue that this form of translation is so technically constrained that it cannot manage even a sense of promise, only destroying (rather than deconstructing) the 'original'. Certainly, dubbing and subtitling fall outside Derrida's purview. However, their concrete limitations do not invalidate his arguments. Derrida never proposes that *all* translation error or failure should be celebrated. Rather, both Derrida (1985b: 123) and Benjamin (1968 [1923]: 69) maintain a distinction between 'good' and 'bad' translation, yet they allow these categories to remain abstractly defined. Significantly, Derrida (1985b: 100) teaches that the identification of translation flaw or fault (of 'essential loss') should neither put an end to discussion nor provide grounds for dismissal.

Following Derrida, I argue that the impurities of screen translation cannot ultimately be opposed to the 'purity' of film, as the Invisible Cinema proposed. Rather, the impurities of translation are conditional to film and other screen media. Indeed, translation 'disarticulates' the purity of film 'originals', alerting audiences to the risky, contaminating process of circulation and translation upon which 'originals' depend. For Benjamin (1968 [1923]: 71), it is the 'original' that is indebted to the translation, and not the other way around, for it is translation that enables the 'original' to be marked as such (as an 'original'), to be canonised, and to live on, in transformation. According to de Man (1986: 85), translation 'decanonises' and 'desacralises' the 'original'; it constitutes 'a making prosaic of what appeared to be poetic in the original' (97). In this way, translation exposes that the 'original' is also *actual* and grounded – reliant upon specific contexts, politics and contingencies. Indeed, it is translation that both marks and produces the 'original's' purity (its connection to 'pure language') and ensures its survival. Similarly, the risks that attend screen translation processes keep screen culture moving, mutating and 'living on'.

Today, on its website, Anthology announces itself 'an international centre for the preservation, study and exhibition of film and video, with a particular focus on independent, experimental and avant-garde cinema'. Its screening programme is 'innovative and eclectic', encompassing a wide range of media and genres beyond the Essential Cinema collection. As Kristen Alfaro (2012a: 57) reveals, Anthology's current, expansive vision now covers 'lesser known experimental filmmakers and also orphan films: home movies, unfinished student films, and behind-the-scenes porn footage'. Additionally, since 2010, Anthology has been increasing online access to its collection, making selected moving-image content available through streaming channels (Vimeo and YouTube) and providing free access to rare documents and specially commissioned publications (56–7). For Alfaro, its developing online archive is proof of the fact that accessibility has always been high on Anthology's agenda. Noting how Mekas was arrested and convicted in 1964 for screening *Flaming Creatures* (1963) as part of the Film-Makers' Cinematheque programme, Alfaro claims that Anthology was partly established in reaction to this form of censorship, with the aim of providing ongoing access to avant-garde and experimental film via a permanent, legal home (48–51).

Anthology advocates for access as a strategy of preservation, particularly for digital media. For Mekas, the 'open and democratic' nature of much digital reproduction can enable experimental media to remain in circulation through 'fresh copies' (quoted in Alfaro 2012a: 59). This transformative afterlife that Anthology seeks to ensure for avant-garde, experimental and marginalised screen media cannot be disassociated from translation. Tellingly, in its current configuration, Anthology (mostly) embraces subtitling along with digital technologies and online accessibility. In contrast to its 'frozen', prematurely petrified and preserved monument to the essentials of cinematic art,[9] it is this open, evolving engagement with experimental screen culture that has enabled Anthology to endure, becoming more than just a dream.

Muted Voices

Although Anthology sought to distance itself from the international art cinema movement by repudiating its reverence for the subtitle, it nevertheless reiterated with further vehemency the demand for *audible* foreignness. In this sense, art house and avant-garde unite in the resolve that foreignness must be *heard to be believed*. According to John Mowitt (2005) a similar demand was espoused by the America's Academy of Motion Picture Arts and Sciences (AMPAS). In his institutional history of AMPAS and the rules governing its Foreign Language Film Award, Mowitt (2005: 45) interrogates 'how the relation between language and foreignness has been forged within the cinematic domain'. Within this regulatory discourse, he identifies an ideology at work that is similar, I contend, to that informing the Invisible Cinema's translation-free screenings. This discourse insists that the authenticity of foreignness lies in its aural inscription: in its audible non-English ('original') dialogue. For Mowitt, this prescriptive equation serves to severely delimit and impoverish cinematic engagement with both foreignness and language *per se*.

Mowitt (2005: 47–52; 182n3) charts the historical development of the Foreign Language Film Award from its beginnings in 1944, when 'motion pictures from all countries' became eligible for Special Award consideration and 'English subtitling was included among the traits of foreignness', through to 1956 when it became an award in its own right. In 1949, for instance, foreign films were defined as 'films first made in a language other than English', thereby excluding those from Anglophone countries like Australia and the UK, which the Academy thus intended to treat as American films (54). Additionally, eligibility was restricted to foreign films released in *commercial* theatres. The rules set out in 1956 specify that eligible films needed to be: (1) feature-length; (2) 'produced by a foreign company with a non-English soundtrack'; (3) first released during the award year; and (4) 'shown in a commercial theatre for the profit of the producer and the exhibitor' (52). Neither a US release nor English subtitles were required. These stipulations were revised in 1958 when the Academy advised that it would be glad to have prints submitted for voting with English subtitles if available, and explicitly stated that dubbed films, or films not in their 'original' language, would not be accepted (53). In the early 1970s, inclusion of English subtitles became mandatory (see 183n3).

Mowitt deems the Academy's insistence upon *audible* foreignness fetishistic and objectifying. He argues that it effectively renders cultural difference into an exotic sound-effect. 'Once foreignness is reduced to the speech of foreigners, the vocal sounds delivered as dialogue on the soundtrack and translated in the subtitles,' Mowitt (2005: 63) states, 'language is, as it were, spoken for'. To demand that foreignness be audible on the sound track 'in the speech of those "foreigners" recorded there', facilitates its elimination from all other aspects of the film: 'Once expelled from the cinema, foreignness echoes, that is, it returns, as sound' (62–3). Consequently, foreign speech is not afforded the full signifying force or status of language and comes to function instead as an aesthetic object (perhaps resembling the manner in which foreign accents have often functioned within Hollywood).[10]

For Mowitt (2005: 63), the AMPAS stipulation that foreign films be 'in a language other than English' acts as decoy, drawing attention away from the fact that, ultimately, to be eligible for an award, they must 'look and *sound* like the sorts of films perceived to be appropriate for commercial distribution and exhibition in the United States'. Mowitt's (60) inference is that although dialogue must be non-English, in all other respects (such as its sound-effects, musical scoring and technology), the sound track is expected to conform to Hollywood's 'standardization of practices'. Further, by stipulating that foreign-language films be 'shown in commercial theatres, and produced for profit', he writes, 'AMPAS was implicitly intervening in the domain of indigenous cultural practices not only to impose the capitalist logic of standardization, but also, in effect, to eliminate foreignness from the cinema' (62). To be eligible for an award, Mowitt concludes, films could not exhibit foreignness in any regard other than their language (narrowly interpreted as dialogue). Ultimately, Mowitt contends that the processes of capitalist consumption so central to mass culture and globalisation (epitomised by Hollywood) function to construct foreignness in the image of the same, implicating screen translation modes and preferences in these socio-political machinations.

Despite insisting upon English subtitles, the AMPAS attitude to foreign-language films is not significantly distinct from that promoted by the Invisible Cinema, demonstrating that although Anthology utilised issues of translation to differentiate itself from what it deemed a more commercial, art house sensibility, it never strayed far from this more conventional position, effecting more of a sideways step than any major departure. While Anthology's practice of screening foreign films in their 'original' language aimed to expose audiences to otherness and cultural difference, providing a distinctly foreign and defamiliarising experience, this radical strategy ultimately involved inherent forms of domestication. By refusing to subtitle or dub, the Invisible Cinema reduced language to sound effect – elevating its acoustic surface over and above any expressive or communicative depth. In banishing translated text from the screen and repositioning it on the page, the language of foreign films was rendered mute. Keeping in mind Mowitt's analysis of the Academy's Foreign Language Film Award, the Invisible Cinema's rejection of both subtitling and dubbing suggests a rejection of language itself, conceived as inessential to film meaning.

Distinctions between sound, language and speech are crucial to the growing discipline of Sound Studies as well as screen translation. Many film sound specialists, such as Rick Altman (1980: 63) and Michel Chion (2009 [2003]: 73), present language as a privileged, dominant subset of sound. Mowitt offers a different perspective, asserting that language amounts to more than sound alone, and that neither represents a subset of the other. To reduce language to dialogue or speech is to compartmentalise and contain its overall significance. In contrast, for Mowitt (2005: 80), language in cinema is an 'apparatus of enunciation' that shapes 'the way images, sounds, and events get assembled' (57). For Mowitt, the reduction of language to sound has enabled Anglo–American film culture to effectively dodge meaningful engagement with foreign cinematic codes, actual language difference and, the question of 'how foreign languages ... have been represented within Western cinemas' (45).

Dionysis Kapsaskis (2008: 48) reads cultural resistance to subtitling in 'geopolitical terms'. When dominant cultures and language communities refuse to read subtitles, he suggests, they exhibit the 'pathology of national narcissism... linguistic essentialism, and a mechanism for perpetuating cultural dominance'. But is it fair to view the Invisible Cinema's denunciation of subtitling and dubbing in this light, as simply an exaggeration of mainstream resistance to translation within Anglo–American culture? In constructing the Invisible Cinema as the physical manifestation of its 'critical enterprise' (Sitney 1975: v), Anthology set out to do something quite oppositional and 'tentative' (Sitney quoted in MacDonald 1994: 34). Nevertheless, in its desire to provide a direct, unmediated experience of the foreign, Anthology may well have unwittingly put into effect exoticising strategies that effectively reduced the meaning of foreign words to surface acoustics. Ironically, the Invisible Cinema's controversial zero-translation stance took to the extreme the *pro*-subtitling mindset and its preoccupation with purity and authenticity. Paradoxically, in the process, subtitling itself was rejected alongside dubbing.

The Invisible Cinema's short lifespan signifies its ultimate failure – further reinforced by the fact that, following its demise, Anthology renounced its objection to subtitling. If failure and impossibility are preconditions of all translation, as Derrida suggests, it is interesting to plot how the Invisible Cinema's fall and fortune developed hand-in-hand with issues of translation. The cinema's extreme stance against screen translation effectively denaturalises more conventional approaches towards foreign film reception and translation. As I have plotted in this chapter, mainstream attitudes towards subtitling and dubbing invest in the same cultural distinctions operating within more self-conscious cultural institutions belonging to art house and avant-garde circuits. All partake in the regular elision of foreignness through prescriptive notions of authenticity and originality. The cultural status of translation methods and practices points to the significance of such operations beyond a purely functional realm. For film theory, the challenge remains: how to account for translation's influential yet largely uncharted role?

Notes

1. According to Kristen Alfaro (2012b: 76), Anthology was not as exclusive as is often suggested. Referring to the Invisible Cinema's affordable ticket price, Alfaro writes: 'Anthology was less a dictatorship and more of a pedagogical community center for the experimental film; the primary goal remained access, and through access, Anthology developed goals of preservation and pedagogy' (83). While admitting that the Essential Cinema canon and the Invisible Cinema exuded more than a whiff of 'avant-garde film hierarchy' (Alfaro 2012a: 46), she counters that Anthology now prioritises online access over canons and has ceased to call itself a museum (62n25).

2. In Howard Thompson's review (1970) he quotes film student Vincent Joliet: 'Those partitions by your ears, they're great. To me the very silence was something like music itself. It made the visual image even stronger.'

3. In June 2011, for instance, a collection of Hollywood musicals from the 1970s and 1980s were screened – a genre of film notorious for post-synchronised sound tracks and ghosted singing.

4. As Vincent Canby (1970) notes in his review, the only other organisations screening translation-free foreign-language films at the time were cultural institutions like the Alliance Français.

5. Noam Elcott (2008: 19) stresses that Kubelka conceived the Invisible Cinema in 1958, well before the idea of Anthology had been formed. For more on the early conception of the Invisible Cinema, see Kubelka (1974: 35).

6. Significantly, John Sallis (2002: 6) links ideals of translation transcendence to conditions of globalisation, underlining 'a certain complicity between the spread of English almost everywhere and the dream of nontranslation'.

7. See also Tessa Dwyer (2005) and Torey Liepa (2008).

8. Notable directors who advocated for 'film as universal language' include Carl Laemmle, D. W. Griffith and Dziga Vertov. See Rossholm (2006: 51).

9. As Adams P. Sitney (1975: vi) explains, the Essential Cinema collection was never conceived as something 'finished' or 'fixed' as 'new films or newly discovered old films, have the potential of modifying the whole history of cinema'. Hence, he promises, 'new films will be added each year as they are made' (x).

10. Writing on the early sound era, Anna Sofia Rossholm (2006: 73) states: 'For foreign actors in Hollywood, the task was to learn to speak intelligible "Hollywood English" with a slight accent adding a touch of the exotic', which involved an 'adjustment of differences into "sameness"'.

CHAPTER 3

Dubbing Undone:
Can Dialectics Break Bricks? (1973)

Can Dialectics Break Bricks? opens with a long shot of its hero (played by Jason Pai Piau) staring intently into the camera framed in black. As the shot draws closer, a French voice-over announces: 'Le premier film entièrement détourné de l'histoire du cinema' [The first entirely detourned film in the history of cinema].[1] The title appears (*La dialectique peut-elle casser des briques?*) and the credits begin to roll. When the name of the producer (Yeo Ban Yee) flashes on screen, the subtitled voice-over continues: 'A film produced by the person listed here, who naturally has no idea what has happened to his film.' After a series of stares, punches and kicks accompanied by more tongue-in-cheek commentary ('He looks like a jerk, true, but it's not his fault. It's the producers'), the voice-over identifies itself as translation device, pronouncing the film a 'French language version of 1973 by the Association for the Development of Class Struggle and the Propagation of Dialectical Materialism'. The final credit goes to director Doo Kwang Gee (aka Tu Guangqi).

In this convoluted opening, humour, irony, disjuncture and appropriation are everywhere felt, and the viewer is left somewhat adrift. Is

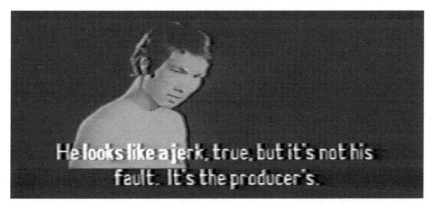

Figure 3.1 Opening credits of *Can Dialectics Break Bricks?* (1973).

the film's title to be trusted? Does this martial arts film really concern the philosophical programme of dialectical materialism? And what is it to 'detourn' a film? Despite identifying as interlingual transfer (from Chinese to French), this extended sequence makes it clear that, as translation, this dub is far from typical. Indeed, this French-language 'version' of a Hong Kong martial arts film set in South Korea constitutes a *sub*-version – a wilful, playful mode of 'non-translation', translation that is deliberately erroneous. This is translation exposed as mistranslation.

To date, *Can Dialectics Break Bricks?* has received scant scholarly attention. Despite a wealth of research on the Situationist International movement with which it is associated, this film is typically passed over or dismissed as curious, amusing side note – an oddball experiment rather than an authentic creation. Most writing on Situationist films focuses upon those of the movement's leading figure Guy Debord. In this chapter, I give this film its due, focusing on the way that its particular mode of cultural mis/appropriation or *détournement* hinges upon a markedly self-reflexive dubbing. In doing so, it massages a link between the Situationist programme of 'devaluation-revaluation' (see 'Captive Words' 2006 [1966]: 230), the strategy of 'détournement' and the deconstructive dynamics of translation. In the following discussion I bring to the surface the productive implications of this link. I use this serious/parodic (see 'Détournement' 2006 [1959]: 68) film to think through the politics of deliberately wayward or errant translation and consider how this early example of 'culture jamming' engages with many of the pressing concerns that arise today from participatory modes of media engagement including piracy, sharing, fansubbing and remix.

De-authorisation

What does the opening sequence of *Can Dialectics Break Bricks?* tell us? And what does it pointedly not say? What remains unsaid? By paying attention to its modes of articulation and *dis*articulation, it is possible to find in this opening scene multiple prefacing statements. Naturally, it introduces the film to come – its narrative thrust and lead character as well as its themes, terms and mode of address. Additionally, it condenses key elements of the Situationist project. Upfront, the film links itself unmistakably with the radical programme of the Internationale Situationniste (known in English as the Situationist International). By declaring itself a 'detourned' film, *Can Dialectics Break Bricks?* aligns itself with this signature concept, which the Situationists defined as the 'reuse of pre-existing artistic elements in a new ensemble' ('Detournement'

2006 [1959]). Hence, despite its boldly declarative style, which 'breaks the fourth wall' by addressing the spectator directly, it links itself to the Situationist movement only indirectly, without naming it outright. This tactic of subtle evasion gains in momentum as the sequence continues. The film announces itself a derivative, second-order mode: a translation. And, in keeping with the lowly status of translation (in comparison to 'originals'), its authorship is hence denied proper authority: it is attributed to a collective with a comically long-winded name, the Association for the Development of Class Struggle and the Propagation of Dialectical Materialism. Additionally, as is immediately apparent, the film's status as translation 'proper' is radically unstable – it is blatantly unauthorised and unfaithful.

Hence, the 'author-function' is dodged on numerous levels. *Can Dialectics Break Bricks?* declares itself a de-authored translation, while also exploring how the process of translation itself wrests control away from authors and is thereby inherently de-authorising, destabilising and unauthoritative. Already, it is evident how much this film speaks through gaps and omissions as much as words – a fact that is brought to the fore through techniques of dubbing and subtitling. These everyday operations of screen translation necessitate points of erasure, condensation and sub-stitution, as discussed in Chapter 1. They are also literally moulded by the lip movements, words and syntax of underlying languages that are absent yet indirectly present. Hence, the film's central, crucial deployment of dubbing draws attention to the intricacies of de-authorisation. Ultimately, however, *Can Dialectics Break Bricks?* has proved unable to success-fully unshackle itself from the constrictions and propriety of author-ship. Nowhere in the opening credits does René Viénet's name appear. Nevertheless, irrespective of this careful, deliberate evasion, the film is routinely attributed to Viénet (and to his agency alone) and pronounced a Situationist film – despite the fact that Viénet left the movement in 1969 and it disbanded a few years later in 1972, a year before this film was made.

In acquiring a 'proper' author in this fashion, *Can Dialectics Break Bricks?* proves how strong is the cultural pull towards fixed points of meaning and individualism, especially in relation to the ownership and consumption of creativity and cultural production. To make sense of this excessive film, audiences seem to demand sites of anchorage, affixing it to a 'proper name' and thereby restoring the sense of cultural legitimacy and authority that the film itself pointedly rejects through its none-too-subtle attack on all such forms of containment and recuperation. This denounce-ment of the 'author-function' was central to the Situationist project, which promoted plagiarism over citation or quotation:

> Anything can be used. / It goes without saying that one is not limited to correcting a work or to integrating diverse fragments of out-of-date works into a new one; one can also alter the meaning of those fragments in any appropriate way, leaving the imbeciles to their slavish reference to 'citations.' (Debord and Wolman (2006 [1956]: 15)

Hence, the Situationists made a point of not copyrighting their texts. In fact, they 'were typically accompanied by an inscription encouraging the use of the text, "even without mentioning the source" ', notes Edward Ball (1987: 23).[2] They decried the proprietorial nature of consumer society as well as its alienating effects, and set out to smash through social norms and legal regulations (see 'Détournement' 2006 [1959]: 67). Viénet himself was especially interested in 'guerilla tactics in the mass media', and promoted illegal actions and media piracy (Viénet 2006 [1967]: 274). Authorship and copyright were aligned with authority, bureaucracy and the deprivation of class-consciousness. Instead, they called for direct communication, participation and collective actions.

In its layered, circuitous opening sequence, *Can Dialectics Break Bricks?* sets itself up as a veritable assault against authorship, enacting a process of unauthorised *détournement* by denaturing a pre-existing film – overwriting it by supplying a new soundtrack of 'know-all French voices' (see Morris 2004: 182). This core act of cultural violation is supplemented by a suite of similarly de-authorising tactics noted above, yet, despite this explicit denunciation of the author-function, critics and scholars mostly refer to *Can Dialectics Break Bricks?* as 'Viénet's film' (Knabb 1997: 362), occasionally acknowledging his alleged collaborator and/or pseudonym Gerard Cohen (see Sanborn 1991: 93). Apart from Meaghan Morris (2004: 182), who registers the collective nature of the Situationist enterprise by referring to 'Viénet's group', commentary on this film invariably falls back upon the solidity of Viénet's 'proper name' and the authority of his Situationist credentials. Regrettably, this move obscures much of the punch the film delivers under the banner of *détournement*, missing (or at least compromising) its essential devaluation of authorship.

Détournement

The Situationists declared *détournement* their signature practice ('Détournement' 2006 [1959]). In short, *détournement* is appropriation to the point of hijacking. In most English-language Situationist scholarship, this French word is left untranslated, suggesting its special function in the vein, perhaps, of Derridean word-twisters like 'différance'. *Détournement* is not a word that exceeds normal usage, however. Rather, it is a common

Figure 3.2 Publicity poster for *Can Dialectics Break Bricks?* (1973).

term that the Situationists set about capturing, bending it to new, revolutionary purposes. The Situationists delighted in taking everyday words
(like 'situation') and bestowing upon them special significance, making the
ordinary extraordinary. Moreover, although common, *détournement* is also
complex, and no single English word proves its equivalent. It translates,

most literally, as 'diversion', but also suggests 'deviation', carrying illicit, subversive undertones (see Ball 1987: 32). Additionally, the word stem 'detour' continues to exert influence. Ken Knabb (2006: 480) defines it as 'deflection, diversion, re-routing, misuse, misappropriation, hijacking or otherwise turning something aside from its normal course or purpose'. For the Situationists, the 'two fundamental laws of *détournement* are the loss of importance of each detourned autonomous element – which may go so far as to completely lose its original meaning – and at the same time the organization of another meaningful ensemble that confers on each element its new scope and effort' ('Détournement' 2006 [1959]: 67).[3]

Significantly, *Can Dialectics Break Bricks?* constitutes the only known Situationist example of an 'entirely detourned film' in that it takes the pre-existing film *The Crush* and derails it via revoicing.[4] In doing so, it follows Guy Debord and Gil J. Wolman's step-by-step guide for film *détournement*, which they envision in relation to D. W. Griffith's *The Birth of a Nation* (1915). Debord and Wolman advise that the best way to detourn this film would be to simply add a new, resistant 'soundtrack that made a powerful denunciation of the horrors of imperialist war and of the activities of the Ku Klux Klan' (2006 [1956]: 14–21).[5] As Patrick Greaney (2010: 75) notes, *Can Dialectics Break Bricks?* actualises this idea, putting into practice the notion of detourning a film 'as a whole, without necessarily even altering the montage' (Debord and Wolman 2006 [1956]: 19). Granted, McKenzie Wark (2013: 86) notes that some slight re-editing has occurred. Additionally, *Can Dialectics Break Bricks?* forsakes the 1970s colour palette of *The Crush* (preserved nevertheless in the promotional poster) in favour of black and white.

Along with the French-language voice-over, these alterations produce a 'new combination' that distorts and hijacks, signalling the culture work of *détournement*. The next film attributed to Viénet, *The Girls of Kamare* (1974), diverges from this route, cutting together (at points, embellishing) two Japanese 'pinky violence' sexploitation films, Teruo Ishii's *Female Yakuza Tale* (1973) and Norifumi Suzuki's *Terrifying Girls' High School: Lynch Law Classroom* (1973). This time, Japanese-language dialogue is preserved, with *détournement* occurring through subtitling rather than dubbing. At one point the subtitles even make an intertextual reference to *Can Dialectics Break Bricks?* during a scene in which Japanese schoolgirls discuss the subtitles overlaid on a sequence showing two women having sex. 'Nicely put, huh?', one states. They continue: 'I think that's the first time a Japanese director has said that / *Can Dialectics Break Bricks?* probably at least did that / Gotta make some more films with those guys / For sure. We'll even show our asses some more, in order to say even more intelligent things.'

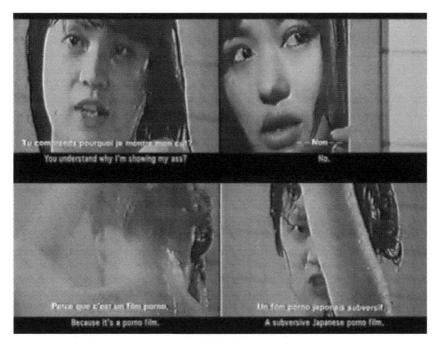

Tu comprends pourquoi je montre mon cul ?
You understand why I'm showing my ass?

— Non.
No.

Parce que c'est un film porno.
Because it's a porno film.

Un film porno japonais subversif.
A subversive Japanese porno film.

Figure 3.3 Film stills from *The Girls of Kamare* (1974).

In declaring itself 'the first entirely detourned film in the history of cinema', and by following so closely Debord and Wolman's guidelines, *Can Dialectics Break Bricks?* warrants attention by Situationist scholars. On this front, however, even Greaney fails, referring to the film only once, in a purely introductory vein. As I elaborate below, this neglect is symptomatic. Within Situationist scholarship, *Can Dialectics Break Bricks?* is typically relegated to the sidelines, accounted for only in parentheses or footnotes, where it languishes, subject to inaccuracies and oversight. In his footnotes, for instance, Simon Ford (2005: 137n7) refers to it as the 'most famous' of Viénet's 'series of détourned Kung-Fu movies', when, in fact, other film *détournements* attributed to Viénet are not composed of martial arts movies at all. Here, Ford collapses nationalities and genres, mistaking Japanese Yakuza and 'pinky violence' films, as well as documentary footage from Mainland China (remixed in the 1977 film *Chinese, One More Effort if You Would Be Revolutionaries* aka *Peking Duck Soup*), as Hong Kong martial arts films.[6] Thomas Levin (1989) also mentions *Can Dialectics Break Bricks?* only in passing, as colourful appendage to the more 'serious' or 'significant' works of leading Situationist figure Debord. In a footnote, it is dismissed as merely an 'amusing example' of *détournement* (111n24).

Such treatment not only downplays the significance of *Can Dialectics*

Break Bricks? but also overlooks the central importance that the Situationists placed on cinema as a whole. For Debord and Wolman (2006 [1956]: 19), cinema constituted the realm in which *détournement* could 'attain its greatest effectiveness and, for those concerned with this aspect, its greatest beauty'. Likewise, Viénet (2006 [1967]: 275–6) declared cinema 'the newest and undoubtedly most utilizable means of expression of our time', lending 'itself particularly well to studying the present as a historical problem, to dismantling the processes of reification'. The centrality of cinema within the Situationist movement as a whole is affirmed by the fact that Debord himself produced six films, while film was a frequent topic of discussion and debate in the *Internationale Situationniste* journal – with Jean-Luc Godard subject to repeated attack.[7] The critical role that the Situationists envisaged for cinema as 'a present-day technology' (Debord and Wolman 2006 [1956]: 18) aligned with their project to re-route mass media forms, and hence disorientate society in the most immediate, accessible and pervasive way possible. For the Situationists, news was considered 'the mediated falsification of what exists' ('All the King's' 2006 [1963]: 150). To expose this level of falsification or propaganda, and to wake up society, it was necessary to take up its means of production. Hence, Viénet's (2006 [1967]: 275) call for pirate radio stations, situationist comics and filmmakers. Consequently, *Can Dialectics Break Bricks?* is a vital artefact for reconstructing and unpacking the concept of *détournement*. The way in which it links *détournement* with dubbing also lends this film a particular novelty and force that especially recommends it for my current exploration into the value politics of screen translation.

Parodic-serious Dubbing

The critical neglect of *Can Dialectics Break Bricks?* stems from a tendency to pit its politics against its comedy, missing how the Situationists sought precisely to politicise the seemingly humorous, trivial and superficial. Asper Jorn (2006 [1958]: 57), for instance, proposed that the Situationists, unlike the Surrealists, were not worried about ' "upsetting the balance" between the frivolous and the serious, but to changing the nature of both'. Indeed, the Situationists argued that it was precisely the 'combination of parody and seriousness' that reflected the contradictions of present society, and confronted them 'with both the urgent necessity and the near impossibility of initiating and carrying out a totally innovative collective action' ('Détournement' 2006 [1959]: 68). The marginalisation of *Can Dialectics Break Bricks?* within Situationist scholarship suggest that this message has not been taken to heart, with scholars consistently trivialising

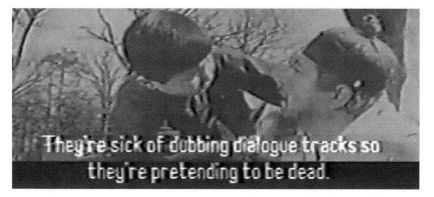

Figure 3.4 *Can Dialectics Break Bricks?* (1973)

the film's politics due to its parody. Meanwhile, a reverse trend is observable within Screen and Cultural Studies where the film's association with the critical weight of the Situationists imbues it with a seriousness that tends to overshadow its absurdity. Emrah Irzik (2011: 145) goes so far as to interpret the film as a literal, humourless call to action, stating: 'the expectation is that at least some viewers will end up entertaining ideas of taking over schools or workplaces and establishing workers' councils', while David Ray Carter (2011: 103) deems it 'far removed from the light-hearted humor of *Mystery Science Theater 3000*'.

Ultimately, *Can Dialectics Break Bricks?* is judged either as too comedic to be political or as too political to be any fun. Both judgements oppose the film's humour to its polemics, whereas, for the Situationists, no such separation is possible. Rather, *détournement*, as they explain, is precisely a 'parodic-serious' process in which 'the accumulation of detourned elements, far from aiming to arouse indignation or laughter by alluding to some original work, will express our indifference towards a meaningless and forgotten original, and concern itself with rendering a certain sublimity' ('Détournement' 2006 [1959]: 68). Humour is paramount in *Can Dialectics Break Bricks?* Yet, at the same time, its deliberate deployment of mistranslation testifies to the seriousness of its parody. The comedic is forcefully wielded to poke fun at taboo sexualities (homosexuality, masturbation, paedophilia, sex between minors), functioning as a form of anti-censorship. In one scene, a small boy addresses a young woman: 'You could be with a girlfriend or masturbating. You've got two good arms.' Often, the humour is particularly self-reflexive. In a climatic scene near the end, an old man explains of the bodies lying around him: 'They're sick of dubbing dialogue tracks, so they're pretending to be dead. It seems that it's hard and that it's not worth the trouble.' According to Knabb, the 'humour comes not so much from its satire of an absurd film genre as from its undermining of the spectacle–spectator relation at the heart of an absurd society' (see 1997: 362).

As an almost unsurpassed example of parodic translation, I propose that *Can Dialectics Break Bricks?* is important for Situationist scholarship, Screen Studies and Translation Studies alike, helping to identify the flavour and substance of Situationist concepts while launching a series of critical, re-evaluative forays into the nature and relation of screen media to translation. Although the concept of *détournement* has been much discussed and defined in critical circles, its connection to issues of translation has been all but ignored. *Can Dialectics Break Bricks?* is particularly notable for activating the unauthorised and re-authoring dynamic of *détournement* under the specific guise of screen translation. Nevertheless, the significance of this film for audiovisual translation is as yet virtually uncharted.[8] Subsequently, the various subtle ways in which this film destabilises and disorients many of the entrenched hierarchies of translation discourse (and praxis) have also been largely passed over, in particular the way in which it effortlessly sidesteps issues of quality, drawing attention to an equally powerful organising principle within translation processes: control. It is here that this film's critical relevance for the current project emerges. By deploying interlingual subtitling and dubbing precisely to foreground the politics of parody, *Can Dialectics Break Bricks?* draws attention to the inherent capacity of translation to appropriate and abuse. In selecting dubbing as its chosen method of *détournement*, *Can Dialectics Break Bricks?* interrogates not just the problem of language and how words necessarily 'coexist with power' ('All the King's' 2006 [1963]: 149) but also the specific nuances that attenuate language difference and transfer.[9] By capturing, erasing and substituting words through dubbing, *Can Dialectics Break Bricks?* indicates how 'the discourse of power establishes itself at the heart of all communication' ('Captive Words' 2006 [1966]: 223) yet it also extends the Situationist critique of language and the supposed 'innocence of words' (224) towards the realm of the inter-cultural and the interlingual. By consciously detourning a foreign-language film that is culturally 'other' in terms both of its ethnicity and 'lowbrow' genre, *Can Dialectics Break Bricks?* imbues the violence of the linguistic with socio–cultural and aesthetic significance. The Marxist-derived notion of alienation so important to the Situationists is reconceived beyond notions of class and the representation of false desires, towards a more global outlook, examining how some languages speak for and above others, and how alienation can be thought in national as well as individual terms. In *Can Dialectics Break*

Bricks?, screen translation makes palpable the violent power of language – its will to co-opt, falsify and tyrannise, yet also its capacity to subvert and resist. In this way, it extends and solidifies the Situationists 'liberation' of language by demonstrating how effortlessly words exert control and how easily meaning is deformed and parodied via the mundane pragmatics of dubbing.

Re-Dubbing

Of course, *Can Dialectics Break Bricks?* is itself not exempt from further translation and mistranslation. Experimental filmmaker Keith Sanborn (2010; 1991: 96), who prepared the English-language subtitles for the film 'without Viénet's help and without his permission', reports that at least two different French versions were produced. The dubbed version was preceded by a Chinese-language version with French subtitles that Viénet reportedly preferred (Sanborn 2010). Jonathan Rosenbaum (1997) suggests that, along with French subtitles, this earlier version might have conceivably featured a redubbed Chinese-language sound track, considering that Viénet was fluent in Chinese and lived in Hong Kong and Taiwan for a number of years (see Hazara 2004). Moreover, these language intrigues continue to multiply. Unsure whether the French dub 'was

Figure 3.5 Publicity poster for *The Crush* (1972). © Yangtze Film Company Ltd.

Figure 3.6 Publicity poster for *The Crush* (1972). © Yangtze Film Company Ltd.

altered from its original subtitled version', Sanborn (2010) notes that an English transcript of the film is rumoured to exist within anarchist circles, which may or may not be based on his English-language subtitles.

The further one probes, the more radically fluid the identity of this film appears, and the more obscured notions of 'origins' become. This identity

Figure 3.7 *Can Dialectics Break Bricks?* (1973).

crisis is further pronounced when one considers the earlier un-detourned Hong Kong production upon which *Can Dialectics Break Bricks?* is based. As Morris (2004: 182) notes, even the Chinese-language film *The Crush* cannot secure claims to authenticity. After expressing a desire to 'see or rather "hear" the first, Chinese film ... erased by these know-all French voices blasting out of the past', Morris reports that director Tu Guangqi was himself known for appropriating 'successful left-wing dramas and themes from a right-wing nationalist perspective', suggesting that *The Crush* may itself constitute an unauthorised remake or *détournement*!

The complications underscored via *Can Dialectics Break Bricks?* as multiple, changeable site of translation add to its humorous, self-reflexive deployment of dubbing and subtitling. Throughout the film's ninety-minute run, during which even admirers admit that 'the joke does wear thin' (Morris 2004: 182), audiences are constantly alerted to the effortless way in which translation can re-route, subvert and hijack meaning. As the hero prepares to fight an opponent, the narrator refers to Viénet's *Enragés and Situationists in the Occupations Movement* (1968),[10] re-contextualising this martial arts fight in relation to the May 1968 protests in Paris. In this way, *Can Dialectics Break Bricks?* exposes the potential for violence, mis-appropriation and abuse that inhabits even the most everyday and unre-markable forms of translation like dubbing, while also parodying serious, political film readings by pushing such practices to a point of ridicule, even specifying page numbers and publishing details ('the Gallimard edition'). The idea that translation is inherently détourning (de-authoring and destabilising) suggests a profitable connection to the concept of 'transla-tion abuse' developed by Derrida and retrofitted specifically for subtitling by Abé Mark Nornes in his seminal article 'For an Abusive Subtitling'

(1999). In the remainder of this chapter, I examine this connection and consider how *Can Dialectics Break Bricks?* might strain the conceptualisation of translation abuse, calling instead for a theory of *mis*-use.

Abusive Translation

In 'The *Retrait* of Metaphor,' Derrida (2007 [1978]: 67) makes brief mention of translation as a form of abuse, stating that 'a "good" translation must always commit abuses' ['une "bonne" traduction doit toujours abuser'], and likening it to a type of 'abduction' or 'transformative capture' (62). He also introduces the notion of 'violent fidelity' (63), suggesting that translation is 'at once violent and faithful' – it necessarily violates even as it devotedly follows or respects the 'original'. As James Smith (2005: xvi) notes, for Derrida, 'remaining faithful to a thinker will require a certain break; being an authentic "follower" will require that one part ways, at some point, in the name of fidelity'. Following Derrida's brief allusion to abusive translation, deconstruction and translation theorists have seized upon this phrase, expanding its possibilities and debating its definition. In 1980, Philip E. Lewis presented a seminar paper ('Vers la traduction abusive') on Derrida's use of this term, which was published shortly afterwards and later translated into English as 'The Measure of Translation Effects' (1985) – turning 'abusive translation' into a veritable topic in its own right. In 1995, Lawrence Venuti (1995: 23–4) remobilised the concept, emphasising its link to fidelity and aligning it with translation foreignisation or 'resistancy'.

In 1999, Nornes altered the course of this conceptual lineage by conjoining abuse to subtitling. His article 'For an Abusive Subtitling' draws upon both Lewis and Venuti, while attempting to sidestep Derrida and deconstruction – denounced as elitist and inaccessible. In contrast to Derrida, Nornes locates translation abuse within populist practices like anime fansubbing and television programmes like *Iron Chef* (1993–9), two examples I discuss further in Chapter 5. For now, my focus remains more narrowly fixed on *Can Dialectics Break Bricks?*, which Nornes discusses fleetingly and indirectly, expanding the reference in his footnotes (where this film so often finds itself placed). Along with a range of other films and television shows, Nornes deploys *Can Dialectics Break Bricks?* in order to refine his re-conceptualisation of abuse – and it is this project to which I now turn. Does this film ultimately support or challenges his agenda? On what basis does he denounce it, and how might this dismissal point to ways in which this film troubles theories of abuse by pushing towards the 'too-abusive' ['trop abusif'] (Derrida 2007 [1978]: 81)?

In analysing screen translation, Nornes maintains a central distinction between abuse and corruption. He asserts that 'all subtitles are corrupt' (Nornes 1999: 17), explaining that corruption is inevitable because all subtitles necessarily involve a degree of 'violent reduction' that is 'demanded by the apparatus' (Nornes 2007: 155). The number of lines and characters used per subtitle, for instance, is determined as much by the multimodal constraints of screen media and reading speeds as by source dialogue. The difference, for Nornes, between abuse and corruption lies in how such violence is managed. While corrupt subtitlers 'conspire to hide their repeated acts of violence through codified rules and a tradition of suppression' (156), abusive subtitlers expose and revel in it (Nornes 1999: 18). Hence, for Nornes, abusive subtitling is neither pure nor *un*corrupt. Rather, it foregrounds its necessary corruption, self-consciously alerting viewers to its degree of complicity (Nornes 2007: 166). Moreover, for Nornes, corruption equates to domestication, a translation strategy he aligns with cultural imperialism (177) and disingenuous engagement with foreignness ('divested of otherness') (179). Corrupt subtitling, he explains, 'is a practice of translation that smooths over its textual violence and domesticates all otherness while it pretends to bring the audience to an experience of the foreign' (155). He also asserts that corruption describes the present state of the subtitling and dubbing industries and that it has done so since sound film became a standardised commodity.

To aid in his explanation of corruption, Nornes (2007: 177) plots it in relation to three key epochs he identifies within film translation practices. Although he insists these epochs are not synchronic, the first corresponds quite neatly to the early sound period of 'talkies', the second came into effect following industry regulation, standardisation and professionalisation and continues into the present where it overlaps with the third, emergent epoch: the abusive (177–8). Nornes (1999: 28) characterises the first epoch as functional and material, 'straddling the theoretical paradigms of sense for sense vs. word for word'. The second epoch is classed as unmistakably corrupt and 'solidly sense for sense', while the third era moves toward the 'word-for-word end of the spectrum' (29). In the second epoch, corruption coincides with professionalisation and institutionalisation (Nornes 2007: 178). Professional modes of screen translation, Nornes (156) asserts, are dominated by corrupt, domesticating strategies whereby 'all forms of difference are suppressed and troublesome texts are fitted into the most conservative of frameworks', while all 'that cannot be explained within the severe limits of the regulation subtitle gets excised or reduced to domestic meanings that are often irrelevant or inappropriate' (178).

In his discussion of abusive subtitling, Nornes (2007: 180) mentions

Can Dialectics Break Bricks? in parentheses, without naming it outright. Referring to 'Situationist René Viénet's appropriations of kung-fu films in post-1968 France' (and hence lumping together all film *détournements* attributed to Viénet as Kung-Fu), he counts *Can Dialectics Break Bricks?* alongside Woody Allen's *What's Up Tiger Lily?* (1966) and Donald Richie's translation of Kurosawa's *Ran* (1985) as one of the 'most abusive translations ever undertaken in the second epoch'. Although ultimately identifying *Can Dialectics Break Bricks?* as belonging to this second 'corrupt' phase of film translation, Nornes nevertheless acknowledges its 'abusive' design. Notably, it does fulfil his 'first step' of 'abusive translation': to 'simply expose the act of translation' and 'release it from its space of suppression' (157). Nevertheless, it fails to qualify as abuse 'proper'. Although rule-breaking and highly self-reflexive, the parodic mistranslation of *Can Dialectics Break Bricks?* overtly disrespects and violates its source. This level of disregard constitutes an insurmountable obstacle for Nornes, distinguishing the revolutionary fervour of the Situationists from the more subtle and constrained abuse he promotes. Refusing to follow or even acknowledge the signification (abusive or otherwise) of *The Crush*, *Can Dialectics Break Bricks?* sets its own abusive agenda instead, expressing 'indifference toward a meaningless and forgotten original' (Debord and Wolman 2006 [1956]: 16).

Devaluation–Revaluation

The concept of translation abuse is re-evaluative. It unsettles and upturns distinctions between 'good' and 'bad', valorises non-standard modes of translation practice and positions translation as productive and performative. For Derrida, all translations commit abuses. They abuse language by stretching it and straining it in response to another, absent tongue that remains only virtually present. Moreover, the abuses translations commit are wide and far-reaching. Translations also abuse meaning, context, culture, history, hierarchies, boundaries, audiences and publics: they abuse in intangible and invisible ways too. They alter and re-route, even as they strive painstakingly to remain faithful. The line between these divergent demands is never clear-cut or stable. It is negotiated anew each time, and is subject to concrete contingencies. Hence, for Derrida, the concept of abuse signals translation's 'double bind' (1985b: 102) and its inevitable failure or necessary impossibility (1985a: 171). As Walter Benjamin proposes, this defeat is precisely translation's task – in German, both words are translated as one: '*Aufgabe*'. Benjamin, Derrida and other deconstructionists place great value on translation's necessary failure and defeat, mining it to develop an extensive framework of negative dynamics and 'negative analytics' (Berman 2000 [1985]: 286).

This reassessment of translation as *dis*articulation (de Man 1986: 84) – encapsulated by the concept of abuse – presents a major theoretical precedent for the re-evaluative aims of this book. The negative dynamics of deconstruction provide a particularly appropriate means of highlighting, challenging and interfering with translation's systemic devaluation (as derivative, secondary, supplementary, inessential), which is particularly pronounced and over-determined in relation to subtitling and dubbing. It is here that Nornes steps in. Following deconstruction theory to a degree, yet also departing from it, Nornes (2007: 176–7) attaches positive value to abuse via subtitling and dubbing that violates normative rules of language, grammar, screen–spectator relations and technical conventions precisely to bring audiences closer to the foreign 'original'. Abusive principles are applied in order to upset standard attributions of translation value. Under the banner of the abusive, Nornes proposes that disruptions to translation fluency should be regarded as a measure of success rather than failure.[11] According to this logic, the more that subtitling and dubbing deviate from the norm of invisibility whereby their fact and function are effaced, the more value they accrue. For Nornes, abusive translation creatively resists the rules and conventions of language use and cinematic address in order to tune audiences in to the foreignness of its source. Unlike the fluent, invisible style of much professional screen translation, modes of abusive subtitling desist from 'smoothing the rough edges of foreignness' or 'convening everything into easily consumable meaning' (Nornes 2007: 185).

Although my own project is indebted to Nornes and his book *Cinema Babel*, which is both ground-breaking and inspiring in the way it brings screen translation upfront in analyses of global screen culture and circulation, it nevertheless finds his theorisation of translation abuse wanting. *Can Dialectics Break Bricks?* helps to explain how and why. For Nornes (2007: 180) and deconstructionists alike, abuse amounts to a 'new notion of fidelity'. In contrast, my interest lies with subtitling and dubbing that is errant and improper, in ways that exceed the boundaries of abuse set down by Nornes. I argue that amateur, non-professional, parodic and censoring screen translation troubles definitions of translation abuse while exposing the ultimate uncontrollability of this term. As translation practices generally become more communal and less controlled in the era of digital, networking technologies (see Tymoczko 2005: 1088–9), errant modes of subtitling and dubbing are becoming increasingly prevalent and paradigmatic, calling for broader terminologies and discursive parameters. *Can Dialectics Break Bricks?* models this type of practice. Although particularly idiosyncratic and exuding a revolutionary fervour specific to the Situationist movement of 1960/70s France, it nevertheless connects to broader cultural shifts and currents of thought, and underlines a practicable link between screen translation, censorship and media piracy – a theme that I address in Chapter 4. Foremost, *Can Dialectics Break Bricks?* refuses to abide by rules (social, legal, filmic, translational), and in this way it exposes the rule-bound limitations inherent within much theorisation of translation abuse.

The gap that emerges between *Can Dialectics Break Bricks?*' mistreatment of its source and theories of 'abusive fidelity' underscores how the Situationist concept of *détournment* fundamentally challenges the authority of authorship and 'originals'. In this way, *Can Dialectics Break Bricks?* exposes both limitations and untapped potential within notions of abuse. In contradistinction to Nornes, I revalue the parodic excess of this film's unfaithful translation as interventionist, unsettling value systems in a manner that surpasses any simple opposition or reversal. For the Situationists, simple reversal 'is always the most direct and the least effective' form of *détournement* (Debord and Wolman 2006 [1956]: 17), whereas for translation foreignists and 'abusists', notes Douglas Robinson (1997: 109–13), it remains indispensible. Flaunting its departure from professional subtitling and dubbing conventions, *Can Dialectics Break Bricks?* self-consciously performs its mis/translation, rejecting quality criteria like accuracy and authenticity in its undisguised will to dominate. Consequently *Can Dialectics Break Bricks?* alerts audiences to the ease by which screen translation makes a bid for power. It demonstrates that the control of meaning through language is radically up for grabs as the capture of words is tentative and temporary rather than conclusive. As 'words are insubordinate', they make it 'impossible for power to totally coopt created meanings, to fix an existing meaning once and for all' ('Captive Words' 2006 [1966]: 223). The Situationists identified this 'insubordination of words, their desertion or open resistance ... as a symptom of the general revolutionary crisis of ... society' ('All the King's' 2006 [1963]: 150), and propose that 'language is the house of power' ('Captive Words' 2006 [1966]: 222). For Viénet (2006 [1967]: 274) moreover, parodic screen translation forms part of the Situationist 'promotion of guerrilla tactics in the mass media', combating censorship and conformity alike. It also challenges Nornes's notion of abuse, by illuminating both its divergence from, and its commonality with, deconstruction.

Re-titling

The title of Nornes's *Film Quarterly* article ('For an Abusive Subtitling') directly appropriates the 'original' French title ('Vers la traduction abusive') of Lewis's 'The Measure of Translation Effects'.[12] This debt to Lewis is openly acknowledged by Nornes. However, despite resuscitating Lewis's earlier French title, Nornes (2007: 179) is at pains to distance himself from Lewis's 'Derridean approach to translation'. In *Film Quarterly*, this dismissal is explicit: 'while the notion of abusive translation originates from a Derridian [*sic*] perspective, the third epoch of subtitling I am identifying also rejects poststructuralism's endless play of signification', continuing, 'this abusive turn ... is also a turn from Lewis' (Nornes 1999: 29). Although this denunciation of Derrida via Lewis is less direct in *Cinema Babel*, it is by no means mitigated or revoked. The intention remains unchanged and it is left for the reader to join the dots, with Derrida and deconstruction linked to Eurocentrism, elitism and distancing effects (Nornes 2007: 179). Nornes views deconstruction as inaccessible and out-of-touch, and hence as deterrence rather than tool.

In resurrecting the earlier French title of 'The Measure of Translation Effects', Nornes blatantly ignores Lewis's (1985: 33) advice. Lewis proposes that, in English, the term 'abuse' 'fails to ring true' as it misses one 'connotation of the French cognate: false, deceptive, misleading'. Consequently, when he self-translates his French essay into English, Lewis drops this term altogether from the title. Lewis finds that in order for it 'to "work" in English', his essay must accommodate itself to the specific 'characteristics of English that serve to contrast it with French' (35) while also taking account of the 'Anglo–American intellectual environment that is circumscribed by the language' (33). He argues that, by avoiding the less playful, more explicitly violent ('injurious', 'insulting') connotations of the English term 'abuse' (38), his transformed title is able to compensate for the translation's unavoidable violation of the 'original'. In light of these comments by Lewis as author-translator, Nornes's subsequent decision to reinstate Lewis's discarded title, knowingly inviting the injurious English-language connotations of 'abuse', appears an instance of misuse.

The mis/appropriation of 'abuse' within translation theory is discussed at some length by Edwin Gentzler (2002), particularly in relation to Lawrence Venuti's seminal publication *The Translator's Invisibility* (1995). Gentzler (2002: 203) examines how Venuti appropriates the notion of 'abusive fidelity' for his own ends, 'to support arguments for resistant theories of translation'. Venuti (1995: 19–21) associates abuse with

Schleiermacher's foreignising approach, whereby 'the translation leaves the author in peace, as much as possible, and moves the reader towards him' (Lefevere quoted in Venuti 1995: 19–20). Interpreting foreignisation as inherently political, Venuti (1995: 18) proposes that notions of fidelity and freedom are always historically determined and that, hence, 'appeals to the foreign text cannot finally adjudicate between competing translations'. Traditional notions of fidelity, equivalence and accuracy, he continues, typically suppose that meaning is fixed and able to be controlled by the target-language culture (18). In contrast, *abusive fidelity* offers a strategy of '*resistancy*' that 'avoids fluency' and thereby 'challenges the target-language culture even as it enacts its own ethnocentric violence on the foreign text' (24).

Identifying this 'ethnodeviant' (Venuti 1995: 20) interpretation of the abusive as part of a 'violent turn' within Translation Studies, Gentzler (2002: 202) deems it a misreading. He accuses Venuti of transposing the term into English, and in the process eliminating 'the play, connotations, tricks, and deception of the term in Lewis's context'. Critiquing Venuti's forceful delineation of abusive translation, he instead applauds the 'carefully written, tentative' tone of Lewis. In actual fact, however, it is not Venuti but Lewis himself who carries Derrida's phrase over into English and develops its conceptualisation. Gentzler's (2002: 201) statement that Lewis 'avoided the term *abusive* in English for fear of its being misappropriated by English-speaking scholars' is simply untrue. Lewis repeatedly employs this term throughout 'The Measure of Translation Effects'. What Lewis avoids is not the English term itself but, rather, the English *title* 'Towards Abusive Translation', which Nornes later resurrects. Venuti *does* effectively fix the meaning of abusive fidelity to foreignising translation and the 'rejection of fluency', as Gentzler (202) notes, yet the *violent* connotations of abuse are invoked as much by Lewis (and Derrida) as Venuti.

Lewis's (1985: 33) decision to avoid 'a stilted transfer of meanings' in his English translation ('The Measure of Translation Effects') and instead 'to endow it with the texture of a piece written in English for an English-speaking audience' (in order to make it 'fit in better, go down and over better') follows, in part, the conventional '*us*-system' ('the *us*ual, the *us*eful, and common linguistic *us*age') that characterises fluent translation (40) – denounced by Nornes and Venuti alike as corrupt and domesticating. Admittedly, Lewis's decision is justified somewhat by the additional commentary function he assumes as author-translator and his decision to shift the tone, meaning and message (along with the title) of his essay from a 'theoretical excursus' to a 'discussion emphasizing the practical processes and concrete results of translation' (33). Nevertheless, this accommodating effort towards English linguistic and cultural norms partly defuses his conception of abuse. It seems to contradict outright Lewis's denunciation of the *us*-system, which 'domesticates or familiarizes ... at the expense of whatever might upset or force or abuse language and thought' (41). Certainly, Lewis creates 'an ambivalent relation' between his translation and 'original', yet its language and texture show no sign of 'forcing the linguistic and conceptual system of which it is a dependent' (42).

On the other hand, when Lewis proceeds to analyse F. C. T. Moore's translation of Derrida's 'La mythologie blanche' (1974 [1971]), his theorisation of 'the abuse principle' runs into problems of another kind. Here, in analysing the translation of a text that is itself already abusive in regards to the French language, Lewis stresses foremost the need to preserve the force of Derrida's performative, textual knots, in order to 'rearticulate analogically the abuse that occurs in the original text' (43). For Lewis, Moore's translation fails on this front. Its 'well-formed sentences' that 'tie ... together much more tightly than does the French' serve to anglicise and flatten Derrida's project – they prioritise and 'respect the use-values of English' (50). Hence, for Lewis, Moore's translation does not 'measure up to the standard for abusive fidelity' (56). Here, as Jane Gallop (1994: 94) comments, Lewis produces a 'very traditional critique of translation, bemoaning the loss of the force of the original French text'. Specifically, she notes how 'the other side of abusive translation ... which actually is abusive as a translation rather than a translation of abuse – it just drops out of his argument'. Indeed, in delineating his programme for abusive translation Lewis insists that as well as forcing language by seeking 'to match the polyvalencies or plurivocities or expressive stresses of the original', it must, at the same time, aim to 'displace, remobilize, and extend this abuse ... directing a critical thrust back toward the text that it translates' (43). When it comes to Derrida, however, the requirement that abusive translation 'goes beyond – fills in for – the original' seems to retreat in importance. Douglas Robinson (1997: 134) reiterates this point, suggesting that, by focusing on the translation of already abusive texts like Derrida's, abuse often devolves into a servile form of fidelity. Robinson queries: 'wouldn't an abusive translation of that sort of text, especially one that returned abuse for abuse, actually be conforming to source-language usage rather than deviating from it, and thus be a contradiction in terms ...?'

Deconstruction Detourned

For Gallop (1994: 48), it is only the 'second function' of abuse (its unsettling of the 'original') that is actually deconstructive and it is this function that is repeatedly lost in its practical application. She notes how defaulting back to a traditional notion of translation that privileges the 'original' is a particularly common characteristic of supposedly deconstructive texts, including those of Derrida himself (52). Referring to 'Plato's Pharmacy' (1972), Gallop (1994: 53) comments, it 'does not seem a very deconstructive notion of translation: Derrida bemoans what has been "obliterated" by translators and takes us back to what is in the original text'. As she point out, the task of displacing the 'original' is far harder to achieve in practice than in theory.[13] A similar argument is made by Pym (1995), who takes Derrida and deconstructionist texts to task for a tendency to 'inferiorize translation, even when they have no real interest in doing so, even when they proclaim they are doing precisely the opposite'. In these texts, notes Pym, 'actual translations are ... mostly seen in a rather traditional way, often saying less than their antecedents', while Derrida's 'chief source of delight' in *La dissémination* (1968) 'is his ability to correct the authority of the previous translators' of Plato.

Returning to Nornes, I contend that his appropriation of the term 'abuse' while concomitantly turning away from deconstruction is more violent and violating than Venuti. However, if violation constitutes an integral part of abusive translation, as evoked 'in that twist or skewing signalled by the prefix *ab* that is attached to the dominant c(h)ord of use' (Lewis 1985: 41), then how can the charge of mistranslation be sustained? To claim that either Venuti or Nornes misappropriate the deconstructive project of abusive translation is to rely on the possibility of an authentic or correct interpretation. However, as Venuti (1995: 18) reiterates following Derrida, interpretation is always contingent, historically determined and shifting. Gallop's (1994) critique suggests that even the authority of the author or author-translator cannot guarantee authenticity, arguing that Derrida's own iteration of abusive translation proves unable to transfer into the concrete. As there is 'no fully determined original in the first place', states Davis (2001: 90), the question of fidelity is the wrong one to be asking.

I revisit the deconstructive origins of 'abusive subtitling' not in order to show how this concept mistranslates or misinterprets either Derrida or Lewis, but, rather, to note how it registers a deliberate desire on the part of Nornes towards misappropriation and misuse. This is to agree with Spivak (1976) and Gallop (1994: 53) that the possibilities of *mis-*

translation should not be underestimated and that the force of translation may well lie in its uncontrollability and unauthorised chaos – a concept explored in detail in the second half of this book, in chapters that focus on media piracy and censorship, fan translation and the localisation of online video streaming. While Nornes's titular adoption of the term 'abuse' returns it to the limelight that Lewis specifically sought to avoid via his measured strategy of non-equivalence, it is potentially more in line with its 'original' force summoned in 'The *Retrait* of Metaphor', where Derrida refers to abuse as 'a kind of quasi-catachrestic violence' (2007 [1978]: 67).

By rejecting the deconstructivist critical thrust of abusive translation, Nornes enacts an appropriation that is ultimately more violent and extreme than Lewis would like. Far from discrediting Nornes, however, the force of this abuse uncovers a productive undercurrent. In contrast to the hesitant warnings of Lewis and Gentzler, Nornes demonstrates that disparity between the French and English connotations of 'abuse' generates an incommensurability that is more productive than inhibiting. When conjoined to subtitling (with its mundane associations), the excessive violence of the term 'abuse' is only further accentuated. The disparity between the two terms produces precisely the connotations of play and trickery that Lewis refuses to risk. This exaggerated disconnect provides an excessive drama to Nornes's delineation of 'abusive subtitling' – making the phrase both unexpected and memorable. Indeed, it is precisely due to this *mis*appropriation that the 'abuse principle' has managed to break beyond the confines of post-structuralist critical theory and gain widespread interest across Screen and Translation Studies where it has mostly been linked to fansubbing practices, as I discuss in Chapter 5.[14]

If we think of Nornes parting ways with deconstruction theory in order to align abuse with populist, playful modes of foreignisation and rescue it from the wasteful excesses of Eurocentric post-structuralism, it is clear that unauthorised usage is key to this process. In this way, *Can Dialectics Break Bricks?* may have more in common with the possibilities of abuse than Nornes recognises. Moreover, Nornes's decision to abuse the abusers, to deliberately misappropriate the term 'abuse' by defusing its deconstructive force and thereby violating its authorised usage, cannot, in the end, be separated from the project of deconstruction itself. Ultimately, it is impossible to discern where the abuse of abuse begins and ends, or to distinguish victims from perpetrators (see Robinson 1997: 137; Gentzler 2002: 206).

Lewis, Venuti and Nornes all attempt to control and constrain Derrida's brief allusion to abusive translation within 'The *Retrait* of Metaphor'. Each also attempts to introduce abusive strategies into their own translations and interpretations, seeking to concretise their abusive thinking. In doing so, however, they overlook the degree to which the value of abuse resides more in the impurities of practice than any ideal of fidelity. That is, abuse has less to do with fidelity than with the contingencies of the actual and the errors of the concrete. Hence, where Nornes falters most notably is, I argue, in this transition from practice to theory. Nornes's practical concerns are interesting and insightful, whereas his conceptual schema reverts to prescription over open-ended possibility. Dismissing the abstraction of deconstruction theory and post-structuralism as elitist, Nornes's own theoretical traversals tend towards conceptual lock-down. As I discuss further in Chapter 5, Nornes pinpoints instances where others like Viénet and the Situationists go astray, while elevating isolated instances of screen translation that, when put to the test, uncover a plethora of holes. Ultimately, Nornes judges *Can Dialects Break Bricks?* as corrupt due to its excessive domination over and disrespect for its source. In this regard, he *follows* Lewis rather than departing from him. Together with Venuti, Nornes accepts and reaffirms Lewis' (1985: 42) claim that abuse amounts to 'a new axiomatics of fidelity.'

For Nornes, fidelity is not forsaken via abusive translation but rather, reconceived and strengthened. Furthermore, like Lewis, he largely ignores the two-way, theoretical complexity of abuse, opting instead to explore a uni-directional abusive drift that affirms entrenched hierarchies between original and translation. Here, a gap emerges between saying and doing. In practice, Nornes's appropriation (and retranslation) of abuse constitutes a wilful act of critique and *mis*-use. This critique is partly performed through language experimentation and texture, with the words 'abusive' and 'subtitling' playing against one another to create dissonance. Ultimately, I suggest that Nornes's remobilisation/recalibration of the term 'abuse' more closely resembles the de-authoring and unauthorised appropriations of the Situationists than the type of respectful play to which he restricts abusive subtitling 'proper'. Moreover, by wilfully misusing the concept of abuse, Nornes gives it new life, as becomes evident in relation to the phenomenon of fansubbing explored in Chapter 5. Ironically, Nornes also manages to partially evade the constriction of his own conceptual schema through the contradictions that surface via his filmic and televisual examples. At times these examples seem to work against his arguments by detailing abusive situations that do not easily fit his theoretical definition. Concrete instances of translation abuse, such as the parodic mistranslation of *Can Dialectics Break Bricks?*, point to contexts and tactics that prove far less containable than Nornes suggests.

Overall, Nornes's illustrative examples demonstrate how the concrete can defy control in its irreducible specificity and contingency.

Foremost, Nornes rallies against the demonstrable impracticality and inaccessibility of deconstruction, obsessed as it is with complicated textual intrigues, laboured word play and neologisms born from graphic/grammatical intervention (such as Derrida's signature term *différance*).[15] This response rehearses the common complaint that Derrida focuses myopically on the textual to the exclusion of all that is *con*textual or *extra*-textual. While this argument is eruditely discredited by the likes of Smith (2005), Kathleen Davis (2001) and Ross Benjamin (2004), it continues to exert influence nevertheless. Even Derrida acknowledged the power of this argument, referring to it as the 'Derrida' myth, and responding, in his defence, that, on the contrary, his work attempts 'to understand what is going on precisely *beyond* language' (quoted in Smith 2005: 16). While I agree with Davis (2001: 4) that deconstruction 'argues for the inescapable importance of attending to history' and that it is 'deeply political' (46), the enduring strength of the Derrida myth suggests that there may be something in his 'tortuous, precious, language-straining French' (Lewis 1985: 57) almost predisposed to put readers offside. Hence, it is understandable that practising translators in particular might find Derridean deconstruction frustratingly impractical. However, in rehearsing this surface response, Nornes overlooks the possibility that deconstruction may actually aid in the crucial project of bridging or, at the least, exploring and interrogating theory/practice gaps. By adopting Derridean terminology while nevertheless neglecting its theoretical impetus, Nornes effectively misses an opportunity – one that this book seeks to reclaim.

Notes

1. Henceforth quotations from the French-language version of *Can Dialectics* are reproduced in English translation only, using subtitles prepared by Keith Sanborn. Following Sanborn as well as Ken Knabb's translation of Guy Debord and Gil J. Wolman (2006 [1956]), when the concept of *détournement* is used as a verb, it does not retain an accent.
2. Consequently perhaps, many discrepancies plague attributions of Situationist authorship. In the French-language reprint of the collected issues of the *Internationale Situationiste* journal, 'Captive Words' is attributed to Mustapha Khayati whereas in Knabb's translation it is anonymous, and in Michael Kelley and Yvan Tardy (2008) it is attributed to Debord.
3. In 'The Use of Stolen Films', Guy Debord (2003 [1989]: 233) writes: 'these stolen fiction films, external to my film but brought into it, are used,

regardless of whatever their original meaning may have been, to present the rectification of the "artistic inversion of life"'.

4. As I go on to discuss, Keith Sanborn (2010) and Jonathan Rosenbaum (1997) claim that *Can Dialectics Break Bricks?* was produced in at least two language versions, one dubbed and the other subtitled.

5. This quote is from 'A User's Guide to Détournement' published just prior to the official formation of the Situationist International (SI) in 1957. The SI grew out of the earlier Paris-based Lettrist movement which itself bore links to Surrealism and Dadaism. Debord joined the Lettrists in 1950 and formed part of its breakaway left-wing faction, the Lettrists International. Marxist politics were pre-eminent within the SI and radical, public actions, such as protests and demonstrations, were promoted along with cultural and artistic interventions. These actions culminated in the Paris May 1968 student and workers revolts. See Elizabeth Sussman (1989: 2–15).

6. These include *Les Filles de Kamare / The Girls of Kamare* (1974), based on two Japanese sexploitation films, and *Chinois, encore un effort pour être révolutionnaires / Chinese, One More Effort if You Would Be Revolutionaries* (1977), which remixes documentary footage. See Joel Kuennen (n.d.) and Sean Welsh (2011). Andrew Uroskie (2011: 30) is another Situationist scholar who refers to *Can Dialectics* exclusively in his footnotes.

7. Interestingly, Ken Knabb's English translation of excerpts from the collected journals omits many notable entries on cinema. On cinema and the Situationist movement, see Thomas Y. Levin (1989).

8. Other than an extremely brief mention in Ella Shohat and Robert Stam (1985: 48) and Nornes (2007: 180; 269n43), see Welsh (2011) for a preliminary consideration of the translational dynamics of *Can Dialectic*'s *détournement*.

9. The Situationists continually stressed the importance of language and terminology, providing lists of definitions and even a preface to a Situationist Dictionary. 'Captive Words' (2006 [1966]: 222) refers to the need for every 'revolutionary theory' to 'invent its own terms, to destroy the dominant sense of other terms and establish new meanings' as it is 'impossible to get rid of a world without getting rid of the language that conceals and protects it'. See also Michael Kelley and Yvan Tardy (2008).

10. *Enragés et situationnistes dans le mouvement des occupations* (Paris: Gallimard, 1968).

11. On the ideological implications of translation fluency, see Venuti (1995: 19–25). On fluent/non-fluent translation in relation to notions of 'good' and 'bad,' see Douglas Robinson (1997: 108–11).

12. The 'literal rendering' in English offered by Lewis (1985: 33) of his French title is 'Toward Abusive Translation.' Interestingly, in *Cinema Babel*'s publication details, Nornes adopts Lewis' translation instead of his own when acknowledging his *Film Quarterly* article, mistakenly citing it as 'Toward an Abusive Subtitling: Illuminating Cinema's Apparatus of Translation,' and

thereby proving Debord and Wolman's (2006 [1956]: 20) assertion that 'all titles are interchangeable.'

13. For Gallop, Spivak's 1976 translation of Derrida's *De la Grammatologie* (1967) goes some way toward achieving this leap from the abstract to the actual. In her translator's preface, Spivak summons a reader 'who would fasten upon [her] mistranslations and with that leverage deconstruct Derrida's text beyond what Derrida as controlling subject has directed in it'.

14. Nornes's concept of 'abusive subtitling' has received widespread interest within Screen and Translation Studies, so much so that Nornes revisited the concept in a 2016 public lecture in order to engage with critiques. See, for example, Giorgio Hadi Curti (2009), Colm Caffrey (2009), Dwyer (2005), Kofoed (2011), Kwai-Chung Lo (2005), McClarty (2014), Massidda (2015), Colleen Montgomery (2008), O'Hagan (2011), O'Sullivan (2011), Pérez-González (2006, 2007), Michael Raine (2015), Amresh Sinhar (2004), Schules (2014), Secară (2011), White (2010) and Woods (2011).

15. According to Jonathan Rée (1994: 42), when transposed into English as 'an unmodified French word', *différance* loses its philosophical meaning to become a symbol of 'translationism', indicating how philosophical English 'has been fashioned by the translators'. As Rée explains, Derrida created this term 'so that the difference between difference and differance could be seen but not heard. But everything that may be gained by this device is destroyed in English if the word is left in French, since the difference between difference and *différance* is all too painfully audible.'

Part 2

Errant and Emergent Practices

CHAPTER 4

Media Piracy, Censorship and Misuse

This chapter aims to rethink the topic of media translation by focusing on its faults. It argues that translation faults – errors, failures, mistranslations and misrepresentations – signal pressure points or cracks vital to the re-evaluative objective of this book as a whole. Specifically, I am interested in examining 'errancy' as a fault line that is rapidly spreading across the surface of the contemporary AVT landscape, becoming increasingly relevant to the ways in which screen translation is produced and received. The rise of amateur translation and media piracy, for instance, indicates vast areas of practice largely defined in terms of illegality and non-professionalism. This chapter does not deplore, celebrate or seek to remedy wayward forms of screen translation. Rather, it examines their mechanisms, causes and effects, acknowledging their unwieldy productivity and politics: how they bring into relief the unequal power dynamics that attend screen media in the global era. It concentrates on two areas of practice where mistranslation is dominant: censorship and the 'guerrilla translations' (see Dwyer 2012a) of media piracy. Consistently challenging professional norms and standards, these two areas of activity testify to the prevalence and persistence of non-qualitative criteria in translation practice and politics.

Since the emergence of mass media forms and increasingly in the global era, translation provides a routine yet little discussed mode through which media censorship operates. While censorship itself is often identified as a negative, repressive practice, it can also, conversely, be promoted as a defence against harmful elements and influences, as I explore in relation to screen regulating bodies and ratings systems. These shifting evaluations concern the *why* of censorship practice. By concentrating instead on *how* censorship operates – through deliberately erroneous instances of translation – I approach this thematic from a different angle. In focusing on concrete practices and pragmatic considerations, I explore how censorship pervades professional subtitling and dubbing operations, expanding

notions of translation errancy and intimating new conceptual possibilities.
I then proceed to examine the types of amateur, unskilled translations
that commonly aid and abet piracy operations. Pirated screen translation accrues multiple layers of errancy, contravening copyright laws and
regularly failing in attempts to mimic professional norms. On the other
hand, pirate translation can include fansubbing, discussed in the following chapter, which has proved able to produce highly skilled, specialised
results. In this chapter, I introduce the umbrella term 'guerrilla translation'
to refer to both fan and non-fan modes of pirate translation, underscoring
the commonality that underlies such distinctions while drawing attention
to non-Western and non-English speaking contexts as sites of geopolitical
contestation. Censorship and piracy deploy subtitling and dubbing to radically different ends, intersecting with errant value politics in both unregulated and over-regulated contexts. Together, they indicate the excessive,
far-reaching impact of errancy on everyday practices of screen translation.

The Censor's Toolbox

Censorship and/as translation is a vast topic that deserves to be charted
according to different national, historical and political contexts. My aim
here is more modest however, as such a task falls beyond the scope of this
book. Focusing on how this relationship plays out in the context of screen
media in particular, the present discussion veers towards generalities
punctuated by specific examples and practices. Primarily, it engages with
the negative, value-laden nature of censorship operations and how they
affect screen translation as a whole, perhaps even signalling a dominant
strain within professional practice. The subject of censorship cannot help
but conjure associations with the negative. It is either seen in itself as
repressive and 'bad' or, alternatively, as a form of defence against 'bad',
harmful influences. When censorship proceeds via translation its adverse
associations are further accentuated. Censoring translation is wilfully
wayward, deliberately misrepresenting its source, deliberately *mis*translating. In this sense, censoring subtitles and dubs are excessive to translation
'proper', they exceed proper or legitimate usage. Moreover, this excessive
errancy is neither oppositional nor subversive but, rather, regulatory and
repressive. In this way, the errancy of censoring translation suggests a new
interpretation of translation 'abuse' that strains against its deconstructive and foreignising definitions mooted in Chapter 3. Destabilising the
primacy of 'quality' within translation practice, censoring subtitles and
dubbing indicate grounded instances of translation errancy that are inherently re-evaluative.

One of the first things to note about the interrelation between censorship and translation is ambivalence. These two modes or operations are at once friends and foe, alike and oppositional, and the degrees to which they come to either resemble or repel each other constantly shift. On one level, censorship and translation appear at cross-purposes: translation facilitates where censorship frustrates. While censorship blocks or restricts access, translation enables and expands it (see Stephenson 2007: 235). However, although such a dynamic is certainly possible, it is naive to assume that it describes a natural or stable state, or even that these two functions are necessarily always distinguishable. As the example of *Can Dialectics Break Bricks?* highlighted in Chapter 3, translation inevitably involves a bid for control, and here lies its commonality with censorship: both involve power play. As I go on to explore, translation can both service and subvert censorship, and degrees of similarity persist between these operations. Significantly, censoring impulses can infiltrate even the most benign or innocuous operations of translation, demonstrating the broad relevance of categories of errancy and excess to translation scholarship and practice as a whole.

Censorship has been closely linked to screen media since its emergence as the 'first form of mass entertainment' (Grieveson 2004: 14).[1] As Philip French and Julian Petley (2007: 25) note, 'cinema provided the politicians and guardians of morality with the paradigm for censorship in the twentieth century'. The public, accessible and popular nature of film drew it to the attention of regulating bodies from the start, and it has long been recognised as a powerful form of propaganda and, concomitantly, as something requiring strict control. While many volumes have been written on the subject of media censorship, however, far fewer consider the central role that translation often plays in its operations.[2] Along with the prominently publicised technique of cutting, translation constitutes an indispensible component of the screen censor's toolbox. Forming part of screen censorship's techniques and technologies, translation directs attention to practical processes and 'productive effects' (Cather 2009: 61). This approach takes a cue from Foucault, whose detailed rethinking of power mechanisms and operations of control has been particularly influential within media censorship discourse, and is especially evident in the notion that censorship *creates* as much as it *regulates*, producing and shaping the very discourse it ostensibly censures.[3] In the following discussion, I consider screen translation as a tool in this process, outlining various ways in which translation is deployed as a censoring and anti-censorship tool via regulations, ratings and diverse informal and industry practices.

Bad Influences, Moral Goods

French and Petley (2007: 27) argue that 'at every societal level we have been inculcated with the idea that censorship is necessary–to preserve the social order, to protect "us" from "them" and to keep in check what the censorious regard as our baser instincts'. Patrick Garry (1993: xvii) observes that censorship operations often treat speech as action, indicating 'a social desire to impose certain quality standards on ... public speech'. For Garry (11), this 'fear of the destructive power of certain speech' is closely linked to the predominance of mass media and the image, and also relates distinctly to notions of 'quality'. Consequently, 'bad language' is a frequent focus of film and television censors (see Jay 1992: 195–234). Censorship decisions can be made on the basis of ideological or cultural agendas, or due to market and economic imperatives. Often, censorship regulators seek justification by appealing to notions of protection and the 'greater good'. As do anti–censorship advocates, although with a distinctly different sense of where the 'greater good' lies. In this analysis, I am interested less in ideological arguments for or against censorship, and more in its practical processes and effects. Discussions that focus on *why* censorship occurs often involve an evaluative objective, considering for instance whether certain types of censorship can be justified or not – seeking to examine their ideological basis, rationale and context. The present discussion, on the other hand, focuses on the minutiae of censorship operations and their impact. As Kirsten Cather (2009: 61) notes, 'considering what remains of a text after the censor's scissors do their work is crucial, since this is the text that audiences consume'.

The significance of censorship for the re-evaluative aims of this book relates to its near ubiquity. As I go on to detail, censorship in translation, particularly within mass media subtitling and dubbing, is almost inescapable, and can take the form of personal decisions made by translators, adherence to professional norms or conventions, commercial pressures and state-imposed regulations. Peter Fawcett (2003: 153), for instance, refers to the pervasive 'Americanisation of the original' that occurs in much English-language film translation. In such cases, he claims, the 'creeping colonisation' of much mainstream Anglophone screen translation silences and thereby censors culturally specific references.[4] The nigh-inevitability of some form of censorship infiltrating media translation suggests that errancy and excess are likewise, ubiquitous to the field. Consequently, censoring subtitles and dubbing indicate the broad relevance of errancy for translation as a whole, beyond niche and non-professional practices. Nevertheless, it is critical that variances in levels and degrees of censorship are acknowledged. The fact that certain forms of censorship appear a necessary component of socialisation (as when parents censor their conversation and behaviour in the presence of children, or when individuals censor their interactions with others in order to avoid causing offence) does not mitigate the extremity of measures used by autocratic or totalitarian regimes. In these very distinct modes of censorship, categories of errancy vary considerably. Censorship in film translation occurs at both ends of the spectrum, and everywhere in between, as the examples below demonstrate.

Censoring translation intentionally misrepresents or mis-communicates source material. Misrepresentation can occur at the level of words, images and other non-verbal forms of signification, under either internally or externally imposed conditions. Moreover, boundaries between internal and external forms, between self-censorship and state censorship, often blur, as personal decisions reflect broader political, historical and social contexts (Fawcett 2003: 161–3). Filmmaker Andrzej Wajda (1997: 107), for instance, distinguishes between constraints that filmmakers or translators might place upon themselves and those that are enforced by outside institutions, bodies or regulators. While this distinction is useful, it also oversimplifies matters, as it is not always clear where such boundaries lie. Should professional translation norms or conventions, for example, be considered internal or external factors? Although such conventions may not be enforced by punitive measures, nonconformity can result in loss of income, employment or respect (see Díaz Cintas 2012: 283). Similarly, how does technology complicate the picture? How do subtitling and dubbing practices feed into the inbuilt regulatory dynamics of different digital and online formats such as VCDs, DVDs, downloadable files and streaming? Brian Hu (2006) argues that DVD region coding functions as a form of geo-blocking or censorship that implicates translation processes in its operations, as one way 'territorial rights and geographic windows are maintained via DVD is through subtitles and audio channels'. Certainly, such technological parameters affect issues of access, and often the only way to avoid their inbuilt inequalities is to opt out of the system altogether by pursuing alternative, illegal practices such as piracy (see Hu 2006; Hu 2010).

Another way to approach the topic of censorship and translation is by distinguishing between self-censorship, state censorship and industry censorship. While self-censorship can take many forms, ranging from politeness (Hatim and Mason 2000) to depoliticisation, industry censorship can include professional, commercial and technological factors. When examining the specifics of different national media regulation systems, significant zones of co-implication emerge between these various categories. The British Board of Film Classification (BBFC), for instance, boasts its independence from government on the basis that it receives no government funding and the government plays no role in its appointments. However, the government retains the power to de-designate the board at any point (French and Petley 2007: 94). Moreover, the UK ratings system, like that of the United States, provides a market incentive for distributors, filmmakers and translators to self-censor. As the BBFC's David Cooke explains (see French and Petley 2007: 102–4) a '12A' rating (suitable for 12 years and over) ensures film distributors a far greater market share than a '15' rating (suitable only for 15 years and over).

One major distinction between ratings categories that cover minors relates to the use of the word 'fuck' (French and Petley 2007: 102–4; see also Pujol 2006). In Australia, the 'MA15+' rating (restricted to those 15 and over) was used to classify the Swedish-language film *Fucking Åmål / Show Me Love* (1998). Although the 'MA15+' rating covers films that feature 'strong impact coarse language', the change of title that occurred when the film was exhibited in Australia followed the Anglophone trend to tone down or eliminate strong language (here, used to express teenage frustration with small-town life in Sweden's Åmål). In this case, the title *Fucking Åmål* was replaced with a far less shocking, more upbeat title (*Show Me Love*) alluding to the film's coming of age/coming out story. Ironically however, the Swedish title does not actually require translation at all, as it contains only an internationally recognised English-language expletive and a Swedish place name. Moreover, the softening of the language that occurred in its English retitling suggests that further censorship could lie concealed within this film's interlingual translation.

In Turkey, the distinction between state-regulated censorship, commercial imperatives and self-censorship is particularly blurred. As Asli Takanay and Sirin Baykan (2009) explain, the judiciary bodies that regulate TV broadcasting in Turkey (according to special laws introduced in the early 1980s and 1990s and amended in 2002) are insulated by the Radio and Television Supreme Council, which consists of ten members, the majority of whom represent the ruling party and includes the President. Although the Supreme Council can impose fines for violations of national media transmission laws, block broadcasts for limited periods, alter subtitles without consultation and even shut down TV channels, they do not see themselves as a censorship body because they respond post-broadcast, refrain from intervening during the production phase and play no part in broadcasting decisions. However, as Takanay and Baykan note, the Supreme Council can block entire programmes on the basis of a single line

Figures 4.1 and 4.2 Publicity posters for the Polish (upper) and US (lower) releases of
Fucking Åmål / *Show Me Love* (2002). © Memfis Film.

of dialogue, exerting pressure to self-censor on translators and television channels. In Turkey, banned words and topics include references to genitalia and acts of defecation, slang terms such as 'arse', negative comments regarding religion and references to homosexuality (Takanay and Baykan 2009).

In other national contexts, the relationship between government and media censorship is more direct. In many cases, state-regulated media censorship enlists translation in its services. As discussed in Chapter 1, the mandatory dubbing of both foreign and domestic films in fascist Italy aimed to defend the Italian language from foreign influence and internationalism, and to 'purify from within' by insisting on a shared, standardised national tongue (Ben-Ghiat 1997: 441). According to Betz (2009: 90), 'the official Tuscan' that became the only acceptable language of Italian film production 'forged a synthetic unity' amongst the populace, superficially smoothing over the country's regionalised fragmentation. While today regional dialects remain strongly represented within Italy (Gendrault 2010: 229), when Mussolini came to power in 1922, around 30 per cent of the population communicated solely in dialect (Ben-Ghiat 1997: 439).[5] This evident regionalism jarred with Mussolini's nationalist agenda and eventually policies were developed to prohibit dialects and homogenise regional cultures (439–40).[6] The popular and accessible mass medium of film was seized upon as a vehicle for promoting national and linguistic unification. Described as a form of 'cultural levelling' by Shohat and Stam (1985: 50), the Mussolini dubbing decree saw the regional accents and dialects of local films erased by standardised Tuscan Italian. Other laws at the time saw dialects removed from the school curriculum and the daily press in 1932, and foreign words banned from advertising and business in 1940 (Ben-Ghiat 1997: 440–1).

To date, research into the specifics of fascist-era Italian dubbing is sparse although the research project Italia Taglia (www.italiataglia.it) is leading the way with its vast database of films subject to official censorship in Italy since 1913.[7] One such film is the Hollywood feature *The Adventures of Marco Polo* (1938), which was released in Italy as *Uno Scozzese alla corte del Gran Khan* ['A Scot at the Court of the Great Khan'] following Mussolini's protests over its 'frivolous' portrayal of the national hero, who was subsequently stripped of his Italian heritage to become the Scottish 'MacPool' in a concession to lip-sync considerations (see Whitman-Linsen 1992: 161; Ranzato 2016: 36). Detailed scholarship is also emerging on screen translation censorship in Franco's Spain, where a similar insistence on dubbing both local and imported films occurred (see Gutiérrez Lanza 2002; Vandaele 2007; Gómez Castro 2016).[8] Seeking

Figure 4.3 Italian poster for *The Adventures of Marco Polo* (1938). © MGM.

to uphold 'traditional national values' (Gutiérrez Lanza 2002: 151) as promoted by the Church, the Spanish censors promoted 'dictatorial moralistic principles' and political propaganda. In addition to banning scenes depicting or referring to adultery, promiscuous relationships, any

behaviour that eroded the sanctity of marriage and anything disrespect-
ful of the clergy, foreign influences were eradicated, as far as possible.
Dubbing eased this task. However, censored dubbing could produce
comical effects, as when *Love in the Afternoon* (1957) was released as *Ariane*
in a version that attempted ludicrously to conceal the adulterous nature of
the central character's relationships by replacing words such as *hombres*
[men] and *amigos* [friends] with the more chaste and 'socially acceptable'
connotations of *novios* [boyfriends] (149). Ironically, by seeking to conceal
the adulterous relationship at the heart of *Mogambo* (1953), the Spanish
censors introduced the subject of incest by turning the husband of Linda
Nordley (played by Grace Kelly) into her brother (Gutiérrez Lanza 2002:
148; Shohat and Stam 1985: 47).

At the other end of the political spectrum, Communist Romania
presents an interesting case study on the interrelationship between censorship, media and translation. In pre-1989 Romania, the Communist
state controlled all official broadcasting, film production and exhibition,
along with the importation of foreign-language media and its translation.
Subtitling was the preferred translation method adopted by the state. In
some ways, this choice jarred with its censorship objectives, as 'original'
dialogue remained accessible to those with the requisite language skills (see
Dwyer and Uricaru 2009). On the other hand, as Televiziunea Româna
employee Margareta Nistor notes, subtitling suited the 'changeable nature
of the censor's agenda by allowing for speedy, last minute alterations'
(quoted in Dwyer and Uricaru 2009: 47). In Communist Romania, film
and television subtitling was routinely subjected to ideological 'cleansing'.
For example, all references to religion were excised: 'God' was translated
as *Cel-de-Sus* [the one above], 'Church' became the nondescript *edificiu*
[edifice] and the religious holidays 'Easter' and 'Christmas' were replaced
by the all-purpose nomenclature 'holiday'.

Interestingly, while producing censoring subtitles in her professional
duties, Nistor also moonlighted as an underground, 'guerrilla' translator,
producing quick, cheap voice-overs for illicit media, demonstrating how
censorship can produce unintended by-products (Dwyer and Uricaru
2009: 49). In Romania, black-market, voice-over translations of pirated
media were often prepared without prior viewing and tended to be more
approximate than accurate. Sometimes a scene's dialogue would merely
be summarised in the passive voice. Translation errors were commonplace
as were technical shortcomings such as muffled sound tracks, bleeding
images and colour alteration. These pre-recorded voice-overs were supplemented by more desirable translations performed on the spot by audience members. 'The live translator would often be called upon to repeat

the performance for further viewings, sometimes up to fifty times, thus recalling the film-interpreting traditions that proliferated in the silent and early sound eras' (48). In both these modes of informal anti-censoring translation, errors and mistranslations were understandably common. However, in contradistinction to more professional, state-based subtitling practices, such flaws were largely unintentional. Consequently, in Romania, the failures and limitations of state-resistant screen translation were quite distinct from the deliberate excesses and mistranslations that characterised state-produced, censored subtitling.

Many threads of connection can be traced between state censorship, like that of Communist Romania and fascist Spain, the semi-state-imposed censorship of Turkey and supposedly independent industry censorship, like that of the UK and Australia. According to French and Petley (2007: 13) in the UK during the 1920s and 1930s, films were censored if they displayed tendencies judged as anti-monarchy, anti-police, anti-war or anti-white supremacy, and if they contained scenes featuring sexuality, infidelity, base emotions, violence or any 'burning questions of the day'! These days, media censorship pressures are particularly pronounced in relation to TV broadcasting, as this home-based medium reaches a far greater percentage of the population than theatrically released films. While Standards and Practices departments within broadcasting stations tend to be heavy-handed in censorship regulation, self-censorship is equally strong. Delia Chiaro (2007) notes that, although the Italian dubbed version of *Sex and the City* (1998–2004) was broadcast on satellite channel Canale Jimmy, which would normally allow less censorship, the strategies used reflect the *possibility* of the show being shown on mainstream TV and are thus heavily censoring, toning down language and omitting references to genitalia – justified by the dubbing director Luigi La Monica on the basis that Americans supposedly use more bad language than Italians. Chiaro (2007: 258) also notes that when Home Box Office (HBO) sold the series to the Turner Broadcasting System (TBS) – part of the Public Broadcasting Service – the US version was itself heavily censored, at times more so than the Italian version.

In the UK, toning down 'bad language' through revoicing is known as 'funstering', a term that came into use following a TV broadcast of *Lethal Weapon* (1987) in which all uses of the word 'fucker' were replaced by 'funster', creating a ridiculous scenario that culminated in the phrase 'muddy funster' for 'motherfucker'.[9] This example demonstrates how translation devices like dubbing are sometimes deployed irrespective of interlingual need, in same-language English-to-English contexts, to facilitate cultural accommodation and censorship. As subtitler John

Minchinton (see Fawcett 2003: 161) reports, the BBC 're-banned the use by its film translators of the f- and the c- word' in the 1970s. Today, common tactics for translating swear words involve the inclusion of asterisks, strings of typographical symbols (@#$%&!) known as grawlixes and 'obscenicons' (see Díaz Cintas 2012: 290). In France where there is supposedly 'no political censorship' (Wajda 1997: 107), dubbing practices can conceal subtle forms of textual manipulation, as occurred in the French dubbing of US TV series *Dynasty* (1981–89), which aired in France from 1983 onwards. In a scene in which Blake Carrington's son Steven comes out to his family as homosexual, the word 'gay' is translated as *'malade'* [sick], thereby attaching negative connotations to his sexuality.[10]

Censorship and the Abusive

For Nornes (2007), when degrees of misrepresentation become more or less 'accepted' within professional practice (as with self-censorship and the 'toning down' of strong language), it equates to a form of 'corruption'. In such cases, the translator's misrepresentation of the source material is often less easy to detect and more pervasive than with top-down forms of political censorship. While such misrepresentation can seem minor at the level of words, it can substantially change the tone of the source material overall (Mera 1999: 78). 'Cumulative presence and repeated absence build up a world view', states Fawcett (2003: 163) and 'in translated film, that view is dominated by the hegemonic power'. For Nornes and Venuti (1995), it is the invisibility of much translation domestication that is particularly problematic. Conversely, when censoring misrepresentations are overt rather than concealed, they can appear more abusive than corrupt. The euphemisms that littered Televiziunea Româna subtitles marked rather than disguised their level of corruption, and consequently created a destabilising dynamic (see Dwyer and Uricaru 2009). Like the parodic translation of *Can Dialectics Break Bricks?*, such forms of censorship make translation highly visible, drawing attention to its mediating function and introducing a level of self-reflexivity into reception processes.

In Communist Romania, the credit sequences of imported films were routinely removed and their titles transformed beyond recognition, forcing audiences to guess their identity (Dwyer and Uricaru 2009: 45). Hardly subtle, such 'heavy-handed' censorship tactics ironically resulted in particularly active forms of spectatorship, with viewers making calls and consulting reference and theory books to unravel the mysteries of identity. Such forceful and excessive forms of censorship edge very close to the abusive. Moreover, when Televiziunea Româna commissioned censoring subtitles, the foreign source language remained audible and hence fully accessible to multilinguals, almost encouraging deconstruction of the translation–censorship nexus. These overtly censored subtitles also led to alternative forms of politically subversive, informal screen translation operations, such as the black-market dubs produced by moonlighting state employees. Censoring translation defiantly resists demands for textual accuracy or fidelity of any sort – even the specifically 'violent fidelity' theorised by Derrida (2007 [1978]: 63). Hence, it also exceeds the boundaries of the abusive as delineated and debated by translation scholars, proving a *too concrete* and stubbornly normal instance of translation abuse. Derrida, Lewis (1985), Venuti (1995) and Nornes (2007) all develop abusive theories of translation constrained by notions of fidelity and foreignisation to the point that they are unable to engage with such everyday, pervasive forms of manipulation and misuse.

In their wilful unfaithfulness, censored subtitling and dubbing appear to cross the line of the 'not-too-abusive' that Derrida (2007 [1978]: 63) constructs, becoming too abusive to be of any 'good' use and exemplifying how situated practices of screen translation often exceed definitional limits. In practice, however, the overly abusive nature of translation censorship can alert audiences to the power dynamics at stake, leading to unintended, particularly productive effects, such as Romania's underground foreign-film viewing parties (see Dwyer and Uricaru 2009) and fansubbing (discussed in Chapter 5). The way in which censored translation exposes the 'too abstract' tendencies of abusive translation theories echoes Douglas Robinson's efforts to do the same by bringing ordinary notions of abuse and violence (particularly domestic violence) into play (1997: 137). For Robinson, the violence that Lewis (1985) and other translation scholars seek to recuperate through the abusive is itself the problem: the fact that 'translation ... is steeped in a culture of violence, that translation perpetuates and in some cases even glorifies that violence' (173). As with domestic violence, distinctions between perpetrators and victims sometimes blur, as those who experience abuse find themselves repeating abusive behaviours. For Robinson, foreignising theories of abusive fidelity resemble the self-justifying (il)logic of domestic violence perpetrators who claim their abusive behaviour is for the victim's own good (166–8).

Robinson (1997: 164) argues that abusive translation and servile, normative translation are both part of the same system, as 'each harbors a bit of the other'. 'Servility reflects an abusive history,' he continues, 'it is conditioned by abuse and can itself convert into 'a subtle channel of control disguised as neutral instrumentality', as when a translator 'projects her repressed need for stability and consistency and control onto the source text and resolves to find it there even when it is lacking' (163–4). Robinson points out that once the violence of the term 'abuse' is fully unleashed (as it is by Lewis, 'a native speaker of English … certainly aware that abuse is usually considered a bad thing'), it cannot be entirely recuperated (132–3). Hence, he notes, 'the sort of "strong, forceful" translation that Lewis theorises as abusive in his article is in this sense only one expression of abusiveness, one way in which the violence inherent in the system is channelled' (164). Other notions and practices of abuse express this violence in other ways, and cannot simply be dismissed as failing to qualify as abuse 'proper', when this term is itself defined, according to the online *Oxford Dictionary*, as a form of misuse. Rather, the violence and uncontrollability implicit in the term 'abuse' cannot be ignored. As Robinson warns, theorists of abusive translation need to consider the full implications of this term. 'It will do no good,' he warns, 'to protest that you didn't *mean* abuse that way' (173).

Media Piracy and Guerrilla Translation

As already discussed, media piracy is a common by-product of transla-tion censorship. As Laikwan Pang (2004) notes, in the global context, media piracy responds to uneven global flows of production, circulation and reception. While media piracy certainly occurs in Western and Anglophone countries, such locations are generally not identified as piracy 'hotspots', referred to as 'notorious markets' by the Motion Picture Association of America (MPAA) (see McIntosh 2015). Rather, the large majority of global media piracy operations involve the pirating of US media products in non-Western parts of the world. Consequently, the US industry constitutes media piracy's most vocal and litigious denouncer (Pang 2005: 135). With Hollywood reportedly losing over $2.4 billion per year through online piracy alone (see Alemi 2016), and the US economy as a whole losing around $250 billion per year (Scholes 2014), war is currently being waged (see Granados 2015).[11] The MPAA organises large-scale anti-piracy public awareness campaigns and publishes regular information and statistics on its operations. In 2009, the MPAA website asserted that 80 per cent of global piracy originates from outside the United States and that rates are highest in China, Russia and Thailand. Interestingly, this directly combative language has now been replaced by rhetoric emphasising the global, inclusive approach being adopted world-wide against piracy. Nevertheless, it is clear that whether 'hot' or 'cold', the war in which Hollywood is engaged primarily targets non-domestic piracy that, more often than not, involves layers of language difference and translation.

In the following chapter, I discuss at length the phenomenon of fan-subbing, which mostly constitutes a subset of pirate translation (with the exception of recent efforts towards legalisation and commercialisation). In this chapter, I consider the broader genre of pirate translation, characterising it as a 'guerrilla'-type practice that rebels against or resists legal media and translation frameworks. Representing different subsets of guerrilla translation, fan and non-fan pirate translations err in diverse ways. Non-fan guerrilla types, such as those accompanying traditional bootlegging operations, are often highly dysfunctional. Lovingly repro-ducing subtitle mishaps from a pirated DVD of *The Lord of the Rings: The Two Towers* (2002), the 'Engrish [*sic*] Two Towers Subtitles' website (www.anglefire.com/rings/ttt-subtitles/) illustrates how the textual inac-curacies of guerrilla translation can reach a point of unintelligibility (see Dwyer 2014). The cry of 'warmongering!', for instance, is subtitled as 'you are warm hungry'. On the other hand, guerrilla translation can function to subvert media regulation and censorship, as occurred in Communist Romania.

Hence, the shifting value of guerrilla translation further complicates and unsettles understandings of translation errancy and abuse, while also underlining the increasing relevance of such terms within today's global convergence culture. Current screen translation research needs to pay attention to the increasing presence of illicit and substandard sites of practice, and the geopolitical contexts from which they emerge. Guerrilla screen translation in its diversity raises a host of issues relating to the broader social and political context of subtitling and dubbing in the global era. As Hans Vöge (1977: 120) noted already in the 1970s, screen transla-tion likely reaches a larger audience than any other form of translation.

Figure 4.4 'Guerrilla' English subtitle for the line 'Warmongering' in *The Lord of the Rings: The Two Towers* (2002). © New Line Productions.
Subtitle courtesy the Engrish Two Towers website.

With current increases in informal distribution networks, online 'notorious markets' and 'rogue websites', this reach has grown exponentially.
Such forms of unofficial, underground translation effectively map the
routes by which global power relations intersect with language, pinpointing the extraordinary power wielded by entertainment media and its
translation in the exercising of cultural capital.

Bad Imitations

The errors and errancy characteristic of much non-fan guerrilla translation need to be defined and distinguished from other types of improper
and excessive translation discussed so far. As opposed to some fansubbing,
non-fan guerrilla subtitling and dubbing tend to imitate the norms and
conventions of mainstream, commercial practices, exhibiting a conservative formal and textual approach. On a pirated English-language box set
of *The Wire* (2002–8), for instance, the English-language subtitles are
a uniform white font and are conventionally positioned at the bottom
of the screen. They do not actively intervene with the source material
– providing no translator headnotes, glosses or discussion – and make
no attempt to emphasise the graphic or material dimension of spoken
or written language. Perusing a number of other pirated DVDs, similar
observations are made. The Vietnamese subtitle track found on a pirated
copy of *Iron Man* (2008) sourced in Ho Chi Minh City displays an unvarying yellow font and is again positioned at the bottom of the screen. The
DVD also contains a Vietnamese-language version, which consists of a
single voice speaking impassively over the top of the existing audio track
that remains faintly audible in the background.

In these examples, pirate subtitles mimic commercial norms, aiming
'to achieve a one-to-one correspondence between … two different medial
varieties of the same linguistic stimulus', and the 'subtitles only convey an
edited version of the character's speech' (Pérez-González 2007: 75). By
imitating the formal and textual norms and conventions of mainstream,
professional AVT, they attempt to pass as legitimate merchandise. The
profitability of such forms of guerrilla translation largely relates to how
successfully they mimic the strategies and production qualities of official,
legally sanctioned media, replicating (at least superficially) its audio, visual
and translation quality. Through such forms of imitation, guerrilla translation aims to achieve a level of invisibility. Instead, however, the act of
translation is made doubly visible. Despite aiming to pass as professional
and mainstream, guerrilla practices tend to announce themselves via overt
flaws. Citing 'ridiculous subtitles' as 'the one major element defining the

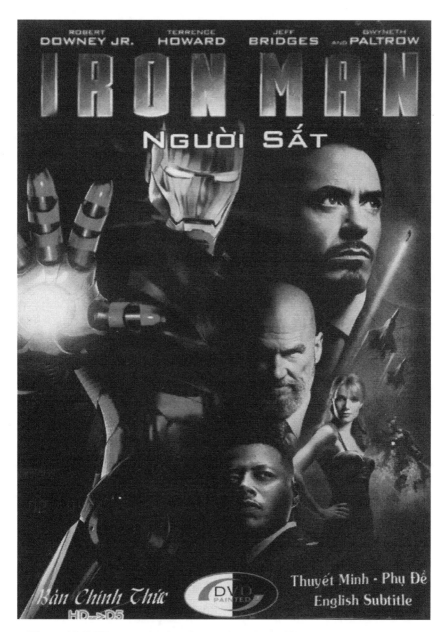

Figure 4.5 DVD cover of a pirated copy of *Iron Man* (2008). © Paramount Pictures.

unique pirated-Hollywood-movie-watching experience' in Hong Kong, for instance, Laikwan Pang (2005: 147) draws attention to the overtness of its dysfunction. Transcribing the English subtitles accompanying a pirated DVD of *Kill Bill: Vol. 1* (2003), Pang (147–8) reports how 'this set of subtitles … corresponds little to the real dialogue, and even suggests incorrect information'. Such errors stand out forcefully in comparison to the institutionalised invisibility of mainstream, professional subtitling. In this way, the imitative, conservative strategies of much non-fan, pirate translation ultimately expose the hidden agendas of professional practice (such as the invisibility effect that fluency facilitates) (Venuti 1995) and how 'translators are programmed to adopt a certain behaviour based on a set of accepted norms' (Díaz Cintas 2012: 283).

While fansubbing is often celebrated as a niche mode of guerrilla translation that is errant in a wilful, subversive sense, the dysfunctional errors of non-fan guerrilla translation are largely thought unredeemable. Despite its grey legality, fansubbing has proved capable of achieving higher levels of foreignising fidelity than its commercial counterpart (see Barra 2009: 519), whereas non-fan, profit-driven guerrilla translation augments what Creative Commons founder Lawrence Lessig (2004: 63) denounces as a non-creative form of 'copy-shop piracy' (62) that he specifically links to Asian counterfeiting practices (see Liang 2010: 359). Unlike parodic or fan translation, the errancy exhibited by pirate, guerrilla-style translation is typically not self-reflexive. Neither is it of a professional quality, as is much censored translation. Rather, guerrilla translation tends to be characterised by sloppiness, substandard expertise, poor working conditions and a 'bottom-line' mentality. Moreover, textual inaccuracy or misrepresentation is generally not its objective (as with both parody and censorship) but an unintentional by-product of lack (of time, care, responsibility or expertise). On the other hand, the diversity and uncontrollability of guerrilla screen translation has much to offer, unravelling the complicated spatial co-ordinates and everyday workings of media distribution systems while also unscrambling some of their messy politics. Despite having 'no political or intellectual calculation', according to Pang (2004: 28) the type of traditional media piracy so prolific within Asia 'may help to reveal the hidden patterns of our ideologically-infused entertainment technology'.

A Digital Frankenstein?

The conflict-ridden scene of media bootlegging is partly a response to the changing technologies of audiovisual media, and aids in delineating an international perspective. The errancy of guerrilla screen translation is experienced on a day-to-day basis by huge segments of the global population, permeating the non-Western, non-English-speaking terrain of the 'Majority World' where media piracy is rife and issues of translation regularly assume a guerrilla-like dimension. Hence, pirate translation interrogates the politics of access and global empowerment embroiled within the wider screen translation landscape. To a degree, this illegal activity simply realises the inbuilt reproductive potential of digital technology, exploring in full its logical repercussions. For Ramon Lobato (2008: 22), digital piracy is '[n]ot only ... a side-effect of technology developed by the major studios, but ... is also made possible in many cases by DVD preview discs secretly copied by U.S. technicians during postproduction.' Such copying itself registers the separation that digitisation forces between content and medium (see Wang 2003: 31). The endlessly reproducible nature of the digital now means that films can be effortlessly copied on to cheap, disposable formats such as CDs, DVDs and VCDs which themselves hold little value. As Liang (2009) states, 'the ordered flow of cinema is constantly frustrated by technologies that enable the reproduction of a 20 million dollar film on a 20 rupee CD'. These pirate economics have been dubbed a form of cockroach capitalism or 'globalization from below' (Baumgärtel 2006a; 2015), taking the decentralisation and deregulation of transnational capitalism to an extreme and uncovering legal loopholes and power inequalities in the process. 'In this type of globalisation,' states Tilman Baumgärtel (2015: 15), 'the participants are not multinational corporations any more, but smugglers, small-time crook and criminal gangs' whose 'organisation is flexible, fast and efficient, and ... crosses national boundaries'. Hence, he wonders if media piracy 'might be the most aggressive and most developed – illegal – version of capitalism' (Baumgärtel 2006b).

According to Shujen Wang (2003, 32), '[g]lobal audiences, more and better informed about new releases in the U.S. by instantaneous Webcasting, have become less willing to wait for local theatrical releases, creating an instant market for pirated products'. For this reason, media piracy and its guerrilla translations can be seen as responding to desire created by the speed of digital networking, one of the trickle-down effects of new technologies. For many in the Majority World, experiences with technology do not so much speed up everyday life as punctuate it with extended moments of delay and breakdown (Larkin 2004: 305). Nevertheless, an expectation of both speed and access sets in. According to Govil (2005), 'the argument within the industry for simultaneous global release has to do with narrowing the time during which piracy can take root in spaces waiting for legal distribution; today, that window is down to less than one day, including subtitling, etc.'.

Where fan and non-fan piracy differ in their use of new technologies is in relation to the Internet and online networking. Although media boot-legging has fully embraced digital DVD and VCD formats, and makes use of digital technologies to add or 'encode' subtitle and voice–over tracks, this deployment remains largely 'off–line' (Pang 2004: 25). In these types of media piracy, the online labour and distribution networks so central to fansubbing practices are almost entirely absent. Instead, bootlegging operations are commonly wedded to tangible objects that require actual distribution and transportation. As Baumgärtel (2006a: 383) notes, 'pirates in the Philippines seem to make little use of the means of digital distribution that are available to them, but seem to rely on more "traditional" methods, that include messengers and personal delivery, and using long distance busses [*sic*] and fishing boats for the delivery of illegal DVDs'. He continues, '[w]hen ... fishermen smuggle illicit movies into the country ... disks are hidden in the belly of tuna fish or in barrels of shrimp' (386).

According to Baumgärtel (2006a) and Rolando Tolentino (2006), these age–old methods underscore the long and complicated history of piracy in the Philippines. Here, on street corners, in parking lots and shopping malls, notes Tolentino, the term 'DVD' (pronounced 'Dividi' in 'a low almost sinister-like whisper') has come to signify both a national type (the Moro) and an entire way of life, rather than simply a technology. With pirates 'hand-delivering the master Dividi copy', media piracy in the Philippines is characterised by the 'anachronistic use of technology' where digital operations proceed hand in hand with more primitive technologies, methods and networks (Tolentino 2006). According to Pang (2004: 26), this 'sub-modern' dimension is often likened to 'guerrilla tactics' and encourages the 'Western stigmatisation of Asian movie piracy', linking it to the low-tech criminal worlds of drugs, theft, porn and terrorism (see also Baumgärtel 2015: 14). The offline nature of piracy in South East Asia reflects the fact that pirated discs 'require almost no technological knowledge' and are thus accessible to a broad demographic 'in terms of class, age, culture and geography' (Pang 2004: 25). Pirated discs can be played on pirated region-free DVD players ('the buyer will be asked ... what brand name he or she prefers to have glued on the generic player') (Tolentino 2006), whereas the even cheaper, 'everyday and user-friendly' VCD format (considered a primitive alternative to the DVD) emerged as particularly prominent within East Asian and Third World contexts (Davis 2003: 166; also see Pang 2004).

Errant Geographies

The anachronistic use of technology displayed by media pirates and guerrilla translators underscores its situated nature. Far from representing a physically liberating, deterritorialising tool, as is suggested by the rhetoric of progress, technology use is always geographically embedded. While VCDs have been referred to as a specifically 'Asian' technology particularly suited to piracy (see Davis 2003: 165–6), the politics of space and place also play out in relation to DVDs. As discussed earlier, Hu (2006) implicates the entire DVD region coding system in 'enforcing economic and political censorship by denying the option to see alternative films or alternate versions with alternative languages':

> When films are sold for territorial distribution, they are typically sold not simply by country, but by language … Region coding can also help enforce these linguistic territorial rights since Chinese-language DVDs (Region 3 and 6) are incompatible with French DVD players (Region 2). (Hu 2006)

For Hu, region coding is currently deployed to entrench US-favoured distribution strategies and regulations and, as a result, directly encourages the emergence of 'notorious markets' beyond US borders.

Although piracy has been likened to a form of 'spatial pathology' (Govil 2005: 43), traversing vast areas of land at surprising speed through shifting underground routes, it remains geographically determined nevertheless (Liang 2009). While commercial subtitling and dubbing processes are implicated in the economics of geographic windowing and region coding, helping to mark territorial borders and control (and cost) aspects of space and time, guerrilla-style translation practices carve out an alternative, subterranean cartography. The amateur subtitles and garbled mistranslations of pirated films and TV series provide telling clues left behind in an otherwise close-to-seamless digital operation. These errant translations function as a mapping device, revealing the 'persistence of the geographic' (Govil 2005: 42) within piracy's shadowy, elusive and decentralised operations.

In the Philippines, pirated films have historically tended to enter the country through one of two routes that are literally inscribed in their translations. Films displaying Malay and Bahasa Indonesian subtitles have usually arrived via 'the …island of Mindanao', explains Baumgärtel (2006a: 386), which is 'characterised by its Muslim population and close connection to … Malaysia and Indonesia'. Those with characteristically Chinese-inflected English subtitles come from Hong Kong or Singapore (389). Alternatively, in Nigeria, as Larkin (2004) discusses, Indian films are very popular amongst the predominantly Muslim Hausa population. These films traditionally arrived through Lebanese and Indian traders via the Persian Gulf and consequently, had Arabic and English subtitles that at times were obscured by scrolling advertisements for video shops in the Gulf. Hollywood films also arrived via the Middle East. Larkin (2004:

295–6) recalls: 'one Jean-Claude Van Damme film I watched had Chinese subtitles superimposed over Arabic ones, providing a visible inscription of the routes of media piracy'.

By bringing the politics of the Majority World into view, non-fan forms of guerrilla translation interrogate notions of access and self-empowerment enmeshed within ideas of technological development. Within the parameters of the Majority World, fansubbing and online technologies are only available to elite (though ever broadening) sectors of society. The rest rely on other, older forms of networking and community interaction. According to Larkin (2005: 114), there is 'a fundamental political question of access embedded in the issue of piracy' as 'there's a massive realm of the world's cultural production that is made off limits to whole categories of society'. 'All the people watching pirated DVDs would never be able to afford [legal DVDs],' he states, 'some 1% at the top might, but for the vast majority of Nigerians, 120 million people, as probably for the vast majority of Indians, the stable commodity price of … a CD is just not feasible'.

Liang (2005: 12) argues that in the age of globalisation and transnational dialogue there is an urgent need to think 'through the problem of understanding the publics which lie outside the assumptions of the liberal public sphere'. He states:

> The impulse behind copying in Asia and other parts of the non-Western world may not arise from … self-conscious acts of resistance, but may instead be understood in terms of ways through which people ordinarily left out of the imagination of modernity, technology and the global economy [find] ways of inserting themselves into these networks. (Liang 2005: 12)

By and large, in this non-Western terrain made up of 'illegal cities', the 'avenues of participation' tend to be non-legal, non-professional and unconventional (Liang 2005: 6). Ravi Sundaram (2001) terms this type of intervention a form of recycling: '[t]his is a world of those dispossessed by the elite domains of electronic capital, a world which possesses a hunter-gatherer cunning and practical intelligence' (96). Here interactivity plays a crucial role – not the predestined interactivity of digital and online media but rather a DIY interactivity that manifests in people's irreverent attitudes towards media. While the technological experimentation and online networking so crucial to fan communities are available to certain sectors of society only (youth, the educated and the upwardly mobile), the cultures of recycling and DIY are age-old and cross-generational. Sundaram notes how 'software pirates, spare parts dealers, electronic smugglers, and wheeler-dealers of very kind in the computer world' are accommodated by Delhi's long history of single-commodity markets that dates back to the Mughal Empire (95). He goes on to detail the way in which second-hand modems and computer manuals, late-night Internet connections and out-of-date software provide an informal technological training to 'those excluded from the upper-caste, English-speaking bastions of the cyber-elite' (95).

According to Liang (2005: 8), 'new media challenges the one-way, monopolistic, homogenising tendencies of old media, as it tends to be decentralised in ownership, control and consumption patterns and hence offer greater potential for consumer input and interaction'. This seems a particularly useful way of framing the type of technological interaction effected via media bootlegging and its translations. Whereas fansubbing exploits the distributed, peer-to-peer interactivity of online networking to obtain ('rip'), collaboratively translate and distribute translated media through file sharing and streaming, exemplifying global trend towards decentralisation, traditional bootlegging deploys an entirely different 'interactivity' that although technologically conservative could potentially prove more subversive and interventionist. For Pang (2004: 30), 'pirated movies provide us with a different perception of Hollywood films that is beyond the producers' control'. She suggests that 'one of the most effective ways to interrogate the power concentrated in the hands of technology producers and information distributors ... is to actively participate in technological processes that reshape the products', thereby challenging the subservience of consumption. Media piracy both feeds off and threatens official channels of media production and capitalist consumption. Characterised as 'Hollywood's own digital Frankenstein' (Lobato 2008: 22), media piracy and guerrilla translation appropriate and repurpose digital technologies and their associated regulatory controls. While fans tend to hold the authority of the 'original' in high esteem, profit-driven pirate translators unwittingly encourage viewers to 'see through' the very workings and illusions woven by 'originals'. Guerrilla subtitles composed of 'Chinese inflected English' or other hybrid language forms alert viewers to the politics of translation in the global era, making visible the institutionalised, powerful *in*visibility of mainstream translation practices as documented by Venuti (1995). The errancy of guerrilla screen translation testifies to the geographically located nature of technology and to the fact that, like translation, technology usage doesn't always play by the rules.

Conclusion

As a product of censorship and piracy operations, screen translation is implicated within diverse socio-cultural, national and transnational dynamics. Such dynamics pinpoint the crucial role played by language mediation within contemporary culture and politics. Additionally, the examples outlined in this chapter collectively underscore how translation can disrupt any notion of 'stable meaning transfer' (Pym 2005), and exceed functional frameworks. Screen translation parody, censorship and piracy are all characterised by mistranslation and error, and remain largely beyond the purview of translation training and much scholarship.[12] However, these modes of screen translation practice are particularly prevalent today, permeating both formal and informal modes of practice and registering the significance of 'errancy' as a critical concept. While quality is undeniably an important consideration for screen translators, I contend that 'errancy' is equally, if not more, significant – not least because many current modes of screen translation (such as fansubbing and pirate, guerrilla translation) are communal, decentralised and anti-regulation.

Alongside parodic translation discussed in Chapter 3, censorship and piracy exemplify the increasing significance of errancy for the current transnational mediascape – underlining how media traversals across cultural and linguistic borders are defined, foremost, by uncontrollability. By focusing on errancy, I instigate a programme of revaluation, directing attention away from endless, unresolvable debates on 'quality', towards the geopolitics that determine and delimit value systems in the first place. The various types of errant screen translation examined in this chapter constitute common, practical examples of translation *misuse* and hence are profitably examined in relation to theoretical conceptions of translation *abuse*. Specifically, they indicate how concrete practices do not necessarily conform to conceptual frameworks. Collectively they articulate points of tension between abstraction and actualisation, exposing the unsustainability of theoretical tendencies towards prescription – clearly evident within evaluative translation discourse advocating for either subtitling or dubbing, domestication or foreignisation.

In contrast, the case studies developed in this chapter indicate the necessity of attending carefully to differences between theory and practice, highlighting that translation theory cannot simply substitute abstraction for actualisation, for, in actualising concepts of abuse and quality, they become unavoidably prescriptive. Instead, theoretical discourse might learn from, and listen more to, the pragmatics of practice, acknowledging the shifting contingencies that govern practical, grounded understandings of both 'good' and 'bad'. In translation practice, quality is not a fixed category; it is constantly being redefined with different problems requiring different solutions. The solutions arrived at by practising translators are not authoritative or definitive. They are subject to change and reinterpre tation, as practising subtitlers and dubbers readily admit (see Rosenberg 2007). Thus, virtuality surfaces even within the concrete pragmatics of subtitling and dubbing. This open, non-prescriptiveness also needs to be preserved at the level of theory.

Notes

1. According to Monika Mehta (2009: 66) the power of cinema as a mass medium continues to influence censorship operations in postcolonial India. After Independence in 1947, formal censorship of art and literature ceased while film censorship continued in order to regulate its 'effects on the citizenry'. On the particular significance of the cinema for censorship in the US, see Lee Grieveson (2004) on perceived dangers resulting from its accessibility to 'lower-class' and immigrant audiences, its realism, and darkened viewing spaces thought to facilitate immoral behaviours.
2. Notable exceptions include Chiara Bucaria (2009), Delia Chiaro (2007), Jorge Díaz Cintas (2012), Tessa Dwyer and Ioanna Uricaru (2009), Peter Fawcett (2003), Camino Gutiérrez Lanza (2002), Ilaria Parini (2014), Chloë Stephenson (2007), Jeroen Vandaele (2007; 2014), Patrick Zabalbeascoa (2016), Xiaochun Zhang (2012) and a special issue of the journal *Altre Modernità* on Ideological Manipulation in Audiovisual Translation, edited by Díaz Cintas, Ilaria Perini and Irene Ranzato (2016).
3. For Foucauldian readings of screen censorship, see Grieveson (2004) and Annette Kuhn (1985). On Foucault and translation censorship, see Francesca Billiani (2007).
4. Peter Fawcett (2003: 163) states: 'Cumulative presence and repeated absence build up a world view. And in translated film, that view is dominated by the hegemonic power.'
5. According to Gendrault (2010: 229): 'In Italy, territorial affiliation is much more powerfully marked by dialectical forms than it is in other countries that have long been heavily centralised.' Gendrault considers the continuing challenges of Italian dialect within domestically produced films in the 1980s and 1990s, noting that films that make extensive use of the Neapolitan dialect often require subtitling for nationwide release (231).
6. As Martine Danan (1991: 612) notes in relation to Spain, 'until Franco came to power, Castilian had failed to eradicate powerful minority language – Galician, Basque and Catalan'. Today, these regional languages retain a presence. On the linguistic diversity of Spanish media translation, see Zabalbeascoa (1997).
7. For exceptions, see Carla Mereu Keating (2016), Ranzato (2016) and Stephenson (2007). On contemporary Italian media censorship, see Bucaria (2009), Chiaro (2007), Denise Filmer (2016), Silvia Monti (2016), Parini (2014) and Annalisa Sandrelli (2016).
8. On Spanish film censorship, see also Díaz Cintas (2012: 287) on research

projects TRACE (TRAnslations CEnsored) and Tralima (Traducción, Literatura y Medios Audiovisuales).

9. See the entry on 'Censorship' in the online *Film Reference* encyclopaedia (www.filmreference.com). A similar phenomenon occurred when *Blue Velvet* (1986) was screened in Australia on the Channel 7 network and the term 'fuckin' was replaced by 'friggin'. Thanks to Mehmet Mehmet for bringing this example to my attention.

10. Thanks to a student from Wendy Haslem's *Censorship: Film, Art, Media* (2010) course at the University of Melbourne for bringing this example to my attention. To see this clip, visit: http://www.dailymotion.com/video/xc1ggb.

11. 'War' terminology also appears in Lawrence Lessig's discussion of piracy (2004: 17).

12. Parodic and pirate translation are particularly under-represented within translation scholarship. Research on media translation censorship is significant, as I have outlined above (see notes 2, 7 and 8 in this chapter).

CHAPTER 5

Fansubbing and Abuse:
Anime and Beyond

Fansubbing constitutes one of the most significant developments to occur within screen translation to date. An amateur form of subtitling done by fans rather than professionals, today fansubbing is predominantly digital and online, utilising vast, geographically dispersed networks to pull off subtitling feats with phenomenally fast turnaround times. Italian fansubbing group ItaSA (Italian Subs Addicted), for instance, provides access to US TV shows like *The Big Bang Theory* (CBS, 2007–) *and Modern Family* (ABC, 2009–) within hours of US airings (Barra 2009: 517–18; Vellar 2011: 6–7). By taking translation into their own hands, fans revalue this vital mediating tool, reversing the usual tendency within screen culture to either ignore or denounce its operations. Instead of approaching translation as unwanted interference, fansubbers respond proactively towards perceived failings, transforming limitations into possibilities and proposing a course of creative reinvention. Through graphic and textual play (which might include unusual fonts or layout, karaoke-style animated subtitles and the inclusion of foreign honorifics), as well as interventionist translator notes and collaborative, technologically savvy working protocols, the fansubbing phenomenon is exploding standard screen translation practices, exposing supposed rules and formal constraints as mere conventions. This celebration of the subtitle's liberation from the chains of normative use is driven from the bottom up, from everyday viewers without formal training, who often flout copyright in order to labour at the mammoth task of translation for no financial remuneration.

In this chapter, I investigate fansubbing as an errant or improper form of AVT that is currently reconfiguring the paradigms and politics of the screen and translation industries. Fansubbing can be identified as errant on the basis that it constitutes a subset of non-professional translating and interpreting.[1] Fansubbers are generally untrained and voluntary. In this way, they are positioned at a remove from the 'ongoing professionalization' (Olohan 2012: 194) of the translation and interpreting industries, and consequently are not bound by industry or institutional modes of regulation and rationalisation.[2] Simply by dint of its non-professional status, I propose, fansubbing is defined as 'improper'. At the same time, however, the errancy of fansubbing exceeds this definitional parameter, also manifesting in more explicit, intentional forms of disobedience and irregularity. Since its evolution within anime subculture, fansubbing has typically contravened copyright laws, and although the example of Global TV streaming service Viki, detailed in Chapter 6, proves that this phenomenon can be legalised, these subversive, culturally resistant origins continue to affect the culture and spirit of fansubbing nevertheless. Hence I argue that, although fansubbing has experienced a recent surge of scholarly interest, insufficient attention has been paid to its demonstrable errancy effects.

In this chapter, I broaden fansub research by drawing attention to its linguistic and cultural diversity and I consider its 'improperness' in relation to the community-based and largely uncontrollable nature of crowdsourced translation. In a similar vein to translation scholar Luis Pérez-González (2006) who sketches a broad social context for fansubbing, likening it to a form of cultural chaos, I position fansubbing as indicative of major social transformations brought about by emerging technologies and processes of decentralisation. In so doing, I pinpoint how fansubbing is currently disrupting and reconfiguring value systems at the intersection of screen media and translation. In order to appreciate and unpack the revaluing dynamic of fansubbing, it is necessary to revisit the concept of 'abusive subtitling' introduced in Chapter 3, which Nornes (2007: 182–3) states took inspiration from the 'spectacular example of anime fandom'. Assessing in detail how this association between fansubbing and the 'abusive' has developed, I ask whether the errancy of fan translation actually challenges the theoretical paradigm of 'abusive subtitling', exposing its limitations and blind spots.

As Mark Duffett (2013: 5) outlines, fandom has a long and complex history closely associated with mechanisms of fame, public life and modes of passionate engagement. With links to seventeenth-century religious fanaticism and US baseball fervour, fandom has grown exponentially with the rise of 'modern capitalist societies, electronic media, mass culture and public performance' (5). As media forms and industries have multiplied, expanding from print publishing to recorded sound and moving image media, fandom has rapidly diversified. In the twentieth century, media fandom in particular emerged as a prolific phenomenon now encompassing myriad practices including fan fiction, cosplay (costume play), mash-up videos, game modification (modding) and fansubbing.

Resonating in relation to the significant role played by fans in the shaping and success of early Hollywood (see Crafton 1999), fansubbing also connects directly with the significant fan community that emerged during the 1930s around science fiction literature and film, as I go on to detail. It also testifies to the central importance of videocassette recording (VCR) and later the Internet, for media fandom, do-it-yourself (DIY) 'participatory' shifts and the globalisation or internationalisation of popular culture (Duffett 2013: 11–12).

Signalling a paradigm shift in attitude on the part of media consumers, fansubbing as part of fan culture generally is indicative of fundamental and far-reaching social transformations, epitomising the increasingly 'participatory' nature of today's popular and public realms alike, as theorised by Henry Jenkins (2006a: 22). Affecting culture as much as economics, Jenkins (2) posits that decentralisation (facilitated by digital and online technologies) enables audiences around the globe to interact with popular culture in new and unpredictable ways that blur distinctions between production and consumption. He terms this process 'cultural convergence' (23). Riding the crest of this participatory wave, fansubbing is centrally positioned in terms of global media and social developments. For Pérez-González (2006: 276), it represents 'only the tip of the iceberg which subsumes all current and future initiatives taken by the viewers to assume more power following the decentralisation of the media establishment'. For Jenkins (2006a: 243) fansubbing is one factor affecting the 'ever more complex relations between top-down corporations and bottom-up participatory culture'. Fansubbing underscores the fact that language and translation are critical, enabling tools for global, transmedia flow and transformation.

Anime Origins

Fansubbing is thought to have originated in the US when comics and science-fiction fans became interested in the medium of Japanese animation, first termed 'Japanimation' and later 'anime' (Patten 2004: 85–6).[3] In Japan, anime refers to all types of animation irrespective of national origin or language (86). Outside of Japan, it is used to refer to Japanese-produced animation primarily intended for Japanese-speaking audiences (Leonard 2005b: 284). Having first materialised during the 1960s and 1970s, US fans of anime mobilised themselves during the 1980s to begin the task of translation, which they found wanting for a variety of reasons that I detail below. Sean Leonard (2005a: 11) dates the use of the term 'anime' by US fans to 1979, by which time dedicated clubs had formed in Boston, New

York and Philadelphia following the founding of the first anime fan club in Los Angeles in May 1977, the Cartoon/Fantasy Organization (C/FO) formed by Fred Patten (2004: 19) and fifteen others. In 1989, the first broadly available fansubs appeared following the accessibility of home computers like the Commodore Amiga and Apple Macintosh that, used in conjunction with additional hardware, were able to overlay a video stream with subtitles (Leonard 2005a: 8).

In the following decades of the 1990s and 2000s, anime fandom went global, whilst fansubbing began to assume a life of its own, crossing into different genres, formats and languages. As Luca Barra (2009: 517) explains, 'following the massive growth of peer-to-peer networks, file sharing programs and broadband', fansubbing has become increasingly widespread, seeping far beyond anime subculture and 'interweaving with other fandoms of single products, specific genres (such as science fiction or fantasy), or American TV series in general'. Beyond anime, fansubbing has developed around Latin American telenovelas like *Marimar* (1994), German soaps like *Verbotene Liebe / Forbidden Love* (1995–) and Korean TV dramas (K-dramas) like *Changnansŭrŏn k'isŭ / Playful Kiss* (2010).[4] For Barra (517), all such fansubbers are 'direct descendants of the anime fans, who in the 1980s and the 1990s, distributed subtitled versions of Japanese animation products that were not broadcast at all or were commercialized only in deeply revised and modified versions'. In this section, I provide a schematic history of anime fansubbing in the US in order to better understand the geopolitical implications of this phenomenon and to consider how its emergence effectively re-evaluates the purpose and means of screen translation. As numerous in-depth studies of this history already exist, I will focus on a handful of salient points relating to an expanded conception of fansubbing and its re-evaluative dynamic.[5]

Leonard (2005a: 8) dates 'the birth of the modern anime industry' to the appearance in 1963 of Osamu Tezuka's *Tetsuwan atomu*, which was bought on-the-cheap that same year by US TV network NBC and translated/adapted by Fred Ladd, who later became a pioneering distributor of anime in the US. Ladd's adaptation *Astro Boy* became a hit on NBC and was syndicated to fifty stations around the country, paralleling the appeal of *Tetsuwan atomu* to 'millions of youth' in Japan (Leonard 2005b: 284).[6] Following *Astro Boy* and the success of other series from the 1960s aimed primarily at children, such as *Tetsujin-28go / Gigantor* (1963–6), *Janguru taitei / Kimba the White Lion* (1965–6) and *Mach GoGoGo / Speed Racer* (1967–8), the reception of anime in the US dived and swerved. Leonard (2005a: 7) notes that US pigeonholing of TV animation as a 'kid-only' medium in the latter half of the 1960s (largely motivated by economics) resulted in increased pressure by groups such as Action for Children's TV to sanitise content, 'keeping violence, sophisticated narratives, and skilled artisans away from cartoons'.[7] Such pressures coincided with the fact that more mature, adolescent-targeted themes were beginning to surface in Japanese productions (Leonard 2005a: 9–10). The mainstream US market for anime eroded in the early 1970s when, according to Ladd, 'you couldn't give away a Japanese-made series ... because of the pressure to reduce the amount of violence on TV' (quoted in Leonard 2005a: 10) and numerous titles were 'dumped' onto Japanese-language cable programmes (see Jenkins 2006b).

The subcultural, US fandom around anime developed partly in response to this sudden cessation of broadcasting on mainstream TV. Elsewhere, on the other hand, at around the same time that it disappeared from US TV, anime was introduced to Europe where it began to flourish, becoming a mainstay of local TV programming. *Speed Racer* was broadcast on German screens in 1971, followed soon after by co-productions *Vicky the Viking* (*Wickie und die starken Männer*, 1974–5) and *Maya the Bee* (*Die Beine Maja*, 1975–6). Italy and France began importing anime in 1973 and 1974. However, in the US at this time, the dearth of readily accessible anime forced fans to become resourceful. The introduction of VCR technology in 1975 in the US and Japan provided the perfect means to do so (Patten 2004: 24).[8] As both countries are on the NTSC TV system, Japanese and American videotapes are compatible (21). For this reason, VCR technology greatly facilitated the informal methods of fan distribution. Science-fiction (sci-fi) fans in both countries began to swap tapes, with those in Japan often receiving copies of *Star Trek* (1966–9) and *Battlestar Galactica* (1978–9) in exchange for anime titles (Leonard 2005a: 5–11; Patten 2004: 44). During this time, US fans also obtained copies of series being shown on Japanese community TV stations (Leonard 2005a: 10–12). Suddenly, with access to Japanese-language anime, US fans became aware of the extent to which anime series had been doctored, re-edited and sometimes entirely transformed for network TV (Patten 2004: 45).[9] From this point onwards, the issue of translation began to trump that of access – or rather, access alone was no longer enough: it had to be trusted access. More often than not, fan networks were the only channels able to inspire such trust, ensuring the 'authenticity' of the anime being distributed. Unaltered anime, referred to as Original Anime Video (OAV), was screened at fan gatherings and conventions such as the Los Angeles Science Fantasy Society in 1975 (24). At these events, groups were exposed to undubbed anime that had not been tainted by US distribution strategies. The level of interference that was routine within

US broadcasting became apparent and new appreciation for anime artistry developed.

The untranslated nature of the anime screened at clubs and conventions led fans to begin this task themselves. Initially, according to Napier (2001: 14) and Jenkins (2006b), screenings at sci-fi conventions and fan clubs tended to be accompanied by live, on-the-spot modes of translation. Typically, a bilingual fan would stand at the front of the screening, calling out lines of dialogue and summarising plot details.[10] Such practices recall the efforts of early film lecturers or narrators – a tradition that was particularly popular in Japan where narrators known as 'katsuben' or 'benshi' often received top billing over film stars (see Komatsu 1996; Anderson 1992). In the late 1980s, with the introduction of home computers, fans began to develop methods of home subtitling, enabling anime a far wider circulation than sci-fi networks alone. The first known fansub was prepared by Roy Black of C/FO Virginia in 1986 (Leonard 2005a: 21). As Leonard reports, this was a 'third-generation copy of a fourth or fifth generation copy of a *Lupin III* episode that someone had genlocked with a Commodore Amiga and had subtitled, scene by scene'. Enabling the synchronisation of two input signals, consumer genlocking or 'generator locking' technology made fansubbing a possibility. However, in the early days, Leonard estimates that it would have taken the 'average fan' over one hundred hours to fansub a single anime episode and cost around US$4000 (21n70).

In 1989, the Ranma Project of San José, California, produced the first widely accessible fansubs of *Ranma nibun-no-ichi / Ranma ½* (1989–92) within weeks of the release of the Japanese laserdisc (Leonard 2005a: 22). Ranma Project fansubs were screened at AnimeCon '91. Throughout the 1990s, anime fansubbing and fan distribution 'exploded' due in large part to the development of digital and online technologies (22). Through the Internet, fan interest and demand grew rapidly, while digital advances significantly improved the quality, speed and efficiency of fansubbing practices. Apart from the fansubbed *Ranma ½* episodes, most of the anime screened at AnimeCon '91 was untranslated. In the following year, almost *all* screenings at AnimeExpo '92 were fansubbed (26). In 1993 and 1994, US companies licensed many of the fansubbed anime series screened at Anime Expo '93. Leonard notes that anime series that were already fansubbed (and hence had a developed fan base) tended to be licensed far more readily than others (26).

The domesticating practices of US broadcasters and distribution companies tended initially to be associated exclusively with dubbing. For this reason, dubbing was largely denounced by anime fans for its deforming tendencies.[11] In response, fan communities began to see themselves as 'guardians of the text' (Cubbison 2005: 54) – a function fulfilled in part by the championing of subtitling over dubbing, with subtitling promoted as a more authentic and respectful method. In this regard, anime subculture followed the general trend amongst Anglo–American audiences to associate subtitling with serious, 'quality' modes of appreciation (as canvassed in Chapter 1), despite the typically low cultural status of animation in the US once it became exclusively associated with children's programming (Furniss 1998: 202–8). As a result of these historical developments, subtitling 'by fans for fans' quickly became the only means of trusted access to anime and, consequently, a central pillar of its fan community.

Fansub Diversity

While fansubbing originated in response to the specific needs and desires of anime subculture, it has not remained limited to this context. Today, fansubbing has spread far and wide and incorporates many different styles and approaches. Much fansubbing activity now revolves around US TV shows, with fans around the world refusing to be left behind by windowed release strategies around hit TV titles. Brazilian (legendas.tv), Chinese (yyets.cc) and Polish (grupahatak.pl) fansub groups are all now converging around popular US programmes like *Game of Thrones* (2011–), producing subtitles in a mere matter of hours after an episode's first airing so as to beat official dubbed or subtitled versions (see Svelch 2013; Mika 2015). Even within anime subculture, fansubbing is hardly homogenous. Distinctions can be drawn, for example, between 'hardcore fans' or 'Japanophiles' (Levi 2006: 44), who foreground Japanese elements within anime experiences, and 'speed subbing' groups that sometimes forsake textual subtleties for speed of access. According to Antonia Levi (2006: 57), 'Japanophiles no longer dominate ... as they once did', while anime is itself becoming more culturally diverse, with Korean manga (*mangwa*) and Chinese animation gaining a limited presence within the scene (61). Presently, anime fansubs come in many shapes and forms, covering a broad spectrum of foreignising and domesticating, literal and liberal approaches. Despite this variance, however, screen and translation scholars have tended to align anime fansubbing primarily with formal experimentation, foreignisation and Japanophile traits.[12] In this chapter, I detail both Japanophile and alternative fansubbing traits and the tensions that arise between them. By attending to such diversity, fansubbing (of anime and beyond) can provide a productive means of interrogating and potentially remodelling the concept of 'abusive subtitling' introduced in Chapter 3.

In general, Japanophile fansubbing eschews the invisibility or fluency that prevails within much professional screen translation where the ultimate goal of subtitling is 'not to be noticed' (Béhar 2004: 85). In contrast, Japanophile anime fansubbers foreground the act of translation through a range of strategies that might include experimental typesetting (fonts, colours, sizing, layout and format), retaining foreign words such as honorifics, and including translator notes and credits. According to Levi (2006: 44), such tactics seek to resist the assimilating impulses of global popular culture. In this way, the Japanophile approach fits the description of fansubbing provided by Nornes (1999; 2007) in his delineation of 'abusive subtitling'. He refers specifically to word definitions and cultural explanations ('footnotes!'), 'different fonts, sizes and colors', and to the fact that fansubbers 'freely insert their "sub"-titles all over the screen' (2007: 182). For Nornes, these traits signal that fansubbing is amateur rather than professional (developed 'quite by instinct') and that it shuns industry norms.

Constituting its most striking, immediately visible characteristic, the formal experimentation of fansubbing has attracted much comment to date within Translation Studies research.[13] The unorthodox phenomenon of translator notes effectively summarises how fansubbing's flouting of formal conventions can draw attention to subtitling processes as a whole. As Jorge Díaz Cintas suggests (2005), in 'breaking old taboos' of professional practice where 'interference and presence of the translator ... has always been out of the question', this particularly unusual feature epitomises fansubbing's formal unconventionality. Usually displayed at the top of the screen and referred to as 'headnotes', or written in the subtitle line, using colour or parentheses to differentiate them, and referred to as a 'gloss' (Díaz Cintas and Muñoz Sánchez 2006: 46), translator notes are used to explain culturally impenetrable terms and concepts, and to provide overt instances of interpretation. For Pérez-González (2007: 76), they signal the 'new space of interaction between the translator and the viewer' opened up by grass-roots, do-it-yourself (DIY) initiatives: 'fansubbers' headnotes introduce a non-diegetic dimension into the interlingual and intercultural mediation process' which 'declares its artifice and allows fansubbers to maximize their own visibility as translators'.

In a fansub of *Yakitake!! Japan* (2004–6) (episode 62), a translator headnote is used to explain the double meaning of a word when written in *hiragana* script, as referenced in the dialogue. Here, the formal device of the headnote is used to provide in-depth textual interpretation and to facilitate a foreignising approach. For Melek Ortabasi (2007: 286–7), fansub translator notes constitute an important step towards realis-

Figure 5.1 Translator headnote from a fansubbed episode (62) of *Yakitake!! Japan* (2004–6). © TV Tokyo. Fansubs courtesy Anime Static.

ing a type of 'thick' translation capable of adding depth to the viewing experience by providing background or contextual cultural/historical information, while also accounting for non-verbal levels of signification so prevalent within audiovisual media. Coined by Kwame Anthony Appiah (2000), the term 'thick translation' draws on Clifford Geertz's ethnographic notion of 'thick description'. Referring primarily to scholarly, literary examples, Appiah (2000: 341) defines 'thick translation' as 'translation that seeks with its annotations and its accompanying glosses to locate the text in a rich cultural and linguistic context'. For Theo Hermans (2003: 387) who discusses the conceptual lineage of this term, one advantage of thick translation is its 'highly visible form' that 'flaunts the translator's subject position, counteracting the illusion of transparency or neutral description'. For Ortabasi (2007: 287), however, fansub headnotes and glosses do not go far enough in this direction, remaining too linear and bound by old technologies and formats, such as books (with their footnotes and prefaces), thereby failing to make use of the interactive, multimodal possibilities of digital media. Ortabasi concedes nevertheless that anime fandom has pushed the industry to take the next 'technological step' of inserting hyperlinked 'capsules' and 'popups' into DVDs in order to 'embed (pop-) cultural, linguistic, and/or historical information into the film track' (288).[14]

A foreignising textual approach is another trait common to much Japanophile anime fansubbing. Foreignisation usually involves a literal or word-for-word style of translation that retains elements of foreign syntax and word order.[15] Fansubbed anime often retains Japanese honorifics like '-sama' [great], suffixes such as '-kun' for teenage boys or '-sensei' for teachers and 'fictive kinship' modes of address like 'ojisan' [uncle] to address middle-aged males to whom one is not related (see Mattar 2008: 368). Foreignisation aims to counteract the flattening, domesticating textual strategies so prevalent within commercial AVT.[16] Many early US TV adaptations of anime, for instance, transformed programmes to an almost unrecognisable degree and, as a result, most viewers were unaware of their Japanese origins (Ruh 2010: 31). Consequently, the foreignising style of much anime fansubbing goes hand in hand with the heightened authenticity it is seen to offer.[17] Although the domesticating nature of commercial anime translation has lessened over recent decades in response to *otaku* demands,[18] many fans (and scholars) insist that Japanophile fansubbing is able to provide a higher level of *otaku*-style quality than offered by professional subtitling (Cubbison 2005; Vellar 2011: 7; Ito 2012a: 197).[19]

Moreover, since the early days of US anime fandom, subtitling was not the preferred translation method of *all* fans but rather appealed to certain 'purist' sectors (Patten 2004: 63). Sales of anime on the US market, for instance, were far higher for dubbed titles than subtitled ones (Cubbison 2005: 46; 50). One of the earliest anime distributors, Streamline Productions, formed in 1988 by Carl Macek and Jerry Beck, distinguished itself from other early fan-led business ventures by releasing dubbed rather than subtitled videos in an effort to reach the broadest English-language audience possible (Patten 2004: 78). Patten explains: '[k]eeping anime so esoteric that a market for it never developed would be bad for everyone' (78). Patten joined Streamline in 1991 in order to oversee the quality and authenticity of these dubbed releases, despite neither speaking nor reading Japanese (77–8). Nevertheless, he recalls the efforts he went to in order to restore 'original' character names left off the 'very rough' translations of scripts provided by the Japanese anime companies that were often 'inaccurate as to minor details that were particularly ethnically Japanese' (77).

While Streamline's strategy sought to grow US audiences for anime beyond a niche subculture, many dedicated fans themselves prefer dubbing, as indicated by the existence of 'fandub' groups such as Figher4Luv (starsfandub) (and German-based Crash Dub Studios (crash-

Before, Saya-chan sensei said this.

Figure 5.2 English fansub of *Burakku rokku shuta / Black Rock Shooter* (2012), episode 3, that retains the honorific 'sensei' for teacher. © Fuji TV. Fansub courtesy Generation NeXt Sub Team.

dub.com).[20] For many fans, dubbing better approximates 'original' or 'source' viewing experiences, courting similar pre-teen audiences. *Anime News Network* columnist Ryan Matthews states, the 'amazing truth is that watching a good dub brings you much closer to the original experience than a subtitle' (quoted in Cubbison 2005: 49). For Mathews, fandubs are more authentic than fansubs because they can convey 'subtle distinctions in a character's language' such as accent and tone.

Evidently, vast differences complicate fan approaches to subtitling and notions of quality. Speed sub groups, for instance, equate near to instantaneous access with a 'quality' viewing experience, whereas for many other groups quality is measured in relation to the accuracy and texture of the translation itself. In some ways, speed subbing is antithetical to notions of 'quality', exemplifying 'the fansub ... at its most market–ized and competitive', with groups racing to release translated titles on the same day they first air in Japan (Denison 2011: 7). Nevertheless, with so many speed groups competing for attention, it stands to reason that those also able to deliver a better product will attract the most viewers. As one fansubber explains, 'usually the group that release first, assuming equal quality, gets the most downloads' ('Razz' quoted in Ito 2012a: 196). Moreover, even Japanophile fansubbing does not necessarily equate to 'high-quality' translation (see Shules 2014). The collective, team nature of much fansubbing makes it especially susceptible to inconsistencies in relation to character names, spellings, pronunciations and the like. Díaz

Figure 5.3 A comparison of three fansubbed versions of *Kôkaku kidôtai / Ghost in the Shell: Stand Alone Complex* (2003) which highlights the textual error made in AnimeJunkies speed sub (see top). © Animax.

Fansubs courtesy AnimeJunkies, AnimeOne and Anime-Kraze.

Cintas and Munoz Sanchez (2006: 48) refer to the common mistakes found in fansubbed anime, such as the infamous Anime Junkies error when the line 'mass abductions … involving overseas mafia' was translated as 'mass naked child events'. Often, they argue, fansubbing errors result when English is used as a pivot or intermediate language (49). In this regard, fansubs can resemble the worst practices of 'one-stop' global translation houses that increasingly demand translation in any language to be based on an English-language spotting list of time-coded subtitles (see Nornes 2007: 235).

As Yasser Mattar (2008: 363) notes, another major point of tension within anime fansubbing concerns the long-running translation debate between foreignisation and domestication. On the basis of interviews with 23 fansubbers, Mattar reports that fansub groups Raven-Classics, Kinoshniki Fansubs and Psychlo-Anime, for instance, all promote domesticating strategies when facing difficult to translate words and references, with the ultimate goal of enhancing understanding (363–71). The Raven-Classics 2004 fansubs for the *Panzer Dragoon* (1995) video game, for instance, ignored the gendered divisions prominent within Japanese language, choosing to translate in a gender-neutral manner instead (367–8). Raven-Classic's 'Asoka' (quoted in Mattar 2008: 368) comments: 'Yes, men and women speak different in Japan. But not in English. So however they say it, we will still translate it in the same way.' Other fansub groups such as Subs Ryougun Setsuzoku, YAC Team and Ripping in Peace advocate for foreignising fansubs that educate viewers about the differences between Japan and the receiving culture by retaining the gendered, polite characteristics of Japanese language, and by explaining dense cultural references through interventionist translator notes (368–71).

Looking beyond anime contexts, Luca Barra (2009: 519) and Serenella Massidda (2015) analyse two Italian groups that fansub mainstream US TV series and identify similar differences between them. Barra suggests that in committing themselves 'strictly … to original interpretation', loyalist fansubbing groups like Subsfactory rely heavily on 'explanations and notes that can weigh down the vision of the series'. ItaSA on the other hand, approach many of the same programmes with a freer, more playful albeit domesticating style. Barra's findings echo those of Mattar, indicating how the foreignisation/domestication debate fractures fansubbing as a whole, and is not confined to Japanophile frameworks alone. Additionally, arguments cited by Mattar in support of domesticating fan*subs* resemble those mounted by some anime fan*dubbing* groups (see Cubbison 2005: 49), demonstrating that the question of familiarisation versus foreignisation can be framed from many perspectives, and used to support widely varying positions. The distinction that Nornes (2007: 176) draws between 'abusive' and 'corrupt' subtitling partakes in this same debate, as do many attempts to pit professional against amateur AVT. In part, it is the similarities of these differences to which we need listen in order to recognise the critical impasse resulting from prescriptive notions of value within screen translation.

As fansubbing has expanded beyond anime subculture, its heterogeneity has become even further pronounced. Facilitated via digital and online technologies, fansubbing now accompanies media from around the world, is linguistically and stylistically diverse, and has even spread beyond popular culture into politics.[21] Fansubbing is now largely inseparable from other types of amateur community translation and, consequently, political activists (see Pérez-González 2010) and corporate conglomerates alike, such as Google Inc., are adopting its tactics.[22] The example of Viki discussed in Chapter 6 demonstrates the extent to which fansubbing has expanded beyond anime, signalling broad societal shifts towards global conditions of 'convergence' (Jenkins 2006a: 23).

Participatory Subbing

According to Maria Tymoczko (2009: 401–2), networked collaboration and decentralisation are increasingly central and transformative aspects of the translation industry as a whole. Fansubbers exemplify this trend, constituting 'lead-users' of digital and online technologies for AVT purposes (Hippel quoted in Mattar 2008: 361). Fansubbers have pioneered the use of decentralised, collective labour, online networking and web-assisted translation, for instance, while staking out a territory located well beyond the confines of Western or Eurocentric thinking.[23] Mizuko Ito (2012a: 187) reports, for instance, that some US-based fansub groups work with 'team members in different time zones to keep the workflow on a twenty-four-hour cycle'. Although individualist fansubbing is certainly possible (see Svelch 2013), the far more common scenario is for fans to produce translations within collaborative, online communities that deploy particularly effective teamwork protocols, producing impressive subtitling feats within short timeframes. Today, fansubs are commonly produced within twenty-four hours after a show's première.[24]

Mattar (2008: 361) distinguishes fansubbers from other types of participatory consumers or *prosumers* by the fact that they 'see their end goal as education and effective understanding' rather than 'originality and creativity'. Seeking to pinpoint the translation-specific nature of this particular fan activity, Mattar argues that fansubbers are 'cultural presenters' more than 'cultural producers' – adding value to screen content rather than creatively reinventing it (360).[25] Like Mattar, I am similarly interested in connecting with the translation-specific nature of fansubbing as prosumer activity, highlighting the role of translation within the conditions of convergence identified by Jenkins. In particular, I posit that fansubbing exposes problems and blind spots within transnational media flows and globalised cultural mechanisms, as much as offering solutions.

The networked, collaborative model of practice common to much fansubbing often involves the testing or development of new software and plugins, from collective authoring platforms to synching tools (see O'Hagan 2008: 179), while pushing ethical and copyright boundaries. Fans use segmenting software to divide a programme's subtitles into manageable chunks (see Henthorn 2016a), and then integrate the translation efforts of individual contributors with those of the group, communicating via email, wiki tools, blogs and Internet chat forums (see Ito 2012a: 186). The distribution of labour amongst fansub groups is 'reaching a *semi-professional* level of specialization and organization' (Barra 2009: 521). Most importantly, along with shifting the agency of translation from the individual to the group, fansubbing communities also emphasise the 'co-creational' (509) nature of their practice, using online forums to access in-depth cultural knowledge and to problem-solve translation issues. According to O'Hagan (2008: 179), the collective nature of fansubbing provides an excellent environment for the acquisition of new translator competences, including genre knowledge, technological expertise, immediate peer feedback and a healthy interactive translator community – leading her to conclude that 'Translation Studies can no longer afford to overlook the fan translation phenomenon'.

In disregarding copyright and industry regulations, fansubbing partakes in broader trends towards community participation and crowdsourcing that are affecting the translation industry as a whole.[26] Many translation professionals are understandably threatened and alarmed by the exponential growth of fansubbing and other amateur translation activities, arguing that it signals a mass *de*valuation of translation from a 'profession' to a socially useful 'skill' (Garcia 2010). This argument is interesting to consider in light of the fact that fansubbing also, incontrovertibly, signifies awareness and appreciation of translation. Ignacio Garcia contends that, although worrying on some levels, the growth of amateur translation nevertheless constitutes 'a sign of social health' akin to literacy. Rather, Garcia (2010) contends that 'mass amateurism' in relation to translation is here to stay and, consequently, translators and scholars need to acknowledge how it reinterprets notions of quality according to subject-matter familiarity, speed and other variables.[27]

Fansub Ethics

Rather than analysing the varied motivations of individuals involved in fansubbing, this book considers the impact of fansubbing on the power dynamics of the global mediascape.[28] In particular, I am interested in how fansubbing continually challenges laws and regulations integral to the exercising and management of screen media copyright – an issue much debated by fansubbers themselves. Although Japanese companies and creators initially tolerated fansubbing's 'grey' legality, thereby lending it a degree of legitimacy (see Patten 2004: 25), Japanese anime companies and US distributors are intensifying litigation against fansubbing, which they increasingly frame as piracy, despite efforts within the subculture to maintain ethical standards (Lee 2011: 1141; Ito 2012a: 185).[29] Certainly, fansubbing is complexly positioned in relation to free-market capitalism and entertainment conglomerates. As Ian Condry (2010: 198–9) explores, it occupies a murky terrain in-between grass-roots activism, media piracy and advanced, market-oriented capitalism. With fansub 'groups behaving competitively and being encouraged to standardize (and professionalize) production to attract greater numbers of fan viewers', the community is becoming 'increasingly market-ized', complicating the situation further (Denison 2011: 9).

The competitive nature of much speed subbing points to tensions within the anime fan community that have actually been present since its inception. Leonard (2005: 28) notes that 'the first major fansub distributor circa November 1990', William Chow of Canada's Vancouver Japanese Animation Society and the Arctic Animation fansubbing group, used to charge for tapes instead of using the stamped, self-addressed envelope (SSAE) system, 'placing him in the eyes of some as a bootlegger'. In Leonard's estimation, it is likely that Arctic Animation made little to no profit from such operations, and in other respects this group adhered strictly to fansubbing ethical codes, sporting the usual 'not for sale or rent' disclaimers on their tapes and ceasing distribution if a title became licensed (see ANN forum on 'Funimation' 2008). While this example shows the extent to which early fansubbing sought to safeguard the not-for-profit nature of activites, it also indicates that this area was in need of protection and policing. The very fact that ethical codes and guidelines feature so prominently within anime fansubbing culture, with websites like *Anime News Network* publishing 'A New Ethical Code for Digital

Subtitling' (2003) and a survey on 'Legal Action Against Downloaders' (2008), demonstrates that this is an area of ongoing contention (see also Lukács 2010, Crisp 2015 and Moriarty 2015).

As the first-hand accounts of Leonard (2005) and Patten (2004) indicate, US anime fans did not set out to contravene copyright laws. Wishing to access content unavailable through legal channels, their first tactic was to try to persuade Japanese anime producers and distributors such as Toei Animation to invest in the US market. In 1978, Toei's US representative Pico Hozumi actually approached C/FO fans for promotional help, and Tezuka also encouraged fan activities when he visited LA earlier that year (Patten 2004: 25). In the late 1970s, Toei supplied videos and merchandising to numerous fan conventions (26). This pattern of co-operation continued into the early 1980s (27–9). When such moves failed to develop commercial interest, fans began to take matters into their own hands, hence growing awareness and appreciation of anime while expanding its potential market within the US (67n18). As they were not gaining financially from their subbing activities, fans reasoned that their infringing of copyright laws might be overlooked. In most cases, this assumption proved correct.

Fans received anime tapes via the SSAE system. In some cases, they were required to pay a subscription cost to the anime club, yet again this tended only to cover the cost of video reproduction and postage. Once fansubbing 'proper' began, fans underscored the not-for-profit nature of their endeavours by including disclaimers and advisory warnings at the beginnings of anime tapes, such as 'Not for Sales or Rent, Subtitled by Fans for Fans', and 'Cease Distribution When Licensed'.[30] This not-for-profit ethos constitutes a significant component of fansubbing's defence under the 'fair use' doctrine of the US legal system. Numerous arguments can be made in defence of fansubbing as 'fair use', including its non-commercialism, its educational and social benefits, and the geographic and linguistic obstacles to access that it underscores (Rembert-Lang 2010). Moreover, some argue that fansubbing highlights the need for legal changes in relation to copyright protection and interpretations of 'fair use' (Daniels 2008: 735).[31]

As fansubbing has developed and spread, threats to its not-for-profit spirit have continued to surface. According to Leonard (2005: 28–9), bootleggers were already prevalent amongst the fansub community by 1990 when Ranma Project fansubs were unscrupulously copied and sold by a Philadelphia-based operator. Bootleggers would sometimes pose as anime clubs at expos and conventions in order to sell pirated fansubs for profit. As Hatcher (2005: 537) comments, in certain contexts, fansubbing can come to resemble 'more traditional forms of counterfeiting and piracy'. Fansubs can easily find their way on to eBay or other websites where they are packaged as legal, commercial products, while both Hatcher and Leonard note that profit-seeking individuals and groups regularly emerge from or infiltrate the anime fansub community.

Denison (2011: 11) considers fansubbing's link to piracy in more depth, identifying it as part of a broader shift in anime fan culture relating to generational differences and changing technologies. She points to fansub group AnimeJunkies that caused controversy amongst the fansub community when it continued to distribute subs for *Ninja Scroll* (2003–) once the series had been licensed in the US. Now disbanded, the group was also renowned for substandard speed translations (12).[32] Although many groups denounced AnimeJunkies, it endured nevertheless until 2014, and Denison (2011: 12) suggests that its popularity may have been 'indicative of a shift in the fan culture from responsible to more profligate piracy'. This shift has provoked some anime licence-holders to institute increased enforcement measures (14). An alternative strategy has been for anime companies to adopt fan practices themselves, competing with the 'viral' scale of fan activities by offering streaming anime titles (Denison 2001: 14; Ito 2012a: 200; Lee 2011: 1142).

Clearly, the 'not-for-profit' nature of fansubbing cannot be taken for granted. Condry (2010: 195) suggests fansubbing can be understood as 'piracy that defers to market principles', pointing out that although 'fan practices clearly pose a challenge to commodification', they are not necessarily 'anti-market' (199). According to ANN's ethical guidelines, fansubbing boosts the anime industry as a whole by growing audiences, testing the marketplace with regards to new titles and encouraging on-sales by providing a type of 'free trial' ('A New Ethical' 2003; Jenkins 2006a: 159). As Leonard (2005: 283) states, from the 1970s to the early 1990s anime fansubbing and fan distribution 'constituted the demand formation phase necessary, but ancillary, to capitalist activity'. The fact that industry players are now beginning to model their activities on fansubbing practices supports Mattar's notion that fansubbers constitute 'the most updated users' of anime, exhibiting 'intimate knowledge' of needs that are 'likely to be required by other users in the market in the near future' (2008: 361). Thus they are proactively involved in creating a 'much improved end product' that can be of benefit to the industry as a whole. Mattar (354) likens this process to economist Eric von Hippel's notion of 'democratizing innovation', while Condry (2010: 203) describes it as a form of 'market disobedience'.

Fansubbing and Abuse

Having explored the anime origins and current diversity of fansubbing practices, I now consider its relevance for theories of the abusive. As flagged at the start of this chapter, fansubbing is centrally positioned in relation to Nornes's notion of 'abusive subtitling'. While Nornes's re-conceptualisation of screen translation was inspired by the example of anime fansubbing, my research developed in the reverse direction. It was Nornes and his engaging exploration of screen translation that brought me into contact with fansubbing. Nevertheless, I discovered numerous threads within this amateur practice drawing me in different directions to those travelled by his *Cinema Babel*. Consequently, in the following discussion, I scrutinise the role Nornes (2007: 183) assigns fansubbing, especially how he collapses this broad phenomenon on to the 'spectacular example' of Japanophile anime fansubs. I also note how he deploys fansubbing strategically to wrest notions of abuse away from deconstruction theory towards popular culture and everyday practices. In Chapter 3, I examined this deliberate turn away from deconstruction in more detail. For now, I explore how an expanded definition of fansubbing might destabilise Nornes's appropriation of abuse.

For Nornes, anime fansubbing exemplifies the emergent, abusive turn in screen translation, bending linguistic and cinematic rules to provide an authentic pathway to the foreign while cueing spectator awareness of the mediating role of translation (1999: 18; 31–2). More specifically, it is the formal innovation, textual foreignisation and irreverent attitude characteristic of *Japanophile* anime fansubbing that epitomises the abusive for Nornes. He suggests that fansubbing's creative use of colours, fonts and formatting draws attention to itself by upsetting subtitling norms and audience expectations relating to fluency and inconspicuousness (Nornes 2007: 182). Visibility is further heightened by the introduction of translator notes to augment the 'authentic' foreign flavour that Japanophile fansubs strive to preserve. By flouting linguistic, cultural and spectatorship norms, such forms of fansubbing display an irreverence that particularly impresses Nornes. Producing subtitles 'with attitude' (27), Nornes characterises fansubbing as abusive yet grounded in the everyday, its unruliness deriving from its populist, grass-roots foundations and thereby ensuring its authenticity and relevance. The mass appeal of this fan translation phenomenon enables Nornes to think abuse in populist terms, beyond the confines of high theory signalled by this term's deconstructionist lineage.

However, as discussed, fansubbing *in practice* cannot be reduced to the activities of anime Japanophiles alone. Fansubbing is a far more diverse and heterogeneous phenomenon. Moreover, this heterogeneity is a central aspect of fansubbing, resulting directly from its characteristic unruliness and overt disregard for legal, cultural and linguistic rules. As a DIY practice, uncontrollability and non-standardisation are built into the fansubbing ethos. Nevertheless, in order to illustrate his notion of abuse and rein in its deconstructive tendencies, Nornes constricts discussion of fansubbing to one type only, prioritising formal experimentation and textual foreignisation over other aspects of this community-based, non-professional mode of practice. Consequently, the concrete is made to conform to the conceptual, and not the other way around.[33] In the process, the concept of abuse is itself constricted. Ultimately, for Nornes, abuse must adhere to strict guidelines: it must assume 'a respectful stance vis-à-vis the original text' (179) by matching and extending abusive nubs already present in the 'original' (176). Above all, for Nornes, abusive AVT demands 'quality, attentiveness, rigor, and cognizance of the ideological dimensions of the practice' (222). By fixing abuse to this particular notion of fidelity, Nornes does a disservice both to this theoretical concept and to fansubbing, bringing each under strict quality control.

Significantly, fansubbing is not the only example deployed by Nornes to illustrate the abusive. In fact, despite acknowledging its central place in the formulation of 'abusive subtitling', *Cinema Babel* devotes only one paragraph to fansubbing and explicitly warns against focusing on this example to the 'exclusion of all other possibilities' (183). Given this lack of attention, the reductive tenor of Nornes's approach is not surprising and is partly excusable. However, the brevity of his discussion of fansubbing is not anomalous but in fact a common thread that links his varying filmic and televisual concretisations of the abusive. In this way, Nornes's neglect of fansubbing's complexity and diversity is indicative of broader tensions. A brief examination of some of these other examples drawn from a diverse range of films and TV programmes aids in pinpointing the tensions that attend Nornes's invocation of the concrete within his theoretical conception of abuse.

In *Cinema Babel*, Nornes discusses abusive subtitling in relation to documentaries, comedies, reality game shows, art house, independent and mainstream Hollywood features. Abusive traits are identified, for instance, in the post-production English translation of *Ryori no tetsujin / Iron Chef* (1993–9) as well as in the 'partial subtitling' (O'Sullivan 2011: 105–9) of multilingual documentaries *Forest of Bliss* (1986) and *Siskyavi: A Place of Chasms* (1991). Examples of comedic subtitling (on 2005 Japanese TV game show *Namare-te / Accent Station*) are praised, as are

Figure 5.4 Animated part-subtitling in *Man on Fire* (2004). © Fox.

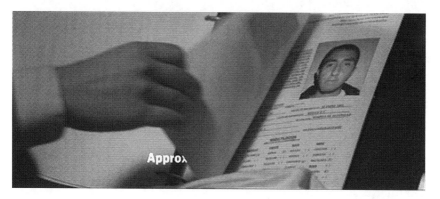

Figure 5.5 Animated subtitles in *Man on Fire* (2004) interact with diegetic objects.
© Fox.

the experimental subtitles of independent filmmaker Jon Jost, the minimal subtitling favoured by Robert Bresson and the integrated subtitles of Hollywood feature *Man on Fire* (2004) that 'move "behind" objects in the image' (159; 183).[34] Additionally, Nornes provides the example of his own English subtitling of the documentary *Aga ni ikiru / Memories of Agano* (2004). For the Japanese dialect spoken in this film, Nornes develops 'a strategy of the fragment', producing subtitles composed of occasional words within 'long strings of ellipses', and bracketed asides (184).

One problem these examples collectively expose is the difficulty of defining a concept like abusive subtitling without becoming prescriptive and hence foreclosing on its very possibilities. While Nornes offers widely varying examples of subtitling abuse taken from diverse contexts, a degree of rigidity enters his definition nevertheless. Some of the subtitling he discusses is ultimately exposed as belonging to his second rather than

Figure 5.6 Chairman Kaga's subtitled speech in the English adapted series of *Iron Chef* (1993–9). © Fuji TV and Food Network.

third epoch, and is summarily dismissed when it proves unable to live up to rather exacting standards. Such is the case, for instance with Robert Young's subtitling of *Tenamonya konekushon* / *Tenamonya Connection* (1991), and with the parodic dubbing of *What's Up Tiger Lily?* and *Can Dialectics Break Bricks?* Nornes goes so far as to provide precise instructions as to how Young's subtitles could have been made 'truly abusive' (2007: 181). At other points, the abusive is less precisely defined, attaching to various examples that seem to contradict any insistence upon attentive rigour and fidelity to the 'original', as with the example of *Iron Chef*. Overall, the brevity with which Nornes discusses his concrete examples of abusive translation enables ambiguities and contradictions to develop, as I discuss below.

The translation of *Iron Chef* presents an interesting case. Nornes (2007: 225) applauds the fact that subtitling is employed *at all* in this show's 'hybrid' English translation, as Anglophone audiences are known for their monolingual viewing habits and resistance to subtitles on primetime television (see Rich 2004; Kilborn 1993: 649). However, the subtitling on *Iron Chef* is notably minimal. Predominantly, voice–over is adopted, with subtitling preserved for the particularly theatrical speech of master of ceremonies *Kaga shusai* (Chairman Kaga). Nornes comments, 'unlike the jury of dummies, the grain of his voice – the materiality of his language – is every bit as important as what he says'. For Nornes, this creative mix of subtitling and dubbing presents an 'impressive' expression of the emergent, hybrid mode of translation (2007: 225). What I find troubling with this example is the ease by which *Iron Chef* seems to pass the abusive test, whereas the experimental subtitling strategies of Young and documentary filmmaker Trinh Minh-Ha, for instance, are held up to intense scrutiny, and ultimately declared unsatisfactory (181; 156). In contrast, Nornes provides no analysis of the textual and formal strategies exhibited by *Iron Chef*'s subtitling and voice-over, both of which are conspicuously lacking in graphic or textual experimentation, conforming in most respects to 'corrupt' fluency norms (see Gallagher 2004). Moreover, as O'Sullivan notes (2011: 116–17), hybrid modes of screen translation are becoming increasingly mainstream and are not necessarily culturally 'resistant' or progressive. As she points out, the mixing of dubbing and subtitling modes is usually motivated by economics and relates to audience expectations regarding 'authenticity' effects (116). The dominant voice-over of *Iron Chef* enables wide audience accessibility, while its occasional subtitles endow it nevertheless with cultural capital. Together, these techniques emphasise rather than downplay the Japanese origins of the programme and draw attention to processes of screen translation. By doing so, *Iron Chef* both displays and disavows its cultural otherness, at one and the same time.[35]

Nornes's critique of Trinh raises further problems in regard to the politics of abuse. Although Trinh theorises about subtitles in *Framer Framed* (1992) and *When the Moon Waxes Red* (1991) and puts this theory into practice, employing experimental subtitling in the short film *Surname Viet, Given Name Nam* (1989), Nornes (2007: 156; 166) judges her approach in a negative light, referring to its overall 'weakness'. Troubled by Trinh's academic language and post-structuralist agenda, Nornes takes issue with her 'implicit call for an oppositional avant-garde ... anchored too deeply in 1970s suture theory' (166). Charging Trinh with 'essentialism', 'Eurocentrism' and 'elitism', Nornes judges the playful yet serious subtitling tactics of *Surname Viet*, in which subtitles deconstruct the authenticity of the ethnographic subject, as overly intellectual and out-of-touch with 'popular reading modes'. At the same time, however, the unconventional approach to translation deployed in *Siskyavi* is celebrated, precisely *because of* its distancing effect (Nornes 2007: 184). In this film, subtitles simply cease when sacred knowledge is discussed on-screen, and audiences are confronted by a frustrating absence of translation. The fact

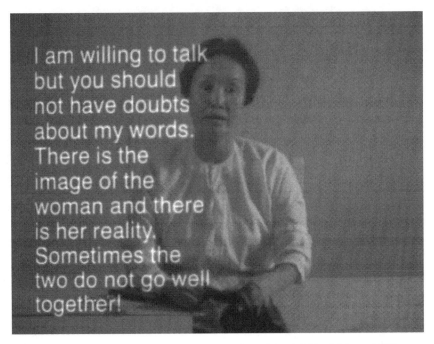

Figure 5.7 Subtitling in *Surname Viet, Given Name Nam* (1989). © Moongift Films.

that Trinh is extremely conscious of subtitling's ideological dimension, as Nornes admits, further troubles his dismissal (166).

On reflection, the diversity of the examples Nornes provides to bolster his theory of abusive subtitling function, in contrast, to expose various weaknesses, underscoring rather than overcoming the gap between theory and practice, abstraction and actualisation. The intellectual, academic tone of *Surname Viet, Given Name Nam* distinguishes it from the type of popular address that Nornes lauds. Although the documentary mode of *Siskyavi: The Place of Chasms* has little in common with *Iron Chef*, in its efforts to 'speak directly to Native viewers' (Marks 2000, 218) it remains rooted in populist, lived modes of knowledge and culture. The fact that *Surname Viet, Given Name Nam* fails (for Nornes), where *Siskyavi: The Place of Chasms* and *Iron Chef* succeed, seems to contradict Nornes's (2007: 177) insistence on the political imperative of abusive subtitling to 'bring the fact of translation from its position of obscurity, to critique the imperial politics that ground corrupt practices'. Although Nornes places ideological critique in a position of upmost importance in his theorisation of abuse, his practical examples do not. Rather, in practice, Nornes seems primarily to value subtitling that draws attention to itself, through formal, graphic, textual or technological means. For Nornes, any such event can become cause for celebration, as rendering translation visible and conspicuous is itself a political act. Indeed, visibility is the one factor that appears to unite Nornes's diverse examples of abusive translation. Whether abusive translation occurs on the festival circuit, in niche screenings, in subcultures, on mainstream television, in Hollywood or online seems of little importance to Nornes, despite the very different politics and paradigms involved.

Concretising Abuse

By prioritising formal experimentation throughout his varied examples of 'abusive subtitling', Nornes fashions this concept to fit a foreignising agenda. Following Lewis and Venuti, he positions the 'abusive' as a new form of fidelity 'with attitude' that combats the cultural imperialism implicit within domesticating modes of translation (Nornes 2007: 177). For Nornes, abusive subtitling amounts to a critique of both 'imperial politics' and 'dominant ideology' (177–9). 'Foreignizing translation in English', suggests Venuti (1995: 20), 'can be a form of resistance against ethnocentrism and racism, cultural narcissism and imperialism, in the interests of democratic geopolitical relations'. As Douglas Robinson (1997: 104) notes, the 'newness' of this particular brand of foreignism involves a shift away from elitism towards a 'multicultural or "ethnodeviant" resistance to ethnocentrism'. With this agenda in mind, Nornes's devaluation of Trinh's post-structural politics begins to make some sense, as a deliberate attempt to resist the elitist tendencies of both post-structural theory and foreignisation. Conversely, Nornes (2007: 179) advocates for foreignisation aligned with grass-roots, populist modes of reading and viewing exemplified by TV game shows and DIY phenomena like fansubbing.

However, for Robinson (1997: 101), foreignism is 'implicitly elitist', as is critical theory: both 'adopt a superior position in regard to the people and the issues one is theorizing' (111). For Robinson (111), Venuti's foreignising tactic of 'getting in the reader's face, enhancing the oddness and alienness and difficulty of a translation in order to thwart hegemonic attempts to assimilate it' is not necessarily any less assimilative or controlling than fluent translation modes. Moreover, he argues that, in the process of making a translation familiar and 'at home' in the target language, an 'air of alterity' can persist (114). Significantly, he critiques the way in which Venuti promotes foreignism as an antidote to domestication, *re*valuing via reversal. By simply reversing the devaluation of non-fluent translation, Venuti (and, by extension, Nornes) fail to sufficiently disrupt translation's evaluative politics. Rather, hierarchies remain firmly in place between the 'original' and translation. As a result, notions of quality remain dependent upon the very value judgements they seek to unsettle.

Ultimately, the diversity of Nornes's examples is located at a remove from his theory. Instead of broadening and strengthening his concept of abusive subtitling, their differences trouble the precision of his definition. Admittedly Nornes does not intend these examples to be steadfast or foundational, offering them as teasers rather than testers, as flashes of potential intended to generate rather than shut down discussion. Nevertheless, they destabilise his theoretical scaffolding by glossing over the stumbling blocks that concretisation can present. By aligning abuse with a particular notion of quality and fidelity, Nornes seeks to control and safeguard this concept. In the process, he undervalues the heterogeneity and unpredictability of fansubbing practices. This effort to dictate and safeguard the parameters of abuse ends up diffusing its aberrant force while engendering gaps between how abuse *should* proceed and the multiple sites of abuse currently surfacing within screen translation practice. The example of Viki detailed in the final chapter of this book presents a contrasting perspective. As a 'monetorized' instance of fansubbing that extends beyond anime subculture and largely conforms to mainstream, professional norms, the example of Viki proves how actual fansubbing operations signal alternative conceptual possibilities.

Notes

1. On non-professional translating and interpreting, see the special issue of *The Translator* edited by Luis Pérez González and Sebnem Susam-Sarajeva (2012).
2. Maeve Olohan (2012: 194) notes that the 'professional' status of translation is by no means secure and varies considerably within different national contexts.
3. On the early reception of anime in the US and Europe, see John Gosling (1996), Teemu Mäntylä (2010), Fred Patten (2004), Frederik L. Schodt (1983) and Olivier Vanhée (2006).
4. On *Marimar* fansubbing, see Janet Hope Camilo Tauro (2002). On the transformative fansubbing of *Verbotene Liebe*, see Karen Hellekson (2009; 2011; 2012). On K-drama fansubbing amongst pan-Asian and Asian American audiences, see Brian Hu (2010), Thandao Wongseree (2016) and Mizhelle D. Agcaoili (2011).
5. On anime subculture history in the US, see Harvey Deneroff and Fred Ladd (1996), Lawrence Eng (2012a; 2012b), Maureen Furniss (1998: 205–9),

Allison Hawkins (2013), Sean Leonard (2005a), Susan Pointon (1997), Susan Napier (2001) and Fred Patten (2004).

6. On the US adaptation of *Astro Boy*, see also Ruh (2010).

7. On the influence of lobby groups such as Action for Children's Television (ACT), see Furniss (1998: 202–9).

8. Carl Macek notes that in the early days, fans were dealing with reel-to-reel videotapes rather than videocassettes (see Patten 2004: 7). Koichi Iwabuchi (2002: 25) emphasises how VCR technology facilitates the transnational circulation of media through both legal and illegal channels.

9. This degree of transformation continued into the 1980s and 90s when anime experienced resurgence on US TV with series such as *Voltron: Defender of the Universe* (1984–5) and *Robotech: The Macross Saga* (1985). See Brian Ruh (2010: 33–8).

10. Jenkins (2006a: 159) provides details of one such screening at the MIT *Anime* Club.

11. Notably, as I go on to explore, dubbing was not rejected *per se* by all fans. See Patten (2004: 78).

12. For an exception, see Douglas Schules (2014). Research on fansubbing has expanded significantly over recent years, and has reached beyond Translation and Media Studies to include disciplines like Sociology (see Mika 2015; Wongseree 2016) and Entertainment Law (see Rembert-Lang 2010; Lee 2011).

13. On the formal experimentation characteristic of much fansubbing, see Jorge Díaz Cintas and Pablo Muñoz Sánchez (2006: 46–7), Jordan S. Hatcher (2005) and Pérez González (2006: 270–2).

14. On formal innovations in DVD subtitling that borrow from fansubbing, see Díaz Cintas (2005). On the use of 'pop-ups' in commercially released anime, see Colm Caffrey (2008; 2009).

15. Venuti (1995: 20) notes that the concept of foreignising translation is evident in the work of Friedrich Schleiermacher (1768–1834) who speaks of translation that seeks to 'register the linguistic and cultural difference of the foreign text, sending the reader abroad'. On the other hand, domesticating translation is often equated to fluent translation, where the target language and culture takes precedence over foreign syntax and foreign cultural references. See also Jeremy Munday (2001: 27–8; 146–8).

16. Sean Leonard (2005b: 289) cites New World Pictures' 1986 adaptation of Hayao Miyazaki's *Kaze no tani no Naushika / Nausicaä of the Valley of the Wind* (aka *Warriors of the Wind*) as 'the most notorious example of rewriting'. However, according to Brian Ruh (2010: 38–43) the domesticating AVT strategies used in *Warriors of the Wind* were quite typical of the time.

17. Schules (2014) troubles this association by interrogating the role played by Japanophile translator notes and glosses refered to as 'linear notes'. According to Schules, anime fansub linear notes do not necessarily provide a more authentic and in-depth mode of translation. Quite the opposite, they

sometimes allow translation errors to go unchecked, conveying the *appearance* of translation proficiency (in order to accrue subcultural status) rather than the 'real thing'.

18. '*Otaku*' is the Japanese term for 'fan' or, according to Cubbison (2005: 45), 'obsessive geek'. Anime fans have appropriated the term for themselves. See Lawrence Eng (2012b).

19. Conversely, Minako O'Hagan (2008: 175–6) reports that Japanophile anime fansubs are not necessarily more foreignising than professional anime subtitles. Instead, she proposes genre familiarity as a distinctive fansubbing quality.

20. On non-anime fandubbing, see Christiane Nord et al. 2015.

21. In July 2006, an amateur, *ad hoc* community of online collaborators provided Spanish-language subtitles for a *BBC News 24* interview conducted in English with Spain's former Prime Minister José María Aznar López (Pérez González 2010).

22. On corporations such as Google, LinkedIn and Facebook utilising crowd-sourced, amateur translation, see Costales (2011), Garcia (2010), Enrique Estellés-Arolas and Fernando González-Ladrón-de-Guevara (2012), Minako O'Hagan (2009; 2011; 2016) and Julie McDonough Dolmaya (2012).

23. On how fansubbing 'challenges basic Western assumptions', see Pérez González (2006: 276).

24. According to Ito (2012a: 187), the timeframe within anime fansubbing is generally eighteen to twenty-four hours.

25. Unlike fansubbing, for instance, fan fiction (fanfic) and AMVs (Anime Music Videos) focus on producing anew. See Mizuko Ito (2012b).

26. See, Ignacio Garcia (2010) and Alberto Fernández Costales (2011).

27. On the importance of subject-matter expertise for screen translation, see Minako O'Hagan (2008). On speed considerations within fansubbing, see Rayna Denison (2011) and Dwyer (forthcoming 2017).

28. For studies that do consider the motivations of individual fansubbers, see Agcaoili (2011), Kamil Luczaj et al. (2014), Yasser Mattar (2008), Bartosz Mika (2011), Ito (2012a), and Wongseree (2016).

29. Gonzo, Funimation and Odex are some of the anime companies that have increased litigation against fansubbers. See Stone and Manry (2011), Burton Ong (2007) and Victoria Ho (2007). While Levi (2006) argues ethics are becoming less important within fansub communities, Ito (2012a: 185) maintains they are still robust. Significantly, ethics are variously defined amongst different generations of fansubbers, as fan desires become more aligned with 'immediacy' (Lee 2011: 1143).

30. See Leonard (2005a: 9), Annalee Newitz (1994) and Jenkins (2006a: 159).

31. Hatcher (2005: 526) concedes that certain defences of fansubbing can be mounted in relation to fair use, yet concludes that this defence is 'too academic in actual practice'. Tushnet (2007) argues that fan fiction fits within fair use guidelines, yet does not extend her analysis to fansub-

bing. Leonard (2005a: 70) supports an interpretation of fansubbing as fair use.

32. On AnimeJunkies and fansubbing ethics, see Christopher MacDonald (2003).

33. Regularly employed throughout this book, the concrete/conceptual divide functions in a similar manner to Deleuze's actual–virtual dyad. It seeks to acknowledge both the distinction and interplay between actual, situated practices, processes and products, and ideas or theories about them. In relation to Nornes, I suggest that his concept of abuse prioritises theory over practice, focusing on a particular *idea* of fansubbing (how it can or should be done) rather than its varied, concrete manifestations.

34. On subtitling in *Man on Fire*, see also Kofoed (2011) and O'Sullivan (2011: 148–89).

35. For a consideration of *Iron Chef*'s translation for Australian TV network SBS, see Gay Hawkins (2010).

CHAPTER 6

Streaming, Subbing, Sharing:
Viki Global TV

Viki, a play on the words 'video' and 'wiki,' is the global TV site where millions of people discover, watch and subtitle global primetime shows and movies in more than 200 languages. Together with its fans, Viki removes the language and cultural barriers that stand between great entertainment and fans everywhere.

(Viki Website, 2016)

In 2016, a subtitle meter featured on Viki's global TV site (www.viki.com). By pulling down the 'Community' menu and clicking on 'Viki Subtitling Community', you could watch in real time as a meter continuously clicked over, calculating the number of words subtitled by users ('fans like you!') in order to power its massive, and mostly free, on–demand video streaming translation service. In contrast to streaming giant Netflix, which began life as a US–only, snail–mail DVD lending service (see Grimes 2002),

Figure 6.1 Official Viki Channel, Episode 19: Where Do Viki Subtitles Come From?

Viki has always occupied the online streaming space, while its vision has remained, from the start, global yet grounded, tackling head-on the day-to-day pragmatics of global distribution: language transfer. As Netflix grew its business, adapting to changing technologies and industry conditions, it came face to face with these pragmatics and has since developed in-platform translation tools to overcome language barriers that stand in the way of global penetration. Launched in 2010, Viki evolved from a not-for-profit class project based around language learning (Wee 2014) and its remit is precisely to break down these cultural and communication barriers by leveraging the affordances of networking technologies while 'unlocking' revenue streams in the process. It licenses titles from media content producers around the world, adds amateur, crowdsourced subtitles and profits from advertising sales and subscriptions.

In this chapter, I present a detailed case study of Viki in order to assess the current state of fansubbing and its links to other means of improper or informal screen translation, such as crowdsourced, community and collaborative translation (CT3).[1] As I go on to explain, Viki's fansubbing status is by no means assured. Most obviously, it flouts the 'not-for-profit' spirit of most fansubbing ventures. In its efforts to 'monetise' fansubbing, it necessarily denatures this traditionally grass-roots practice. However, Viki's focus on revenue generation does not necessarily discount it as fansubbing either, or compromise its politics or ethics. For this reason, it presents a particularly fascinating object of study, registering the commerce/community tensions that arise as modes of cultural engagement become increasingly global, networked and participatory. Combining subtitling, streaming and fandom, Viki is currently positioned at the forefront of media and technological change, acting as a barometer of the seismic industry shifts engendered by social media and sharing platforms, while offering a glimpse into the future interdependence of the screen and translation industries.

Much writing on user-generated content (UGC) and participatory culture is overly celebratory and uncritical, inflating claims of empowerment, diversification and democratisation. Participation in itself does not signify a social good, and online participatory practices often replicate and reinstate offline social inequalities. Viki's atypical fansubbing profile helps to nut out these complexities, indicating the many forms that participation can take in the era of social media as it moves towards the mainstream. Viki's community of fan contributors demonstrates how informal screen translation lies at the centre of current industry shifts relating to streaming and global publics. Translation industry professionals are understandably threatened by such shifts, often reacting negatively to community and crowdsourced translation projects. Yet, as Ray and Kelly (2011) note, fansubbing and crowdsourcing also open up new opportunities for translation professionals in new markets – as is signified, not least, by the recent exponential growth of the GILT (Globalisation, Interpretation, Localisation and Translation) industries (see Anastasiou and Schäler 2010).

The example of Viki demonstrates how informal and/or improper modes of screen translation are constantly evolving and rapidly spreading, indicating a broad area of practice that is now found in corporate, professional contexts as much as not-for-profit, philanthropic or activist activities. Blurring boundaries between fansubbing and crowdsourcing, Viki demonstrates how participatory activity is moving to the core of the media and translation industries alike, and is especially relevant for video on-demand and streaming services. With this transformative shift brought about by the combination of 'clouds and crowds', traditional criteria for evaluating translation 'quality' no longer suffice. As Minako O'Hagan (2011: 30) notes, 'conventional translation quality measures are neither relevant nor productive in assessing fansubs' as 'underlying motivations and intended goals' are quite different. It is for this reason that Viki fansubs are so instructive, elucidating the alternative motivations for amateur, collaborative translation. In this respect, the evident errancy or improperness of Viki fansubs as amateur, collaborative and crowdsourced underscores the growing significance of translation as a mode of cultural participation, responsive to the intensifying multilingualism or language diversity of global media and technologies.

Key Features and Innovations

While only 'a small percentage of fans volunteer to produce content' on Viki, Jamie Henthorn (2016c) notes that millions of fans watch its streamed content, thereby bringing 'advertisement and paid subscription to the site'. Viki platform co-creator Karl Seguin (2013) describes the website as 'read-heavy'. From this perspective, Viki's primary function is to provide video views via 'content delivery networks' or CDNs. On the other hand, Viki's point of difference hinges upon the unique nature of its 'writes': amateur, DIY subtitles in up to two hundred languages. Viki enables users to create their own subtitles while collaborating in real-time using custom-designed software – the Viki Subtitle Editor and Segment Timer. As Seguin (2013: 4) notes, however, this unique subtitling function uses minimal resources compared to the delivery of video content to globally distributed audiences of around forty million per month in 2016, who are mostly behind slow connections.[2] Nevertheless, even at the level of programming and platform architecture, Viki's community of contributors who provide subtitles, segments or comments remains definitive. 'The community aspect of Viki', explains Seguin (2013: 5), 'has different operational requirements than the main website and mobile clients' and, consequently, 'has its own dedicated team'. Specific 'community' requirements include real-time collaboration (whereas the main website can accommodate slow replication) and a more balanced read–write ratio. Although niche in relation to the rest of the platform, Seguin maintains that 'community defines Viki'.

According to anime and manga blog *Reverse Thieves* ('Viki a Small' 2012), the Subtitle Editor 'is really the big special feature of Viki', offering distinctive functionality and inclusiveness. 'This crowd-sourcing of subtitles is a bit different from traditional fan-subbing', *Reverse Thieves* reports, as it offers multiple opportunities for contributing, even for those without second-language skills. Monolinguals can refine subtitles and captions in their own language and do small things 'like fix typos and grammar or make a line sound more smooth'. They can also help with segmenting – an essential and time-consuming first step in collaborative online subtitling, where volunteers prepare and hand-time (within 0.01 seconds of accuracy) text-boxes into which subtitles are inserted (see Henthorn 2016a). 'I myself fixed a couple of little typos in the course of my viewing" states 'Kate' from *Reverse Thieves*, adding: 'as I don't speak Japanese, I can't really help on the actual translation end'. She explains

Figure 6.2 Viki's Ninja Academy training programme, designed and run entirely by volunteers.

that on Viki 'you have free reign [*sic*] to click into any sentence and change it. You can also add a caption to any line as well, I would assume this is for translation notes like explanations of puns/etc. Once you've changed it your username appears next to it.'

In an interview with Henthorn (2016b), a Viki volunteer who established her own segmenter training programme called the Ninja Academy explains how special tools enable Channel Managers to split video into numerous parts that segmenters can then work on simultaneously, dramatically reducing the overall task time. According to this highly skilled volunteer, Viki's software is more user-friendly than open-source programmes like Aegisub, while the company's technical support team is innovative and consultative. 'They keep on implementing new ideas as we give feedback,' she states, noting how one volunteer communicated directly with Viki's CEO of Engineering in order to improve its segmenting software.

'Timed comments' constitute another key Viki feature. This involves an optional pop-up discussion box or band positioned top left on the screen, overlaying the video image. Viewers can add comments as they watch, 'leaving thoughts in real-time' (Russell 2013) and joining a public conversation that contributes to the social engagement offered by the site. These timed comment are stored as part of the video stream, and are available to view whenever that content is accessed. *TheNextWeb* reports that some shows on Viki include over two thousand of these viewer comments. In previous writing on Viki, I erroneously referred to these comments as 'translator headnotes' due to their positioning on the screen and their potential for the provision of 'thick' translation (see Dwyer 2012b: 231). However, as I noted at the time, translation is rarely, if ever, the subject of these timed comments, which instead typically focus on fashion, grooming, plot points and actors, expressing emotional reactions, fannish enthusiasm and a sense of community. Watching the season finale of Chinese drama *My Amazing Boyfriend* (2016), sadface emoticons feature prominently, and people comment on the fact that they will miss the two main actors once the series finishes. Other comments directly address the crowd ('hiii anybody on?') while others reflect on the nature of the comments themselves ('gonna miss all the funny comments, even the whinny comments where yall complain about looks and clothes').

Viki's timed comments are not translator notes, but rather *viewer* notes. They give voice to viewers or 'readers', not subtitle 'writers'. Of course, nothing excludes fansubbers from utilising this commenting function, yet, when they do so, they comment as viewers not translators. This discussion band is about a communal conversation that anyone can join,

Figure 6.3 Timed comment appearing in a pop-up box on *My Amazing Boyfriend*, Episode 28 (2016)

not about expert or authoritative explanation. When Viki removed this function following a site upgrade in April 2013 'because it felt the set up was clunky and didn't add value' (Russell 2013), users felt like they were suddenly 'watching Viki alone' and the backlash was huge, with Viki CEO Tammy Nam reporting that timed comments became 'the most requested feature in Viki history' (quoted in Russell 2013). The feature was promptly reintroduced the following month, underlining how community and social engagement are critical to Viki's success. As Hye-Kyung Lee (2011) notes, it is this aspect of community bonding and belonging within fansub groups that is difficult to replicate in commercial contexts. To its credit, Viki seems to have achieved this feat, successfully transitioning fansubbing from its grass roots to the boardroom. For Neoteny Labs' Joi Ito (2010), it was Viki's rare ability to 'bridge the gap between the media companies and the fan-subbers' that triggered his 'venture capital alerts with a business model that made total sense'.

As distinct from translator notes, timed comments need to be understood in the context of video sharing, forming part of a social media lexicon in which modes of textual interaction (such as Short Message Service texting, tagging and tweeting) are becoming increasingly important. Video sharing platforms like YouTube allow viewers to engage by commenting in a space located beneath the video stream, below a text

Figure 6.4 Bullet-style subtitles on *Tiny Times 3* (2014).

Figure 6.5 Audiences text comments on mobile phones during a screening of *Tiny Times 3* (2014).

box reserved for the poster/publisher. YouTube viewer comments are available for all to view, and, according to Patrick von Sychowski (2014), they are rapidly transforming this video sharing platform into 'the third social media website after Facebook and Twitter'. Viki increases the visibility and functionality of user comments further, overlaying them on to the video image itself and having them link directly to specific content. These on-screen comments have precedents in video sharing practices popular in Japan and China especially. In China, this practice is referred to as 'danmaku' – 'originally a military word, meaning massed artillery fire' (see ' "Danmaku" ' 2014). On video comment sharing sites such as NICONICO (founded in Japan in 2006), ACFun (known as 'A site' in China) and Bilibili ('B site'), viewer SMS comments are overlaid on videos to 'create a chatroom experience'. 'When many users share their comments at the same time, the video screen will be filled with subtitles, and looks like multiple bullets flying across the screen' ('"Danmaku"' 2014). In 2014, this practice migrated from video streaming to one-off theatrical film screenings (see '"Danmaku"' 2014; von Sychowski 2014), attesting to the growing popularity of this interactive mode of screen engagement, and to points of overlap emerging between subtitling and other forms of digital text production.

A Community like No Other

To join the Viki community, one registers as a user by creating a free Viki account. After setting language preferences, users are then able to select content to watch – which is automatically tailored to suit language needs. Viki indicates what percentage of a programme is available in the preferred languages, although 'viewers on the site can see files even when they're partially translated' (Li 2009). Once registered, users can choose to follow shows (each housed on a page referred to as a 'Channel'), introduce new content by applying to start their own Channel, and contribute to the community, by becoming a 'forumer' (posting on a channel or commenting on posts by others), 'segmenter', 'subber' or 'captioner'. Viki officially recognises 'passion' and 'skills' within its community by awarding 'Qualified Contributor' (QC) status to fans who have created at least one thousand subtitles or segments. Other 'quality-control' measures include the specific guidelines created by channel managers or moderators in order to facilitate subtitle consistency on matters such as grammar, capitalisation and character names. Viki staff directly assist in this complex, multi-layered collaborative process by guarding against vandalism (Viki 2011c), by responding to user queries and feedback, and by maintaining and improving technological features on the website such as homepage loading and subtitle entering (Viki 2011d).

The Viki community embraces numerous possibilities engendered via digitisation, virtual networks, creative commons, wiki-models of 'revision history and user-generated edits' and YouTube-style streaming ('Viki Announces' 2010). In this, Viki is part of a massive societal shift 'associated with current developments in information technologies and the media' that Maria Tymoczko (2005: 1088) asserts is transforming translation practice. For Viki, as for other fansub groups, translation has already become a thoroughly 'decentered process conducted by teams of people linked electronically through technological systems' (1089). It is this collective, electronically mediated organization of labour that reportedly enabled Viki to create an unexpected hit with K-drama flop *Playful Kiss*, which by September 2011 was translated into 49 languages, '20 of which were completed in the first 24 hours' (Upbin 2010). Despite its commercial leanings, however, Viki fansubbers remain an entirely voluntary labour force that has actually turned down offers of payment according to Hovaghimian (Kafka 2010). Rather, they are 'doing it for fun' (Hovaghimian quoted in Kafka 2010), contributing to a collaborative translator community that provides lively discussion and feedback from other amateur translators on matters such as fansub policy, character name consistency, capital letters and lower-case usage. Like other fansub initiatives, this interactive translator community exhibits high-level genre expertise and familiarity with the specific demands of the target audience (see Pérez-González 2006: 265).

Largely reproducing the fluent strategies and domesticating conventions of much professional subtitling, Viki has significantly extended fansubbing's impact, even beyond the 'mass niche' (see Barra 2009: 517). In 2016, Viki attracts around forty million users per month. With subtitles being produced in around two hundred languages including 'Endangered and Emerging Languages' like Manx and Cree, Viki has forged significant inroads to many parts of the so-called 'Majority World' often left off the map altogether within the remit of professional, commercial AVT. In this way, Viki facilitates the internationalisation of fansubbing activities, decentring Western and Anglophone media and languages. While English remains prominent on the Viki website, US English-language content (269 titles in 2016) is minimal in comparison to Korean (894 titles), Chinese (720 titles) and Taiwanese (375 titles) shows. While anime fansubbing facilitates the infiltration of non-English-language media into other English-language markets, countering Anglo-American hostility to translation, Japan constitutes a major economic power, with Japanese anime dominating the world animation market (O'Hagan 2008: 160).[3] On the other hand, Viki enables the profusion of diverse non-English language media into an array of different languages, with some shows being translated into fifty languages (Hovaghimian 2011). Additionally, much activity is devoted to the spreading of Asian media amongst other Asian language markets. Although Viki acknowledges that its fansubs often use English as a pivot language, as can occur in anime fansubbing (Díaz Cintas and Muñoz Sánchez 2006: 49), a policy statement posted on Viki in 2011 welcomes the input of people who can translate without reference to English (Viki 2011b). In this way, Viki appears more interventionist than Japanophile fansubbing, as it actively intercepts the language hierarchies typically entrenched by professional subtitling practice.

In its aim to overcome the geopolitical realities that limit the availability of media in many parts of the globe, Viki deploys a legal, business framework that shuns the national and linguistic biases of professional translation for the 'chaos' of fan agency and fansub dreaming.[4] For Lee (2011: 1141), 'fansubbing has clearly demonstrated a new model of anime distribution', which is now being mimicked by the commercial animation industry as it begins to realise and capitalise on the potential of online streaming services. Gonzo and FUNimation exemplify this trend (Denison 2011; Hovaghimian and Bertschy 2012). For Lee (2011: 1142–4), however, legally streamed animation sites, on the whole, remain 'territorially and technologically bounded'. Sites like Viki buck this trend, potentially closing the 'gaps between the territorially bounded distribution of foreign cultural products and the transnationality and immediacy of consumer desire' (1143).

Ethics and Economics

When Viki reintroduced timed comments in response to popular demand, it also announced plans to leverage this desire for connection and social engagement, using it as the foundation for a new, contextual advertising approach, where ads would match sentiments on-screen, 'for example, "happy ads" for a "happy scene" – to help companies connect with audiences' (Russell 2013). Unashamedly commercial, this strategy takes advantage of Viki's trademark community spirit precisely to generate profit. Viki co-founder Hovaghimian (2015) explains how Viki's timed comments offer advertisers a 'direct view into what gets television and movie fans excited, from the fashions to the intricate plot points', providing far richer data than standard social media metrics coming from sites like Facebook and Twitter. This upfront (even aggressive) commercialism sets Viki apart from most fansub groups. Since the company was acquired by Japanese e-commerce giant Rakuten in September 2013, revenue-generation efforts have ramped up further. The Viki Pass was introduced, offering advertisement-free viewing to those willing to pay a monthly ($4.99 in 2016) or annual ($49.99 in 2016) fee. The Viki Pass also guarantees HD quality, members-only content (subject to regional restrictions) and preview access to new releases. In addition, Viki Apps was launched, available for multiple devices including iOS, kindle, chromecast and rokuTV. By the end of 2015, it reported that mobile accounted for 'more than half of total watch

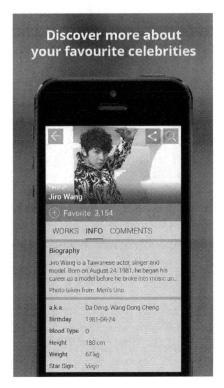

Figure 6.6 Viki App for Apple iOS.

time' (Patel 2015). Also in 2015, Viki made its own acquisition, buying the English-language Korean drama news site Soompi.

Viki's overt commercialism challenges most definitions of fansubbing and defies any easy distinction between fansubbing and crowdsourced translation. Like fansubbing, crowdsourcing is a multifarious phenomenon that can assume many forms. Some have sought to define it, only to prescribe boundaries that are almost instantly outmoded or overturned. Others have sought to avoid this leaky lingo altogether by proposing new, more robust terms such as 'user-generated translation' (O'Hagan 2009; Perrino 2009), 'open translation' (Hyde and Floss Manuals 2011) and even 'massively open translation' (O'Hagan 2016). The market research firm Common Sense Advisory created an umbrella acronym 'CT3' to cover community, collaborative *and* crowdsourced translation, and refers to them interchangeably (see Ray and Kelly 2011: 1–2). Social media giants Facebook and Twitter, on the other hand, prefer the term 'community translation', as they feel it better reflects their brands' investment in users' '*prior* knowledge of the problem space at hand' (original emphasis)

(Twitter's Matt Stanford quoted in O'Hagan 2016: 941).[5] All this terminological complexity and contention makes the task of distinguishing between fansubbing and crowdsourcing not just hard but largely beside the point.

As O'Hagan (2016) demonstrates, crowdsourcing can be dissected according to diverse criteria and agendas. While Daren C. Brabham (2013: xxi) insists that crowdsourcing is 'a shared process of bottom-up, open creation by the crowd and top-down management', Julie McDonough Dolmaya (2012) follows Rebecca Ray and Nataly Kelly's (2011) motivation-based schema and doesn't consider organisational structure at all (see O'Hagan 2016: 941). McDonough Dolmaya (2012: 169) refers to Wikipedia as 'perhaps the best known example of a website whose content has been developed entirely through crowdsourcing', whereas Brabham excludes Wikipedia altogether due to its self-governing 'bottom up' traits. In carefully attending to the overlap and points of contradiction between varying definitions, typologies and terms, O'Hagan's (2016) account registers foremost the degree of discord generated by this emergent mode of participatory translation, even within the narrow disciplinary subfield of AVT. This lack of consensus prompts her to propose a new term, 'Massively Open Translation'. An alternative approach is to embrace the elasticity and ambiguity, noting how words ultimately defy control and definition as they are constantly put to new uses.

The abundant terms currently in use to describe participatory translation practices clearly demonstrate the wide applicability, scope and spread of this activity. Manifesting in many different shapes and forms, this type of practice is common within both corporate and not-for-profit sectors and can incorporate both amateurs and professionals who either work for free or receive forms of remuneration – either products, services or money (see O'Hagan 2016; Ray and Kelly 2011). For some it is a hobby or pastime, for others a form of social interaction and belonging. Many do it to improve their language skills or to exhibit and refine their coding prowess in the case of translation hackers (see Mangiron 2012 and O'Hagan 2009). Some are motivated to 'do good' and 'give back', seeking to redress global access gaps and inequalities. Rather than fine-tune distinctions between these various practices on the basis of motivation, structure, ethics or effect, why not focus on the bigger picture? Seen in their totality, widely diverse participatory translation practices point to the scale of change currently under way. The example of Viki demands such an approach, blurring boundaries between fansubbing and crowdsourcing, community and commerce to such a degree that efforts to separate one from the other are rendered futile.

Viki points to a blurry future, refusing the stability of the status quo. It effortlessly destabilises Serenella Massidda's (2015: 18) proposal that fansubbing can be distinguished from crowdsourced translation on the basis of legal status and ethics (see Dwyer 2017). For Massidda, the fact that fansubbing typically contravenes copyright laws whereas crowdsourcing tends to take place within lawful, commercial parameters obscures ethical considerations. In these contexts, she proposes that legality relates inversely to ethics, linking commercial profitability to capitalist exploitation. Here, Massidda aligns herself with many in the professional translation community who protest against the crowdsourcing initiatives of companies such as LinkedIn and Facebook, forming groups such as 'Translators Against Crowdsourcing for Commercial Business' (see Kelly 2009). According to Ignacio Garcia (2010), however, crowdsourced translation 'may well be good for society, if not for the profession', adding that those who 'take the moral high ground and claim the quality of non-professional translation is low, pointing to ethical or even legal implications that are oversighted ... will do nothing to reverse the process'. Despite any shortcomings, Kelly (2009) notes that CT3 'opens up new multilingual markets that companies might not otherwise enter'.

Not-for-profit crowdsourced translation like that modelled by Wikipedia and the TED (Technology, Education and Design) Open Translation Project (see O'Hagan 2011) obviously challenges Massidda's charge that such practices are necessarily exploitative and unethical. In addition, Viki troubles the idea that fansubbing is, by nature, illegal. Rather, the Viki model is built around licensing, rights and revenue sharing, and consequently much content is subject to geographical restrictions. As I have noted previously (see Dwyer 2016a: 145–6), Viki has changed the face of fansubbing by both legalising and 'monetising' it, providing fansubbing a new level of cultural legitimacy in the eyes of big business and industry, while potentially empowering fans to effect lasting industry change. As Hovaghimiam (2011) puts it, Viki provides 'a legal playground' for pirate-style practices, and many Viki users express relief at being able to access content (free or through subscriptions) and fansub legally. 'I love that I found a way to watch asian dramas in a legal way and practice my languages at the same time!', comments 'OrionsRambling' ('Viki Changes' 2013). *Reverse Thieves* observes that Viki 'is an interesting platform for fansubbers as it is a way for them to work in the light as opposed to the shadows'. As these comments indicate, Viki's commercialism doesn't cancel out community, and those involved still identify as passionate fans and subbers.

Viki's combination of streaming, subtitling and participatory practices positions it at the forefront of changes currently affecting the media industries as a whole. As streaming moves to the centre of online activities, with industry reports predicting video will constitute 80 per cent of all Internet traffic by 2018 (see Shetty 2016), the GILT industries are blossoming, while streaming giants like Netflix and YouTube are instituting in-platform translation tools. In November 2015, YouTube launched a series of new devices designed to facilitate translation of titles, descriptions and subtitles in up to 76 languages, estimating that over 80 per cent of users come from outside the US, while videos from East Asia and Thailand dominate content creation ('YouTube Translation' 2015). YouTube offers diverse translation options at a range of price points, from professional human expertise to machine translation to crowdsourcing. In 2016, Netflix launched in 130 countries, bringing its total to 190. This aggressive global expansion was not matched in terms of language provision, however. Only three languages were added, bringing its total number of supported languages to 21. In contrast, Viki supports around two hundred languages – initially including the fictional *Star Trek* language Klingon. Granted, not all content is available in all languages, while so-called 'tier 1' languages predominate.[6] In 2015, English remained the top viewing language on Viki, followed by Spanish and French and Portuguese (see Omega 2015).

Although Viki's overt commercialism jeopardises its status as fansubbing 'proper', with many users complaining after the 2013 acquisition by Rakuten for US$200 million that Viki has sold out, community remains high on Viki's agenda nonetheless. From its humble beginnings as graduate class project, Viki has always striven to provide social benefit. It evolved from a not-for-profit language-learning project using YouTube videos (see Wee 2014), and, early on, co-founder Jiwon Moon (2008) envisioned it as paving 'the way towards the realization of a grand cultural "Silk Road"'. Funded by investors like Neoteny attracted by its agile business model aiming towards 'social good', and recognised by the Nominet Trust in 2013 as a 'groundbreaking application of digital technology', Viki's commitment to community is core, not tokenistic. Even those on the inside report on the passion that drives Viki's team ('they simply love what they do'), many of whom use their free time developing startups of their own and contributing to open source projects (see Seguin 2013; Cheng 2012). In 2014, Viki strengthened its social and political engagement by launching two campaigns focused on deaf and hard-of-hearing viewers (Billion Words March) and language preservation (Endangered Languages), which I go on to discuss below.

While Viki's status as fansubbing is in no way assured or unchallenged, its contributors and community certainly identify as fans, devoting hours of unpaid labour to spreading, subtitling and segmenting favourite TV shows and movies. Viki volunteers behave like fans, self-organising into channel teams, crediting fan labour, and establishing their own training programmes 'with no interference from Viki' (Henthorn 2016a). In this way, the example of Viki demonstrates just how expansive fansubbing can become, defying prescribed boundaries through continuous evolution. Signalling the current and future state of fansubbing, Viki shows just how far this phenomenon has developed from its anime origins discussed in Chapter 5. Ultimately, it is fan contributors themselves who actively determine the forms that fansubbing can take, not outside commentators. Indeed, evolution is actually in-built within Viki's collaborative translation platform. Back in 2009, Moon (quoted in Jung 2011: 119) explained how the Viki model is about 'evolving subbs', as users decide between multiple translation options and subtitles can always be updated and refined.

While instability and 'mass amateurism' (Garcia 2010) can result in crowd-led chaos, O'Hagan (2016: 942) suggests that vandalism and self-repair, subversion and innovation are two sides of the 'participatory' coin.[7] Users accessing anime on Viki note an absence of quality control and much inconsistency, noting that the site 'has a good deal of rough edges' and advising that 'a lot of the subs really need someone to go through and edit them for typos and grammatical errors'. This reviewer remarks that the subs on *Kotetsu sangokushi* (2007) refer to characters by Korean names. 'You would normally expect either the Japanese or Chinese names ... to be used but the Korean names just come out of left field', he states, attributing this odd choice to the amateur nature of the translation that enables some unusual and idiosyncratic choices, conceding it is only with fansubbing that 'you would usually get such a happenstance on a legally licensed series'. For this user, Viki fansubbing produces non-standard translation along with inconsistency and a fair degree of error. However, while errors and vandalism can be user-corrected Wikipedia-style on Viki channels with open subbing, mistakes are more difficult to fix on channels with limited or restricted subtitling groups (see Viki 2011b; Dwyer 2012b: 238). Moreover, despite this capacity for error, *Reverse Thieves* terms Viki 'a small wonder', bringing 'together the greater fan-sub community with the actual anime they are translating from a company ... without making either obsolete' while providing valued access to older and more difficult-to-find anime titles ('Viki a Small' 2012).

Geopolitics and Deterritorialisation

From its early, not-for-profit days, Viki has always sought to forge meaningful cross-border connections and understanding through the 'soft power' of popular screen content.[8] In doing so, it proactively intervenes within entrenched media distribution channels and translation flows, charting new paths and counter-flows by putting diverse languages communities in touch, as Hovaghimian (quoted in Porzucki 2014) explains:

> We had Egyptian movies that were doing great in Dutch. We have Korean movies that are doing phenomenal in Saudi Arabia. It's actually our number one country for it. And it's in Arabic subtitles.

Hence, Viki's unique style of video-on-demand streaming makes good on its 'global TV' claim, realising the affordances of digital interconnectivity in overcoming cultural and territorial borders, and facilitating language diversity. While streaming services like Netflix and Hulu started as national US services, embarking upon global expansion efforts once established in their home territory, Viki has always been global, 'deterritorial' and expansionist, setting out precisely to bridge communication and distribution gaps, and to spread by infiltrating in-between spaces of connectivity and 'transnational desire' (see Lee 2011: 1144). Its vision, business model and software all reflect this emphasis upon 'scalability'. This courting of new markets and unlikely crossover audiences, proactively intervenes within the language politics of global screen media by rerouting translation traffic, resisting the 'West to the rest' flows discussed by Lawrence Venuti (1995) and forging new, multidirectional currents between diverse countries and language communities – whether big, small or endangered.

This 'big picture' perspective is undoubtedly entrepreneurial – emphasising growth, new markets and revenue generation. Yet Viki's transnational business model also demonstrates an approach to technology and its globalising effects that encourages, rather than restricting, language difference. As the European Union prepares to implement its vision for a digital single market (DSM), it has come face to face with the language barriers that stand in the way of the networked, digital revolution yet that remain nevertheless 'one of the main cultural cornerstones of Europe', with language diversity helping to characterise 'what it means to be and to feel European' ('Strategic Agenda' 2015). Language difference constitutes a natural, inevitable obstacle in the path to digital deterritorialisation, erecting boundaries between cultures, communities and countries that are not easily overcome within cross-border commerce. While digital networking puts people in contact, it requires vast amounts of language support to ensure that effective communication can occur. As 'no single language can address 20% or more of the DSM,' notes a recent report commissioned by the EU's Horizon 2020 programme, all of the languages spoken in Europe need to be supported, as at present 'European citizens are unable to access vast amounts of online content due to *language-blocking*' ('Strategic Agenda' 2015: 1–4, original emphasis). This report also found that 'customers are six times more likely to buy from sites in their native language', pointing to the vital role played by language localisation and translation for online commerce in the audiovisual industry and beyond ('Strategic Agenda' 2015; see also Strömbäck 2015).

Viki is centrally positioned within the industry shifts enabled by technological innovation, offering a crowdsourcing translation service that engages with the practical limitations and pragmatics of globalisation 'on the ground'. Digital technologies are shifting language patterns and hierarchies, with BRIC (Brazil, Russia, India and China) countries set to dominate the online world in the near future (see Sargent 2012). Viki's big picture vision is about this central link that O'Hagan posits between technology, translation and globalisation. Notably, Viki is also joining the dots between fansubbing, media access and digital networking, offering a far broader and more socially engaged context for fansubbing than found within anime groups and other fansub communities based around single programmes, genres or languages. In this way, Viki shows how, rather than depoliticising fansubbing, its broad approach and upfront commercialisation has enabled it to engender social and political awareness around media access and language diversity.

In 2014, Viki launched two major campaigns. Advocating for 'global entertainment access for all', Viki partnered with actor Marlee Matlin to champion the rights of deaf and hard-of-hearing audiences to access timely, mandated closed captions on online media and video streaming (see Washeck 2014). Flagging captioning (as opposed to subtitling) as another core service Viki reached its billion-word target one year on (see Omega 2015). In July 2014 the US Federal Communications Commission (FCC) voted to expand online mandated captioning to cover short videos and clips from live and near-live programmes, while Netflix expanded captioning efforts to cover 100 per cent of its content. Matlin partnered with Viki in 2014 in order to see these changes take effect as soon as possible, driven by the power of the crowd, rather than waiting years for services like Netflix and Hulu to adapt to new rulings (see Mikul 2015; Washeck 2014).[9] Viki's concurrent, ongoing Endangered Languages campaign was established to 'help save endangered and emerging languages' via subtitling, captioning and Viki's Living Tongues documentary channel that explores how new media technologies can foster language revitalisation. Viki publishes a map showing all the languages featured on the website that are classed as either endangered or emerging (37 in total

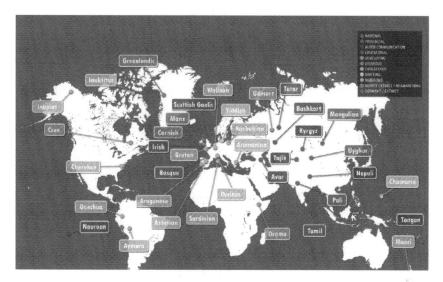

Figure 6.7 Endangered Languages Map on Viki, © 2016.

in 2016), and reports that these languages account for nearly 25 per cent of the two-hundred-plus languages featured on the site.

These two campaigns underline the democratising potential of technology to give voice to underrepresented and underserved language communities through entertainment media, new release films and television, and simple subtitling and captioning software. In doing so, Viki leverages its industry standing and commercial legitimacy to politicise fansubbing, establishing clear links between fandom and media inclusivity in the digital, global age. This type of social, community advocacy is identified by O'Hagan (2016) as a decided advantage that emerges from participatory translation efforts, which typically expand the translator's role and can engender forms of activism. Just as Wikipedia's volunteer translators see their contribution as 'a means of rectifying the inequalities in the way information is made available to various language communities' (quoted in McDonough Dolmaya 2012: 184), so too fansubbers rectify the way in which media content is distributed globally, reaching certain audience sectors and not others, or arriving at different speeds according to windowed release strategies.

With crowdsourced translation and fansubbing, users choose whether or not to participate, yet they are also often involved in deciding *what* gets translated in the first place, particularly in social media and fan contexts where contributors feel part of an active community and hold genre-specific prior knowledge or expertise. On Viki, for instance, users are encouraged to create new Channels for series, movies or recording artists they would like to see subtitled or captioned. These Channels are then self-managed by contributors. In professional contexts, on the other hand, the role and responsibilities assigned to translators tend to be quite restricted (O'Hagan 2016: 940). Of course, volunteer fansubbers are often motivated by 'affective' pleasures rather than politics, primarily seeing this activity as an enjoyable hobby or pastime, and a means of social rather than political engagement. Brian Hu (2010NIB) argues, however, that the emotional tone of much media fandom does not preclude a sense of agency and, as O'Hagan (2016: 943) notes, participatory practices like fansubbing can provide the seed for large-scale shifts in practice and approach, recasting translation as transformative as opposed to normative, while also affecting lasting industry change.

Good Enough?

As noted by McDonough Dolmaya, the Wikipedia model of collaborative translation and self-repair is not foolproof. Some errors go unchecked, leading her to conclude that 'resulting translations can never be definitive but rather evolving texts' (quoted in O'Hagan 2016: 937). As Derrida and Venuti note, however, translation itself is inherently non-authoritative and non-definitive. Rather, translation is a destabiliser. It destabilises or disarticulates 'originals' by bringing to the fore their 'capacity for skidding' (Derrida 1979: 75) and demonstrates how language pulls in multiple directions, opening itself up to various, context-bound interpretations. Translations can always be updated, refined, recalibrated. 'Originals' can always be retranslated. As with Wikipedia and Facebook community translation, Viki brings this instability to the surface, building it into its platform architecture and software that supports multi-authored contributions and real-time collaboration whereby 'subtitles are vetted and edited by many' (Porzucki 2014) 'in a wiki format that enables successive viewers to improve on the previous ones' work' (Healey 2010). On this technological level, Viki prioritises evolution and change over stable or authoritative translation, in the process reconceptualising its merit, impact and outreach – contributing to the 'globalization of film and TV at hyper-speed in rather unexpected places' (Porzucki 2014).

As O'Hagan (2011: 30) concedes, notions of value need to be re-evaluated within the CT3 environment as 'conventional translation quality measures are neither relevant nor productive in assessing fansubs'. As discussed in Chapters 3, 4 and 5, issues relating to access, speed, politics and parody are prominent, recurrent drivers in translation practice, yet to date their

relevance and impact have been little considered within screen or translation scholarship. Fansubbing and its overlap with crowdsourced, collaborative and participatory translation within streaming media distribution
delineates a vast, growing area of practice where 'quality' evaluations
provide little insight, with notions of abuse, resistance, misuse and errancy
better able to productively interrogate the complex value politics at play.
For *Reverse Thieves* ('Viki a Small' 2012), the main problem with Viki is
its lack of 'quality control'. Yet, besides this rather typical flaw in the production of volunteer, collaborative subtitling, the 'quality' of Viki fansubs
can be measured from any number of angles. Typos and grammar are only
two of the many 'errant' properties exhibited. Additionally, Viki fansubs
eschew the typical Japanophile or 'loyalist' (see Barra 2009) approach,
tending more towards mainstream than experimental textual and formal
strategies (see Dwyer 2012b).

   When Ian Condry (2010: 205) asked Studio Ghibli producer Toshio
Suzuki whether he ultimately considered fansubbing 'good' or 'bad,' his
question was met with silence, leading Condry to reflect on fansubbing's
'betwixt and between', love/hate relationship with industry. Perhaps
Suzuki's silence can be interpreted differently, however, signalling that
notions of 'good' and 'bad' are ultimately unhelpful for thinking about this
amateur translation activity that regularly refuses to play by rules, follow
convention or passively submit to language and cultural hierarchies. As I
argue throughout this book, quality debates tend to obscure rather than
interrogate the complexities of screen translation, proving unable to sufficiently engage with the chaos wrought by media piracy, mass amateurism or crowdsourcing. Fansubbing research needs to reflect its widening
transnational co-ordinates and crossover with other modes of informal
community and crowd-driven translation. Furthermore, as Iwabuchi
(2010: 88) notes, fan research must refuse any impulse towards definitional lock-down, as 'the term "fan," even in its positive senses, can easily
become a received taxonomic category that preframes our understanding
and our research questions'. Fansub resistance to set rules and boundaries
needs to be recognised and analysed.

   The example of Viki also reconfigures notions of quality by questioning
the common presumption that amateur, fansubbing is necessarily more
formally experimental or textually foreignising than commercial subtitling. For Viki fansubbers, the authenticity of their practice does not rest
exclusively with textual accuracy or word-to-word fidelity. It also emerges
through concepts of agency and the empowering potential of translation as
both a community-building device and a mode of personal expression. In
this way, Viki provides an equally interventionist model of consumption

as anime fansubbing as described by Pérez González (2006), carving out a similar space of interactivity between highly visible translators (fansub contributors) and their audiences. The fansubbers' subjective voice is aired in discussion threads debating matters of policy and protocol within the fan groups,and in discussing issues of translation with other contributors. Within this environment, authenticity is associated with emotional sincerity rather than textual fidelity, while formal innovation is forsaken for broad accessibility.

Viki fansubbing also demonstrates the productive possibilities of chaos for translation *practice*. In a 2011 policy statement, Viki expresses its commitment to the 'philosophy of open participation', opposing moves to restrict and control the subbing process as a means of preventing vandalism, ensuring consistency and reducing errors resulting from non-serious or credit-seeking contributors (Viki 2011b). Performing a comparative analysis of five randomly selected projects 'done before and after translator participation was limited to small groups of people', Viki found that less controlled translations enable a greater proliferation of options, resulting in 'better and faster subs'. Translation mistakes and vandalisms still occur, yet so too do the user-corrections vital to the success of Internet sites like Wikipedia. In contrast, where subbing is more controlled, interpretation becomes closed-off and translation errors fixed-in-place. Viki states: 'when we found errors in a channel with open subbing (whether due to vandalism or genuine error), we could often find multiple versions of the same subtitle and could revert to the correct one, whereas with a limited group, when the registered translators were wrong because they misunderstood the original language, there was no easy way to correct the subtitles' (Viki 2011b).

Notes

1. Common Sense Advisory groups these three modes of translation together under the acronym CT3. See Rebecca Ray and Nataly Kelly (2011).
2. According to Karl Seguin (2013: 4), the top five cities for Viki visits are distributed across four continents.
3. As Minako O'Hagan (2008: 160), Sean Leonard (2005b) and Jordan Hatcher (2005) note, the global dominance of anime was aided in no small measure by fan translation networks.
4. Viki fansubbing can be compared to the amateur translations of media activists discussed by Pérez González (2010: 11) where the 'very selection of audiovisual simulacra represents an act of resistance against the dynamics of global audiovisual flows, in that the chosen messages would not have otherwise reached the activist's target constituencies'.

5. On Facebook's patent for 'Community Translation on a Social Network', see O'Hagan (2016: 938).
6. Languages are often categorised into 'tier 1' and 'tier 2' groupings, with 'tier 1' generally referring to primary markets and 'tier 2' to secondary markets, which may be assessed according to variables such as size, wealth or language proximity.
7. On the notion of 'chaos' in relation to fansubbing, see Luis Pérez González (2006).
8. For another fascinating project involving film and television subtitling, see Brij Kothari (2015; 2008). Director of PlanetRead, Kothari advocates for the use of same-language subtitles on Bollywood songs on TV to be implemented as part of a national policy to radically improve literacy rates in India.
9. For example, the 2014 FCC ruling covering short online clips was scheduled to take effect only in 2016 and 2017 (see Mikul 2015).

Conclusion: Error Screens

Although translation has proved invaluable to the development of screen culture since the earliest days of silent filmmaking, its centrality is rarely acknowledged within Screen Studies, particularly within English-language frameworks. With translation's value little examined, its politics have consequently remained largely submerged. Redressing this neglect, this book has provided an overview of screen translation practices and politics, and underscored the significance of *improper* or *errant* modes of practice related to parody, piracy, censorship and non-professional participation. These improper sites of subtitling and dubbing provide a key to *revaluing* translation's role within screen culture broadly. I argue that interlingual subtitling and dubbing operations produce errant forms of screen media, constituted by the errors and excesses of mis/translation. I term these *error screens*. Importantly, this book has argued that such 'error screens' are central, not peripheral, to screen culture – as the risks of linguistic and cultural mutation that attend interlingual subtitling and dubbing keep films, television programmes and other screen media circulating, evolving and 'living-on'. I conclude that *mis*-use is central to the *use-value* of screen translation.

Having demonstrated how fixed notions of value and 'quality' are insufficient for analysing contemporary screen translation, I argue attention needs to be directed towards value *politics* and shifting, contextual complexities. Errant screen translation practices indicate that quality and value can be measured from any number of source/target vantage points, thereby destabilising the stability of the 'original'. In this regard, the findings of this book lend concrete support to theories that challenge the status and authority of 'originals'. While practising translators might find attacks on the 'original' difficult to bear, Anthony Pym (1995) notes how such challenges are actually quite practical. 'Users have to believe in meaning transfer,' he explains, while conversely, translators themselves are only too aware of the 'plurality of translation processes' and the 'instability of their sources' (Pym 1995). In screen translator training programmes, for instance, divergent approaches are taught according to genre and audience distinctions. In Italy, explains Christopher Rundle (2008: 4; 11), 'subtitling practices and quality standards differ considerably' between firms, reflecting the varying requirements and market niches of film festivals, DVD localisation and television broadcasting.

The practical instances of screen translation disjunction or excess explored in this book seek to ground the negative analytics of translation theory, keeping them in contact with pragmatics and everyday usage. In this way, the revaluation it offers is not an esoteric, conceptual endeavour irrelevant to practising translators. Rather, it is informed by, and responsive to, concrete shifts observable in the current screen translation landscape. It also broadens the scope of current screen translation research. Whereas parodic and pirate modes of practice have been all but ignored to date within Translation Studies, censoring and participatory translation are receiving burgeoning interest at present. This book has extended discourse on both these phenomena, positioning fansubbing beyond the boundaries of anime alone, and contextualising the misrepresentation that characterises translation censorship in relation to diverse amateur and otherwise 'improper' practices.

Today, subtitling and dubbing are amongst the most ubiquitous translation types of everyday life 'epitomizing emerging modes of translation' associated with globalisation, changing technologies and increasing mediatisation (Tymoczko 2005: 1088–9). Hence, their centrality for Screen and Translation Studies needs to be acknowledged. Moreover, as developments related to digital technologies, online networking and participatory modes of cultural engagement push legal boundaries and nationalist frameworks, these two fields of research must embrace contextual or 'maximalist' (Wehn 2001: 70) multidisciplinary approaches. There is a need to examine how translation is specifically implicated *within* screen dynamics – how it both *shapes* and is *shaped by* screen culture. This book provides a step in this direction. In emphasising error and excess, it also underscores how digital technologies and online networks afford opportunities for unregulated, informal modes of media engagement and how *mis*-use is coming to define participatory modes of screen consumption. This is a major shift that screen and translation scholarship needs to acknowledge and analyse if it is to keep apace of current industry developments.

In developing awareness of translation's integral role within historical and contemporary screen media, culture and discourse, I have indicated how its typical sidelining is diversionary. Translation is dismissed within screen culture because its very centrality challenges the founding illusions upon which screen media are based, while calling into question their value systems. Subtitling and dubbing draw attention to means of production and points of inauthenticity within the audio/visual mix. Most emphatically, they trouble screen culture by exposing the shifting, unstable nature of 'originals' and other signifiers of cultural, aesthetic and linguistic authenticity or purity. Translation submits screen 'originals' to the logic of versioning: the so-called 'original' becomes one sub-category in a broad set of versions distinguished by format (widescreen/letterbox), technology (DVD/VCD/streaming, etc.) and editing ('Director's Cuts', censorship, localisation), in addition to interlingual considerations. Moreover, the very concept of the 'original' is beholden to the facts and framework of translation. Paradoxically, it is through operations of translation that screen 'originals' become marked as such, only acquiring this status through mechanisms of circulation, access and ongoing interpretation.

By emphasising the significance of interlingual 'error screens', this book bolsters efforts to internationalise and diversify screen discourse. Quite literally, my focus on screens viewed in translation gives voice to foreign-language media and audiences. In the process, it draws attention to the grounded pragmatics of the inter-cultural, examining *how*, *why* and *when* screen media travels and in which languages. Such considerations are long overdue within screen discourse. Curiously, even within scholarship specifically focused on inter-cultural screen dynamics, discussion of actual mediating practices like translation remains scarce. By focusing on the material conditions of translation that underpin screen media's global circulation, this book counters this tendency, adding weight to transnational approaches by grounding discussions of national and cultural traversal via everyday pragmatics. The errors and excesses that inevitably structure translated viewing experiences point to the uncertainties and slippages that necessarily attend cultural and linguistic diversification. In this book, I argue that these risks are vital to screen culture's ongoing evolution, and to its theorisation. The importance of translation within screen culture is only set to increase in response to global shifts towards language diversity and multilingualism. Media producers and broadcasters as well as screen audiences and scholars need to take seriously the flawed operations of subtitling and dubbing, recognising how 'error screens' articulate a meeting point between media, multilingualism and misuse that is increasingly coming to define global cultural developments.

Bibliography

Abend-David, Dror (ed.). 2014. *Media and Translation: An Interdisciplinary Approach*. New York and London: Bloosmbury.

Acland, Charles. 2003. *Screen Traffic: Movies, Multiplexes and Global Culture*. Durham, NC, and London: Duke University Press.

———. 2012. *From International Blockbusters to National Hits: Analysis of the 2010 UIS Survey on Feature Film Statistics*. Montreal: UNESCO Institute for Statistics.

Adamou, Christina, and Simone Knox. 2011. 'Transforming Television Drama through Dubbing and Subtitling: *Sex and the Cities.*' *Critical Studies in Television* 6 (1): 1–21.

Agcaoili, Mizhelle D. 2011. 'Hybrid Identities: Filipino Fansubbers of Japanese Media and Self-Construction.' *Asian Studies: Journal of Critical Perspectives on Asia* 47: 1–28. <http://www.asj.upd.edu.ph/mediabox/archive/ASJ-47-2011/agcaoili.pdf> (last accessed 28 June 2016).

Albornoz, Luis A. 2016. *Diversity and the Film Industry: An Analysis of the 2014 UIS Survey on Feature Film Statistics*. Montreal: UNESCO Institute for Statistics.

Alemi, Farnaz. 2016. 'Leading Advertising Agencies and Brands Join Voluntary Initiative to Reduce Ad-Supported Piracy.' Motion Picture Association of America, 10 June. <http://www.mpaa.org/leading-advertising-agencies-and-brands-join-voluntary-initiative-to-reduce-ad-supported-piracy/> (last accessed 26 June 2016).

Alfaro, Kristen. 2012a. 'Moving Cinema: Experimental Distribution and the Development of Anthology Film Archives.' MA Thesis, Film Studies, Concordia University, Montreal.

———. 2012b. 'Access and the Experimental Film: New Technologies and Anthology Film Archives' Institutionalization of the Avant-Garde.' *The Moving Image* 12 (1): 44–64. <http://muse.jhu.edu/journals/the_moving_image/v012/12.1.alfaro.html> (last accessed 28 June 2016).

'All the King's Men.' 2006 [1963]. Translated by Ken Knabb. In *Situationist International Anthology*, edited by Ken Knabb, 149–53. Berkeley: Bureau of Public Secrets.

Altman, Rick. 1980. 'Moving Lips: Cinema as Ventriloquism.' *Yale French Studies* 60: 67–79.

Anastasiou, Dimitra, and Reinhard Schäler. 2010. 'Translating Vital Information:

Localisation, Internationalisation and Globalisation.' *Synthèses Journal* 3: 11–25.

Anderson, J. L. 1992. 'Spoken Silents in the Japanese Cinema; or, Talking to Pictures: Essaying the Katsuben, Contextualizing the Texts.' In *Reframing Japanese Cinema: Authorship, Genre, History*, edited by Arthur Nolletti Jr and David Desser. 259–311. Bloomington and Indianapolis: Indiana University Press.

'A New Ethical Code for Digital Fansubbing.' 2003. *Anime News Network*, June 9. <http://www.animenewsnetwork.com.au/feature/2003-06-08/2> (last accessed 30 June 2016).

Antonini, Rachele (ed.). 2010. Special Issue on 'Child Language Brokering: Trends and Patterns in Current Research.' *mediAzioni: Rivista Online di Studi Interdisciplinari su Lingue e Culture / Online Journal of Interdisciplinary Studies in Languages and Cultures* 10. <http://www.mediazioni.sitlec.unibo.it/index. php/no-10-special-issue-2010.html> (last accessed 22 June 2016).

Appiah, Kwame Anthony. 2000. 'Thick Translation.' In *The Translation Studies Reader*, edited by Lawrence Venuti. 417–29. London: Routledge. Original publication, 1993.

Ascheid, Antje. 1997. 'Speaking Tongues: Voice Dubbing in the Cinema as Cultural Ventriloquism.' *The Velvet Light Trap* 40 (Fall): 32–41.

Ball, Edward. 1987. 'The Great Sideshow of the Situationist International.' *Yale French Studies* 73: 21–37.

———. 1991. 'Reel to Reel: *La dialectique peut-elle casser des briques.*' *The Village Voice*, 4 June: 100–1.

Barra, Luca. 2009. 'The Mediation is the Message: Italian Regionalization of US TV Series as Co-Creational Work.' *International Journal of Cultural Studies* 12 (5): 509–25.

Bassnett, Susan, and André Lefevere (eds). 1990. *Translation, History and Culture*. London and New York: Pinter Publishers.

Baudry, Jean-Louis. 1974–5 [1970]. 'Ideological Effects of the Basic Cinematographic Apparatus.' Translated by Alan Williams. *Film Quarterly* 28 (2): 39–47.

Baumgärtel, Tilman. 2006a. 'The Culture of Piracy in the Philippines.' *Asia Culture Forum* 5: 373–98. <http://www.asian-edition.org/piracyinthephilip-pines.pdf> (last accessed 28 June 2016).

———. 2006b. 'The United States of Piracy.' Asian Edition Conference Proceedings. <http://www.asian-edition.org> (last accessed 28 June 2016).

———. 2015. 'Media Piracy: An Introduction.' In *Pirate Essays: A Reader on International Media Piracy*, edited by Tilman Baumgärtel. 9–23. Amsterdam: Amsterdam University Press.

Béhar, Henri. 2004. 'Cultural Ventriloquism.' In *Subtitles: On the Foreignness of Film*, edited by Atom Egoyan and Ian Balfour. 79–88. Cambridge, MA, and London: MIT Press.

Ben-Ghiat, Ruth. 1997. 'Language and the Construction of National Identity in Fascist Italy.' *The European Legacy* 2 (3): 438–43.

Benjamin, Ross. 2004. 'Hostile Obituary for Derrida.' *The Nation*, 13 December. <http://www.thenation.com/article/hostile-obituary-derrida#axzz2WARK Cwg1> (last accessed 28 June 2016).

Benjamin, Walter. 1968 [1923]. 'The Task of the Translator: An Introduction to the translation of Baudelaire's *Tableaux Parisiens*.' Translated by Harry Zohn. In *Illuminations*, edited by Hannah Arendt, 69–82. New York: Harcourt, Brace & World. Original edition, 1955.

Berger, Verena, and Miya Komori. 2010. *Polyglot Cinema: Migration and Transcultural Narration in France, Italy, Portugal and Spain.* Vienna and Berlin: LIT Verlag.

Bergfelder, Tim. 2005. 'National, Transnational or Supranational Cinema? Rethinking European Film Studies.' *Media, Culture & Society* 27 (3): 315–31.

Berman, Antoine. 2000 [1985]. 'Translation and the Trials of the Foreign.' Translated by Lawrence Venuti. In *The Translation Studies Reader*, edited by Lawrence Venuti. 284–97. New York: Routledge.

Betz, Mark. 2009. *Beyond the Subtitle: Remapping European Art Cinema.* Minneapolis and London: University of Minnesota Press.

Billiani, Francesca. 2007. 'Assessing Boundaries – Censorship and Translation: An Introduction.' In *Modes of Censorship and Translation: National Contexts and Diverse Media*, edited by Francesca Billiani. 1–25. Manchester and Kinderhook, NY: St Jerome.

——— (ed.). 2007. *Modes of Censorship and Translation: National Contexts and Diverse Media.* Manchester and Kinderhook, NY: St Jerome.

Bisson, Marie-Josée, Walter J. B. Van Heuven, Kathy Conklin and Richard J. Tunney. 2014. 'Processing of Native and Foreign Language Subtitles in Films: An Eye Tracking Study.' *Applied Psycholinguistics* 35: 299–418.

Blinn, Miika. 2008. 'The Dubbing Standard: Its History And Efficiency Implications For Film Distributors in the German Film Market.' *DIME Working Papers Series on Intellectual Property Rights*, Working Paper 57. <http://www.dime-eu.org/files/active/0/BlinnPAPER.pdf> (last accessed 28 June 2016).

Bordwell, David, and Kristen Thompson. 2004 [1979]. *Film Art: An Introduction.* 7th ed. Boston: McGraw Hill.

Borges, Jorge Luis. 2004 [1945]. 'On Dubbing.' Translated by Calin-Andrei Mihailescu. In *Subtitles: On the Foreignness of Film*, edited by Atom Egoyan and Ian Balfour, 11–19. Cambridge, MA, and London: MIT Press.

Bowser, Eileen. 1990. *The Transformation of Cinema, 1907–1915.* Berkeley and Los Angeles: University of California Press.

Brabham, Daren C. 2013. *Crowdsourcing.* Cambridge, MA, and London: MIT Press.

Braxton, Jasmine A. 2014. 'Lost in Translation: The Obstacles of Streaming Digital Media and the Future of Transnational Licensing.' *Hastings Communication and Entertainment Law Journal* 36 (1): 193–216.

Bréan, Samuel. 2011. 'Godard English Cannes: The Reception of *Film Socialisme*'s "Navajo English" Subtitles.' *Senses of Cinema* 60. <http://sensesofcinema. com/2011/feature-articles/goardenglishcannes-the-reception-of-film-social ismes-'navajo-english'-subtitles/> (last accessed 28 June 2016).

Bucaria, Chiara. 2009. 'Translation and Censorship on TV: An Inevitable Love Affair?' Paper presented at the 3rd IATIS Conference: Mediation and Conflict: Translation and Culture in a Global Context, 10 July. Monash University, Melbourne.

Caffrey, Colm. 2008. 'Viewer Perception of Visual Nonverbal Cues in Subtitled TV Anime.' *European Journal of English Studies* 12 (2): 163–78.

———. 2009. 'Relevant Abuse? Investigating the Effects of an Abusive Subtitling Procedure on the Perception of TV Anime Using Eye Tracker and Questionnaire.' PhD Thesis. School of Language and Intercultural Studies, Dublin City University.

Canby, Vincent. 1970. 'Now You Can See Invisible Cinema.' *New York Times*, 29 November: 1.

———. 1983. 'A Rebel Lion Breaks Out.' *New York Times*, 27 March: 21.

'Captive Words: Preface to a Situationist Dictionary.' 2006 [1966]. Translated by Ken Knabb. In *Situationist International Anthology*, edited by Ken Knabb, 222–8. Berkeley, CA: Bureau of Public Secrets.

Carter, David Ray. 2011. 'Cinemasochism: Bad Movies and the People Who Love Them.' In *In the Peanut Gallery with Mystery Science Theater 3000*, edited by Robert G. and Shelley E. Barba Weiner. 101–8. Jefferson, NC, and London: McFarland & Co.

Castellano, Alberto. 2005. 'Don't Look Down: In Support of Film Dubbing in Italy.' *Cinemascope* 1. http:// www.cinema-scope.net.

Cather, Kirsten. 2009. ' "I Know It When I Hear It": The Case of the Blind Film Censor.' *The Velvet Light Trap* 63: 60–2.

Cerón, C. 2001. 'Punctuating Subtitles. Topographical Conventions and Their Evolution.' In *(Multi) Media Translation: Concepts, Practices, and Research*, edited by Yves Gambier and Henrik Gottlieb. 173–7. Amsterdam and Philadelphia: John Benjamins.

Chaume Varela, Frederic. 1997. 'Translating Non-Verbal Information in Dubbing.' In *Nonverbal Communication and Translation: New Perspectives and Challenges in Literature, Interpretation and the Media*, edited by Fernandos Poyatos, 315–26. Amsterdam and Philadelphia: John Benjamins.

Cheng, Adrian. 2012. 'About Viki.' Singapore Management University, School of Information Systems, Unit IS427 Wiki Page, 6 April. <https://wiki.smu. edu.sg/1112t2is427g1/Viki> (last accessed 20 May 2016).

Chiaro, Delia. 2007. 'Not in Front of the Children? An Analysis of Sex on Screen in Italy', *Linguistica Antverpiensia New Series* 6: 257–76, <https://lans-tts.

uantwerpen.be/index.php/LANS-TTS/article/view/191> (last accessed 26 June 2016).

Chion, Michel. 1999 [1982]. *The Voice in Cinema*. Translated by Claudia Gorbman. New York: Columbia University Press.

———. 2009 [2003]. *Film, A Sound Art*. Translated by Claudia Gorbman. New York: Columbia University Press.

Chute, David (ed.). 1988. 'Made in Hong Kong.' *Film Comment* 24 (3): 33–5.

Condry, Ian. 2010. 'Dark Energy: What Fansubs Reveal about the Copyright Wars.' In *Mechamedia 5: Fanthropologies*, edited by Frenchy Lunning. 193–208. Minneapolis: University of Minnesota Press.

Costales, Alberto Fernández. 2011. '2.0: Facing the Challenges of the Global Era.' *Tralogy* 1 (4). <http://lodel.irevues.inist.fr/tralogy/index.php?id=120> (last accessed 28 June 2016).

Crafton, Donald. 1999. *The Talkies: American Cinema's Transition to Sound 1926–1931*. Berkeley, Los Angeles and London: University of California Press.

Crisp, Virginia. 2015. *Film Distribution in the Digital Age: Pirates and Professionals*. Basingstoke: Palgrave Macmillan.

Cronin, Michael. 2009. *Translation Goes to the Movies*. London and New York: Routledge.

Crowther, Bosley. 1960a. 'Subtitles Must Go! Let's Have Dubbed English Dialogue On Foreign-Language Films.' *New York Times*, 7 August: 1; 3.

———. 1960b. 'Dubbing (Continued): Reader Interest Draws More Talk About Talk in Foreign Films.' *New York Times*, 21 August: 1; 6.

———. 1965. 'Speaking of Foreign Films.' *New York Times*, 13 June: 1; 14.

———. 1966. 'The Tower of Babel Again.' *New York Times*, 14 August: 93.

Cubbison, Laurie. 2005. 'Anime Fans, DVDs, and the Authentic Text.' *The Velvet Light Trap* 56: 45–57.

Curti, Giorgio Hadi. 2009. 'Beating Words to Life: Subtitles, Assemblage(s) capes, Expression.' *GeoJournal* 74 (3): 201–8.

Danan, Martine. 1991. 'Dubbing as an Expression of Nationalism.' *Meta: Translators' Journal* 36 (4): 606–14.Daniels, Joshua M. 2008. '"Lost in Translation": Anime, Moral Rights, and Market Failure.' *Boston University Law Review* 88: 709–44.

'"Danmaku": The Social Video Sharing Websites in China.' 2014. China Startup, 12 October. <http://chinastartup.tumblr.com/post/99791426566/danmaku-the-social-video-sharing-websites-in> (last accessed 27 June 2016).

Davis, Darrell William. 2003. 'Compact Generation: VCD Markets in Asia.' *Historical Journal of Film, Radio and Television* 23 (2): 165–76.

Davis, Kathleen. 2001. *Deconstruction and Translation*. Manchester and Northampton, MA: St Jerome.

Debord, Guy. 2003 [1989]. 'The Use of Stolen Films.' Translated by Ken Knabb. In *Guy Debord: Complete Cinematic Works – Scripts, Stills, Documents*, edited by Ken Knabb. 222–3. Oakland and Edinburgh: AK Press.

Debord, Guy, and Gil J. Wolman. 2006 [1956]. 'A User's Guide to Détournement.'

Translated by Ken Knabb. In *Situationist International Anthology*, edited by Ken Knabb. 14–21. Berkeley: Bureau of Public Secrets.

De Bruyn, Eric. 2004. 'The Expanded Field of Cinema, or Exercise on the Perimeter of a Square.' In *X-Screen: Film Installations and Actions in the 1960s and 1970s*, edited by Matthias Michalka. 152–76. Cologne: Walther König.

Delabastita, Dirk. 1990. 'Translation and the Mass Media.' In *Translation, History and Culture*, edited by Susan Bassnett and André Lefevere. 97–109. London and New York: Pinter.

Deleuze, Gilles. 1991 [1966]. *Bergsonism*. Translated by Hugh Tomlinson and Barbara Habberjam. New York: Zone Books.

———. 1986 [1983]. *Cinema 1: The Movement-Image*. Translated by Hugh Tomlinson and Robert Galeta. London: The Athlone Press. Reprint, 2000.

———. 1989 [1985]. *Cinema 2: The Time-Image*. Translated by Hugh Tomlinson and Robert Galeta. London: The Athlone Press. Reprint, 2000.

Deleuze, Gilles, and Félix Guattari. 1986 [1975]. *Kafka: Toward a Minor Literature*. Translated by Dana Polan. Minneapolis: University of Minnesota Press.

De Linde, Zoé, and Neil Kay. 1999. *The Semiotics of Subtitling*. Manchester: St Jerome.

DeLuca, Gerald A. 2004. 'Public Theatre' Discussion Thread. Cinema Treasures, 29 December. <http://cinematreasures.org/comments?page=1&theater_id=9741> (last accessed 28 June 2016).

De Man, Paul. 1986. *The Resistance to Theory*. Manchester: Manchester University Press.

Deneroff, Harvey, and Fred Ladd. 1996. 'Fred Ladd: An Interview.' *Animation World Magazine* 1 (5), August. <http://www.awn.com/mag/issue1.5/articles/deneroffladd1.5.html> (last accessed 10 June 2015).

Denis, Claire. 2004. 'Outside Myself: Claire Denis Interviewed by Atom Egoyan.' In *Subtitles: On the Foreignness of Film*, edited by Atom Egoyan and Ian Balfour. 69–77. Cambridge, MA, and London: MIT Press.

Denison, Rayna. 2011. 'Anime Fandom and the Liminal Spaces between Fan Creativity and Piracy.' *International Journal of Cultural Studies* 14 (5): 449–66.

Derrida, Jacques. 1979. 'Living On / Border Lines.' Translated by James Hulbert. In *Deconstruction and Criticism*, by Harold Bloom, Paul de Man, Jacques Derrida, Geoffrey Hartman and J. Hillis Miller, 75–176. New York: Seabury Press.

———. 1982 [1971]. 'White Mythology: Metaphor in the Text of Philosophy.' Translated by Alan Bass. In *Margins of Philosophy*, 207–71. Chicago: University of Chicago Press.

———. 1984. 'Deconstruction and the Other.' An interview with Richard Kearney. In *Dialogues with Contemporary Continental Thinkers*, edited by Richard Kearney. 107–26. Manchester: Manchester University Press.

———. 1985a. 'Des Tours de Babel.' Translated by Joseph F. Graham. In

Difference in Translation, edited by Joseph F. Graham. 165–207. Ithaca and London: Cornell University Press.

———. 1985b. *The Ear of the Other: Otobiography, Transference, Translation.* Translated by Peggy Kamuf and Avital Ronell. Edited by Christie McDonald. Lincoln, NE, and London: University of Nebraska Press. Original publication, 1982.

———. 1987 [1978]. 'Le retrait de la métaphore.' In Psyché*: Inventions de l'autre.* 63–93. Paris: Galilée.

———. 2007 [1978]. 'The *Retrait* of Metaphor.' Translated by Peggy Kamuf. In *Psyche*, edited by Peggy Kamuf, 48–80. Stanford: Stanford University Press.

'Détournement as Negation and Prelude.' [1959] 2006. Translated by Ken Knabb. In *Situationist International Anthology*, edited by Ken Knabb. 678. Berkeley: Bureau of Public Secrets.

Díaz Cintas, Jorge. 1999. 'Dubbing or Subtitling: The Eternal Dilemma.' *Perspectives: Studies in Translatology* 7 (1): 31–40.

———. 2003. 'Audiovisual Translation in the Third Millennium.' In *Translation Today: Trends and Perspectives*, edited by Gunilla Anderman and Margaret Rogers, 192–204. Clevedon: Multilingual Matters.

———. 2004. 'In Search of a Theoretical Framework for the Study of Audiovisual Translation.' In *Topics in Audiovisual Translation*, edited by Pilar Orero, 21–34. Amsterdam and Philadelphia: John Benjamins.

———. 2005. 'Back to the Future in Subtitling.' MuTra 2005 – Challenges of Multidimensional Translation: Conference Proceedings. <http://www.euro-conferences.info/proceedings/2005_Proceedings/2005_DiazCintas_Jorge.pdf> (last accessed 28 June 2016).

———. 2012. 'Clearing the Smoke to See the Screen: Ideological Manipulation in Audiovisual Translation.' *Meta: Translators' Journal* 57 (2): 279–93.

Díaz Cintas, Jorge, and Pablo Muñoz Sánchez. 2006. 'Fansubs: Audiovisual Translation in an Amateur Environment.' *The Journal of Specialized Translation* 6: 37–52. <http://www.jostrans.org/issue06/art_diaz_munoz.php> (last accessed 28 June 2016).

Díaz Cintas, Jorge, Ilaria Parini and Irene Ranzato (eds). 2016. *Altre Modernità: Riviste di studi letterari e culturali / Other Modernities* Special Issue on Ideological Manipulation in Audiovisual Translation.<http://riviste.unimi.it/index.php/AMonline/issue/view/888> (last accessed 26 June 2016).

Di Giovanni, Elena. 2007. 'Films, Subtitles and Subversions.' *Linguistica Antverpiensia New Series* 6: 51–66.

Distelmeyer, Jan (ed.). 2006. *Babylon in FilmEuropa: Mehrsprachen-Versionen der 1930er Jahre.* München: Text + Kritik.

Doane, Mary Ann. 1980. 'The Voice in the Cinema: The Articulation of Body and Space.' *Yale French Studies* 60: 33–50.

———. 1985. 'Ideology and the Practice of Sound Editing and Mixing.' In *The Cinematic Apparatus*, edited by Teresa de Lauretis and Stephen Heath. 47–56. Basingstoke and London: Macmillan.

Dries, Josephine. 1994–5. 'Breaking Language Barriers behind the Broken Wall.' *Intermedia* 22 (6): 35–7.

Duffett, Mark. 2013. *Understanding Fandom: An Introduction to the Study of Media Fan Culture*. New York and London: Bloomsbury.

Durovicová, Natasa. 1992. 'Translating America: The Hollywood Multilinguals 1929–1933.' In *Sound Theory / Sound Practice*, edited by Rick Altman. 138–53. New York and London: Routledge.

Durovicová, Natasa, and Kathleen Newman (eds). 2010. *World Cinemas, Transnational Perspectives*. New York: Routledge.

Dwyer, Tessa. 2005. 'Universally Speaking: Lost in Translation and Polyglot Cinema.' *Linguistica Antverpiensia New Series* 4: 295–310.

————. 2012a. 'Bad-Talk: Media Piracy and "Guerrilla" Translation.' In *Words, Images and Performances in Translation*, edited by Brigid Maher and Rita Wilson. 194–215. New York and London: Continuum.

————. 2012b. 'Fansub Dreaming on ViKi: "Don't Just Watch But Help When You Are Free".' *The Translator* 18 (2): 217–43.

————. 2014. 'B-Grade Subtitles.' In *B for Bad Cinema*, edited by Claire Perkins and Constantine Verevis. New York: SUNY Press.

————. 2016a. 'Multilingual Publics: Fansubbing Global TV.' In *Contemporary Publics*, edited by P. David Marshall, Glenn D'Cruz, Sharon Macdonald and Katja Lee. 145–62. Basingstoke and New York: Palgrave Macmillan.

————. 2016b. 'Mute, Dumb, Dubbed: Lulu's Silent Talkies.' In *Politics, Policy and Power in Translation History*, edited by Lieven D'hulst, Carol O'Sullivan and Michael Schreiber. 157–86. Berlin: Frank & Timme.

————. 2017. 'Audiovisual Translation and Fandom.' In *Routledge Handbook of Audiovisual Translation*, edited by Luis Pérez González. London and New York: Routledge.

Dwyer, Tessa, and Ioana Uricaru. 2009. 'Slashings and Subtitles: Romanian Media Piracy, Censorship, and Translation.' *The Velvet Light Trap* 63: 45–57.

Dwyer, Tessa, and Ramon Lobato. 2016. 'Informal Translation, Post-Cinema and Global Media Flows.' In *The State of Post-Cinema: Tracing the Moving Image in the Age of Digital Dissemination*, edited by Malte Hagener, Vinzenz Hediger and Alena Strohmaier. 127–45. Basingstoke and New York: Palgrave Macmillan.

Egoyan, Atom, and Ian Balfour. 2004. *Subtitles: On the Foreignness of Film*. Cambridge, MA, and London: MIT Press.

Eichelbaum, Stanley. 1971. 'Cinema in Its Purist Form.' *San Francisco Sunday Examiner*, 17 January: 140.

Elcott, Noam M. 2008. 'Darkened Rooms: A Genealogy of Avant-Garde Filmstrips from Man Ray to the London Film-Makers' Co-op and Back Again.' *Grey Room* 30: 6–37.

Elsaesser, Thomas. 2012. 'Is Nothing New? Turn-of-the-Century Epistemes in Film History.' In *A Companion to Early Cinema*, edited by André Gaudreault,

Nicolas Dulac and Santiago Hidalgo. 587–609. Malden, MA, and Oxford: Wiley-Blackwell.

Eng, Lawrence. 2012a. 'Anime and Manga Fandom as Networked Culture.' In *Fandom Unbound: Otaku Culture in a Connected World*, edited by Mizuko Ito, Daisuke Okabe and Izumi Tsuji. 158–78. New Haven and London: Yale University Press.

———. 2012b. 'Strategies of Engagement: Discovering, Defining, and Describing Otaku Culture in the United States.' In *Fandom Unbound: Otaku Culture in a Connected World*, edited by Mizuko Ito, Daisuke Okabe and Izumi Tsuji. 85–104. New Haven and London: Yale University Press.

Ertel, Emmanuelle. 2011. 'Derrida on Translation and His (Mis)Reception in America.' *Trahir* 2: 1–18. <http://www.revuetrahir.net/2011-2/trahir-ertel-derrida.pdf> (last accessed 28 June 2016).

Estellés-Arolas, Enrique, and Fernando González-Ladrón-de-Guevara. 2012. 'Towards an Integrated Crowdsourcing Definition.' *Journal of Information Science* 38 (2): 189–200.

Ezra, Elizabeth, and Terry Rowden (eds). 2006. *Transnational Cinema: The Film Reader*. London: Routledge.

Fawcett, Peter. 2003. 'The Manipulation of Language and Culture in Film Translation.' In *Apropos of Ideology*, edited by María Calzada Pérez. 145–63. Manchester: St Jerome Publishing.

Ferrari, Chiara Francesca. 2010. *Since When Is Fran Drescher Jewish? Dubbing Stereotypes in* The Nanny, The Simpsons *and* The Sopranos. Austin: University of Texas Press.

Filmer, Denise. 2016. '"Did You Really Say That?" Voiceover and the (Re) Creation of Reality in Berlusconi's "Shocking" Interview for Newsnight.' *Altre Modernità: Riviste di studi letterari e culturali / Other Modernities* Special Issue: 21–41. <http://riviste.unimi.it/index.php/AMonline/article/view/6846> (last accessed 26 June 2016).

Fleeger, Jennifer. 2016. 'Tito Schipa, Italian Film Sound, and Opera's Legacy on Screen.' In *Locating the Voice in Film*, edited by Tom Whittaker and Sarah Wright. 31–46. Oxford: Oxford University Press.

Fodor, István. 1976. *Film Dubbing: Phonetic, Semiotic, Esthetic and Psychological Aspects*. Hamburg: Helmut Buske Verlag.

Ford, Simon. 2005. *The Situationist International: A User's Guide*. London: Black Dog.

Foucault, Michel. 1977 [1970]. 'What Is an Author?' Translated by Donald F. Bouchard and Sherry Simon. In *Language, Counter-Memory, Practice: Selected Essays and Interviews*, edited by Donald F. Bouchard. 124–7. Ithaca: Cornell University Press.

Franco, Eliana, Anna Matamala and Pilar Orero. 2010. *Voice-Over Translation: An Overview*. Bern: Peter Lang AG.

French, Philip, and Julian Petley. 2007. *Censoring the Moving Image*. London, New York and Calcutta: Seagull Books.

Frey, Mattias. 2010. 'Cultural Problems of Classical Film Theory: Béla Balázs, "Universal Language" and the Birth of National Cinema.' *Screen* 51 (4): 324–40. doi: 10.1093/screen/hjq028.

'Funimation, Bandai Entertainment Respond on Crunchyroll (Updated).' 2008. *Anime News Network*, 12 March. <http://www.animenewsnetwork.com.au/news/2008-03-12/funimation-responds-to-crunchyroll-us$4m-funding> (last accessed 28 June 2016).

Furniss, Maureen. 1998. *Art in Motion: Animation Aesthetics*. Sydney: John Libbey.

Gallagher, Mark. 2004. 'What's So Funny about Iron Chef?' *Journal of Popular Film and Television* 31 (4): 176–84.

Gallop, Jane. 1994. 'The Translation of Deconstruction.' *Qui Parle* 8 (1): 45–62.

Gambier, Yves. 2003. 'Introduction. Screen Transadaptation: Perception and Reception.' *The Translator* 9 (2): 171–89.

———. 2006. 'Multimodality and Audiovisual Translation.' MuTra 2006 – Conference Proceedings. <http://www.euroconferences.info/proceedings/2006_Proceedings/2006_proceedings.html> (last accessed 28 June 2016).

Gambier, Yves, and Henrik Gottlieb (eds). 2001. *(Multi) Media Translation: Concepts, Practices, and Research*. Amsterdam and Philadelphia: John Benjamins.

Gao, Kun. 2008a. 'Crunchyroll CEO: Making Online Anime Pay: Interview with Kun Gao, Part 1.' *ICv2*, 15 December. <http://icv2.com/print/article/13922> (last accessed 28 June 2016).

———. 2008b. 'Crunchyroll CEO: Replacing Toonami – Interview with Kun Gao, Part 2.' *ICv2*, 15 December. <http://icv2.com/articles/comics/view/13923/crunchyroll-ceo-replacing-toonami> (last accessed 28 June 2016).

Garcia, Ignacio. 2010. 'The Proper Place of Professionals (and Non-Professionals and Machines) in Web Translation.' *Revista Tradumàtica* 8. <http://www.fti.uab.cat/tradumatica/revista/num8/articles/02/02art.htm> (last accessed 28 June 2016).

———. 2015. 'Cloud Marketplaces: Procurement of Translators in the Age of Social Media.' *Journal of Specialised Translation* 23 (January): 18–38. <http://www.jostrans.org/issue23/art_garcia.pdf> (last accessed 30 June 2016).

Garncarz, Joseph. 1999. 'Made in Germany: Multiple-Language Versions and the Early German Sound Cinema.' Translated by Brenda Ferris. In *'Film Europe' and 'Film America': Cinema, Commerce and Cultural Exchange 1920–1939*, edited by Andrew Higson and Richard Maltby. 249–73. Exeter: University of Exeter Press.

Garry, Patrick. 1993. *An American Paradox: Censorship in a Nation of Free Speech*. Westport and London: Praeger.

Gaudreault, André. 2012. 'The Culture Broth and the Froth of Cultures of So-Called Early Cinema.' In *A Companion to Early Cinema*, edited by André Gaudreault, Nicolas Dulac and Santiago Hidalgo. 15–31. Malden, MA, and Oxford: Wiley-Blackwell.

Gaudreault, André, Nicolas Dulac and Santiago Hidalgo (eds). 2012. *A Companion to Early Cinema*. Malden, MA, and Oxford: Wiley-Blackwell.

Gendrault, Camille. 2010. 'Dialect and the Global: A Combination Game.' Translated by Geoffrey Michael Goshgarian. In *Polyglot Cinema: Migration and Transcultural Narration in France, Italy, Portugal and Spain*, edited by Verena Berger and Miya Komori, 229–40. Vienna and Berlin: LIT Verlag.

Gentzler, Edwin. 1993. *Contemporary Translation Theories*. Clevedon: Multilingual Matters.

———. 2002. 'Translation, Poststructuralism, and Power.' In *Translation and Power*, edited by Edwin Gentzler and Maria Tymoczko. 195–218. Amherst: University of Massachusetts Press.

Gerow, Aaron. 2000. 'One Print in the Age of Mechanical Reproduction: Film Industry and Culture in 1910s Japan.' *Screening the Past* 11. http://www.latrobe.edu.au/screeningthepast/.

Godard, Barbara. 2005. 'Sign and Events: Deleuze in Translation.' *Semiotic Review of Books* 15 (3): 3–10.

Gómez Castro, Christina. 2016. 'Ideological Manipulation in the Form of Official Censorship: Audiovisual Tie-Ins of Bestselling Novels in Spain under Franco,' *Altre Modernità: Riviste di studi letterari e culturali / Other Modernities* Special Issue: 42–57, <http://riviste.unimi.it/index.php/AMonline/article/view/6847> (last accessed 26 June 2016).

Gosling, John. 1996. 'Anime in Europe.' *Animation World Magazine* 1 (5), August. <http://www.awn.com/mag/issue1.5/articles/goslingeuro1.5.html> (last accessed 10 June 2015).

Gottlieb, Henrik. 1994. 'Subtitling: Diagonal Translation.' *Perspectives: Studies in Translatology* 2 (1): 101–21.

———. 1997. 'Quality Revisited: The Rendering of English Idioms in Danish Television Subtitles vs. Printed Translations.' In *Text Typology and Translation*, edited by Anna Trosborg, 309–38. Amsterdam and Philadelphia: John Benjamins.

———. 2004. 'Language-Political Implications of Subtitling.' In *Topics in Audiovisual Translation*, edited by Pilar Orero. 83–100. Amsterdam and Philadelphia: John Benjamins.

Govil, Nitin. 2004. 'War in the Age of Pirate Reproduction.' *Sarai Reader* 4: 378–83. <http://archive.sarai.net/files/original/12a426735ae41b79f72edf763898a624.pdf> (last accessed 28 June 2016).

———. 2005. 'Media Empires and the Figure of the Pirate.' Paper presented at Contested Commons/Trespassing Publics, 7 January. Saria–CSDS, New Delhi. < http://sarai.net/contested-commons-trespassing-publics/> (last accessed 28 June 2016).

Graddol, David. 1997. *The Future of English?* London: British Council. <https://doanbangoc.files.wordpress.com/2012/07/the-future-of-english.pdf> (last accessed 28 June 2016).

———. 2006. *English Next*. London: British Council. <https://doanbangoc. files.wordpress.com/2012/07/english-next.pdf> (last accessed 28 June 2016).

Granados, Nelson. 2015. 'The War Against Movie Piracy: Attack Both Supply and Demand.' Forbes Media and Entertainment, 31 August. <http://www. forbes.com/sites/nelsongranados/2015/08/31/the-war-against-movie-piracy-attack-both-supply-and-demand/#62d57b71772b> (last accessed 26 June 2016).

Greaney, Patrick. 2010. 'Insinuation: Détournement as Gendered Repetition.' *The South Atlantic Quarterly* 110 (1): 75–88.

Grieveson, Lee. 2004. *Policing Cinema: Movies and Censorship in Early Twentieth-Century America*. Berkeley, Los Angeles and London: University of California Press.

Grillo, Virgil, and Bruce Kawin. 1981. 'Reading at the Movies: Subtitles, Silence, and the Structure of the Brain.' *Post Script: Essays in Film and the Humanities* 1 (1): 25–32.

Grimes, Christopher. 2002. 'David Meets Goliath in True Hollywood Style: There Is a Positive Side to Having Wal-Mart Move on to Your Turf, as the Netflix Founder Tells Christopher Grimes.' *Financial Times*, 13 November; 32.

Guardini, Paola. 1998. 'Decision-Mking in Subtitling.' *Perspectives: Studies in Translatology* 6 (1): 91–112.

Gutiérrez Lanza, Camino. 2002. 'Spanish Film Translation and Cultural Patronage: The Filtering and Manipulation of Imported Material during Franco's Dictatorship.' In *Translation and Power*, edited by Edwin Gentzler and Maria Tymoczko. 141–59. Amherst: University of Massachusetts Press.

Hajmohammadi, Ali. 2004. 'The Viewer as the Focus of Subtitling: Towards a Viewer-Oriented Approach.' *Translation Journal* 8 (4). <http://translation-journal.net/journal/30subtitling.htm> (last accessed 30 June 2016).

Halligan, Fionnuala. 2000. 'A War of Words.' *Screen International*, 24 March: 12.

Hansen, Miriam. 1985. 'Universal Language and Democratic Culture: Myths of Origin in Early American Cinema.' In *Mythos und Auklärung in der Amerikanischen Literatur*, edited by Dieter Meindl and Friedrich W. Horlacher. 321–51. Nuremberg: Nürnberg Universitätsbund Erlangen.

———. 1991. *Babel & Babylon: Spectatorship in American Silent Film*. Cambridge, MA, and London: Harvard University Press.

Haslem, Wendy. 2004. 'Neon Gothic: Lost in Translation.' *Senses of Cinema* 31. <http://sensesofcinema.com/2004/feature-articles/lost_in_translation/> (last accessed 30 June 2016).

Hatcher, Jordan S. 2005. 'Of Otakus and Fansubs: A Critical Look at Anime Online in Light of Current Issues in Copyright Law.' *SCRIPT-ed* 2 (4): 514–42. <http://www2.law.ed.ac.uk/ahrc/script-ed/vol2-4/hatcher.asp> (last accessed 28 June 2016).

Hatim, Basil, and Ian Mason. 2000. 'Politeness in Screen Translating.' In *The*

Translation Studies Reader, edited by Lawrence Venuti, 430–45. London: Routledge.

Hawkins, Allison. 2013. 'Piracy as a Catalyst for Evolution in Anime Fandom.' Honours Thesis, University of Michigan.

Hawkins, Gay. 2010. 'Multiculturalism on Screen – Subtitling and the Translation of Cultural Differences.' *The Otemon Journal of Australian Studies* 36: 97–109.

Hawkins, Joan. 2000. *Cutting Edge: Art-Horror and the Horrific Avant-Garde*. Minneapolis: University of Minnesota Press.

Hazara, Helene. 2004. 'René Viénet: The Bad Boy of Sinology.' Translated by Not Bored! Radio France. <http://www.notbored.org/vienet-radiofrance.html> (last accessed 28 June 2016).

Healey, Jon. 2010. 'ViKi: Making Online Video Speak in Tongues.' *Los Angeles Times*, 10 December. <http://latimesblogs.latimes.com/technology/2010/12/ViKi-making-online-video-speak-in-tongues.html> (last accessed 28 June 2016).

Hellekson, Karen. 2009. '"Verbotene Liebe," Soap Operas, Fansubbing, and YouTube.' *MediaCommons: A Digital Scholarly Network*, 8 May. <http://mediacommons.futureofthebook.org/content/verbotene-liebe-soap-operas-fansubbing-and-youtube> (last accessed 28 June 2016).

———. 2011. 'Bulgarian Version of *Forbidden Love*.' *MediaCommons: A Digital Scholarly Network*, 2 February. <http://mediacommons.futureofthebook.org/content/bulgarian-version-forbidden-love> (last accessed 28 June 2016).

———. 2012. 'Creating a Fandom Via YouTube: *Verbotene Liebe* and Fansubbing.' In *New Media Literacies and Participatory Popular Culture Across Borders*, edited by Bronwyn Williams and Amy Zenger, 180–92. Hoboken: Taylor and Francis.

Hemmungs Wirtén, E. 2011. *Cosmopolitan Copyright: Law and Language in the Translation Zone*. Uppsala: Uppsala Universitet.

Henthorn, Jamie. 2016a. 'What Is Segmenting? Learning the Technical Skills of Online Translation at Viki (Part 1).' *MediaCommons: A Digital Scholarly Network*, 15 February. <http://mediacommons.futureofthebook.org/question/what-ways-do-internet-tools-and-culture-recursively-affect-both-international-and-localiz-5> (last accessed 27 June 2016).

———. 2016b. 'What Is Segmenting? Learning the Technical Skills of Online Translation at Viki (Part 2).' *MediaCommons: A Digital Scholarly Network*, 15 February. <http://mediacommons.futureofthebook.org/question/what-ways-do-internet-tools-and-culture-recursively-affect-both-international-and-localiz-6> (last accessed 27 June 2016).

———. 2016c. 'Fan-Translation and Developing Literacies Outside the Classroom.' *MediaCommons: A Digital Scholarly Network*, 20 February. <http://mediacommons.futureofthebook.org/question/what-ways-do-internet-tools-and-culture-recursively-affect-both-international-and-localiz-7> (last accessed 27 June 2016).

Herbst, Thomas. 1996. 'Why Dubbing Is Impossible.' In *Traduzione multimediale per il cinema, la televisione e la scena*, edited by Christine Heiss and Rosa Maria Bollettieri Bosinelli' 97–115. Bologna: CLUEB.

———. 1997. 'Dubbing and the Dubbed Text – Style and Cohesion: Textual Characteristics of a Special Form of Translation.' In *Text Typology and Translation*, edited by Anna Trosborg. 291–308. Amsterdam and Philadelphia: John Benjamins.

Hermans, Theo. 2003. 'Cross-Cultural Translation Studies as Thick Translation.' *Bulletin of the School of Oriental and African Studies, University of London* 66 (3): 380–9.

Higbee, Will, and Song Hwee Lim. 2010. 'Concepts of Transnational Cinema: Towards a Critical Transnationalism in Film Studies.' *Transnational Cinemas* 1 (1): 7–21.

Higson, Andrew. 2010. 'Transnational Developments in European Cinema in the 1920s.' *Transnational Cinemas* 1 (1): 69–82.

Himpele, Jeffrey D. 2009. 'Film Distribution as Media: Mapping Difference in the Bolivian Cinemascape.' In *The Contemporary Hollywood Reader*, edited by Toby Miller. 355–73. London and New York: Routledge. Original publication, 1996.

Hindmarsh, Roland, and Georg-Michael Luyken. 1986. 'Overcoming Language Barriers in European Television.' *Multilingua: Journal of Cross Cultural and Interlanguage Communication* 5 (2): 101–7.

Hjort, Mette. 2010. 'On the Plurality of Cinematic Transnationaism.' In *World Cinemas, Transnational Perspectives*, edited by Natasa Durovicová and Kathleen Newmann. 12–32. New York: Routledge.

Ho, Victoria. 2007. 'Odex Softens on Illegal Downloaders.' *ZDNet*, 17 September. <http://www.zdnet.com/odex-softones-on-illegal-downloaders-2062032298/> (last accessed 28 June 2016).

Hovaghimian, Razmig. 2011. 'Interview with Viki's Razmig Hovaghimian: The Power of Crowdsourced Subtitling.' By Martin James. *MIPBlog*, 23 March. <http://blog.mipworld.com/2011/03/interview-with-vikis-razmig-hovaghimian-the-power-of-crowdsourced-subtitling/> (last accessed 30 June 2016).

———. 2015. 'Social Engagement: The New Ad Metric for Millenials.' Adotas. com Newsletter, 25 February. <http://www.adotas.com/2015/02/social-engagement-the-new-ad-metric-for-millennials/> (last accessed 27 June 2016).

Hovaghimian, Razmig, and Zac Bertschy. 2012. 'Interview: Razmig Hovaghimian, Co-Founder and CEO of Viki.com.' *Anime News Network*, 26 April. <http://www.animenewsnetwork.com/interview/2012-04-25/interview-razmig-hovaghimian-co-founder-and-ceo-of-viki.com> (last accessed 30 June 2016).

Hu, Brian. 2006. 'Closed Borders and Open Secrets: Regional Lockout, the Film Industry, and Code Free DVD Players.' *Mediascape* (Spring): 1–9. <http://

www.tft.ucla.edu/mediascape/Spring06_ClosedBordersAndOpenSecrets.
html> (last accessed 28 June 2016).

————. 2010. 'Korean TV Serials in the English-Language Diaspora: Translating
Difference Online and Making It Racial.' *The Velvet Light Trap* 66 (Fall):
36–49.

Hyde, Adam, and Floss Manuals. 2011. *Open Translation Tools*. <http://
en.flossmanuals.net/open-translation-tools/_booki/open-translation-tools/
open-translation-tools.pdf> (last accessed 28 June 2016).

Inghilleri, Moira. 2005. 'Bourdieu and the Sociology of Translation and
Interpreting.' *The Translator* 11 (2): 125–46.

Irzik, Emrah. 2011. 'A Proposal for Grounded Cultural Activism: Communication
Strategies, Adbusters, and Social Change.' In *Cultural Activism*, edited by
Begüm Özden Firat and Aylin Kuryel. 137–56. New York: Rodopi.

Ito, Joi. 2010. 'Viki.' Neoteny Labs, 11 December. <http://neotenylabs.
com/2010/12/viki/> (last accessed 27 June 2016).

Ito, Mizuko. 2012a. 'Contributors versus Leechers: Fansubbing Ethics and a
Hybrid Public Culture.' In *Fandom Unbound: Otaku Culture in a Connected
World*, edited by Mizuko Ito, Daisuke Okabe and Izumi Tsuji. 179–204. New
Haven and London: Yale University Press.

————. 2012b. '"As Long as It's Not *Linkin Park Z*": Popularity, Distinction
and Status in AMV Subculture.' In *Fandom Unbound: Otaku Culture in a
Connected World*, edited by Mizuko Ito, Daisuke Okabe and Izumi Tsuji. New
Haven and London: Yale University Press.

Iwabuchi, Koichi. 2002. *Recentering Globalization: Popular Culture and Japanese
Transnationalism*. Durham, NC, and London: Duke University Press.

————. 2010. 'Undoing Inter-National Fandom in the Age of Brand
Nationalism.' In *Mechamedia 5: Fanthropologies*, edited by Frenchy Lunning.
87–96. Minneapolis: University of Minnesota Press.

Jameson, Fredric. 1997. 'Marxism and Dualism in Deleuze.' *The South Atlantic
Quarterly* 96 (3): 393–416.

Jarvinen, Lisa. 2012. *The Rise of Spanish-Language Filmmaking: Out From
Hollywood's Shadow, 1929–1939*. New Brunswick, NJ, and London: Rutgers
University Press.

Jay, Stephen. 1992. *Cursing in America: A Psycholinguistic Study of Dirty Language
in the Courts, in the Movies, in the Schoolyards, and on the Streets*. Amsterdam
and Philadelphia: John Benjamins.

Jenkins, Henry. 2006a. *Convergence Culture: Where Old and New Media Collide*.
New York: New York University Press.

————. 2006b. 'When Piracy Becomes Promotion.' *Reason Magazine*, 17
November. <http://reason.com/news/printer/116788.html> (last accessed
28 June 2016).

Jorn, Asper. 2006 [1958]. 'The Situationists and Automation.' Translated by Ken
Knabb. In *Situationist International Anthology*, edited by Ken Knabb. 55–8.
Berkeley: Bureau of Public Secrets.

Jung, Sun. 2011. 'K-Pop Beyond Asia: Performing Trans-Nationality, Trans-Sexuality and Trans-Textuality.' In *Asia Popular Culture in Transition*, edited by Lorna Fitzsimmons and John A. Lent. 108–28. London and New York: Routledge,

Kafka, Peter. 2010. 'ViKi Raises Millions for Web Video From Around the World.' *All Things Digital*, 8 December. <http://allthingsd.com/20101208/viki-raises-millions-for-web-video-from-around-the-world/> (last accessed 28 June 2016).

Kapsaskis, Dionysis. 2008. 'Translation and Film: On the Defamiliarizing Effect of Subtitles.' *New Voices in Translation Studies* 4: 42–52.

Karamitroglou, Fotios. 1998. 'A Proposed Set of Subtitling Standards in Europe.' *Translation Journal* 2 (2). <http://www.bokorlang.com/journal/04stndrd.htm> (last accessed 28 June 2016).

Kauffmann, Stanley. 1960. 'Foreign Languages in Foreign Pictures.' *The New Republic* 143, 12 December: 27–8.

Kelley, Michael, and Yvan Tardy. 2008. 'Les Mots Captifs: The Situationist Subversion of Language.' *The European Legacy* 2 (3): 405–10.

Kelly, Nataly. 2009. 'Freelance Translators Clash with LinkedIn Over Crowdsourced Translation.' Global Watchtower, Common Sense Advisory, 19 June <http://www.commonsenseadvisory.com/Default.aspx?Contenttype=ArticleDetAD&tabID=63&Aid=591&moduleId=391> (last accessed 23 October 2016).

Kilborn, Richard. 1989. ' "They don't speak proper English": A New Look at the Dubbing and Subtitling Debate.' *Journal of Multilingual Development* 10 (5): 421–34.

———. 1993. ' "Speak my language": Current Attitudes to Television Subtitling and Dubbing.' *Media, Culture and Society* 15: 641–60.

Kim, L. S. 2006. 'Making Women Warriors: A Transnational Reading of Asian Female Action Heroes in *Crouching Tiger, Hidden Dragon*.' *Jump Cut: A Review of Contemporary Media* 48. <http://www.ejumpcut.org/archive/jc48.2006/womenWarriors/index.html> (last accessed 28 June 2016).

Klein, Christina. 2004. '*Crouching Tiger, Hidden Dragon*: A Diasporic Reading.' *Cinema Journal* 43 (4): 18–43.

Knabb, Ken. 1997. *Public Secrets*. Berkeley: Bureau of Public Secrets.

———. (ed.) 2006. *Situationist International Anthology*. Berkeley: Bureau of Public Secrets.

Kofoed, D. T. 2011. 'Decotitles, the Animated Discourse of Fox's Recent Anglophonic Internationalism.' *Reconstruction* 11 (1). <http://reconstruction.eserver.org/Issues/111/Kofoed.shtml> (last accessed 28 June 2016).

Komatsu, Hiroshi. 1996. 'Mastering the Mute Image: The Role of the Benshi in Japanese Cinema.' *Iris* 22: 33–52.

Koolstra, Cees M., Allerd L. Peeters and Herman Spinhof. 2002. 'The Pros and Cons of Dubbing and Subtitling.' *European Journal of Communication* 17 (3): 325–54.

Korman, Lenny, and Denis Seguin. 1998. 'War of the Words.' *Screen International*, 3 July: 10–13.

Kothari, Brij. 2008. 'Let a Billion Readers Bloom: Same Language Subtitling (SLS) on Television For Mass Literacy.' *International Review of Education* 54: 773–80.

———. 2015. 'Reading for a Billion: A Simple Way to Increase Literacy in India.' *The World Post*, 3 September. <http://www.huffingtonpost.com/brij-kothari/reading-for-a-billion-eve_b_8075964.html> (last accessed 28 June 2016).

Kubelka, Peter. 1974. 'The Invisible Cinema.' *Design Quarterly* 93: 32–6.

Kuennen, Joel. n.d. 'Dialectics of Desire and Revolution: Viénet's *Girls of Kamare*.' Unpublished paper. <http://www.academia.edu/181480/Dialectics_of_Desire_and_Revolution_Vienets_Girls_of_Kamare> (last accessed 28 June 2016).

Kuhn, Annette. 1985. *Cinema, Censorship and Sexuality 1909–1925*. London: Routledge.

Larkin, Brian. 2004. 'Degraded Images, Distorted Sounds: Nigerian Video and the Infrastructure of Piracy.' *Public Culture* 16 (2): 289–314.

Lee, Hye-Kyung. 2011. 'Participatory Media Fandom: A Case Study of Anime Fansubbing.' *Media, Culture & Society* 33 (8): 1131–47.

'Legal Action Against Downloaders.' 2008. *Anime News Network*, 19 November. <http://www.animenewsnetwork.com.au/survey/165/result> (last accessed 30 June 2016).

Leonard, Sean. 2005a. 'Celebrating Two Decades of Unlawful Progress: Fan Distribution, Proselytization Commons, and the Explosive Growth of Japanese Animation.' UCLA Entertainment Law Review, Spring: 1–72. <http://papers.ssrn.com/sol3/papers.cfm?abstract_id=696402> (last accessed 28 June 2016).

———. 2005b. 'Progress against the Law: Anime and Fandom, with the Key to the Globalization of Culture.' *International Journal of Cultural Studies* 8 (3): 281–305.

Lessig, Lawrence. 2004. *Free Culture: How Big Media Uses Technology and the Law to Lock Down Culture and Control Creativity*. London: Penguin. <http://www.free-culture.cc/freecontent/> (last accessed 28 June 2016).

Lev, Peter. 1993. *The Euro-American cinema*. Austin: University of Texas Press.

Levi, Antonia. 2006. 'The Americanization of Anime and Manga: Negotiating Popular Culture.' In *Cinema Anime*, edited by Steven T. Brown. 43–63. New York: Palgrave Macmillan.

Levin, Thomas Y. 1989. 'Dismantling the Spectacle: The Cinema of Guy Debord.' In *On the Passage of a Few People Through a Rather Brief Moment in Time: The Situationist International 1957–1972*, edited by Elisabeth Sussman. 72–123. Cambridge, MA, and London: MIT Press.

Lewis, M. Paul, Gary F. Simons and Charles D. Fennig (eds). 2016. *Ethnologue:*

Languages of the World. 19th edition online. Dallas: SIL International. <http://www.ethnologue.com> (last accessed 28 June 2016).

Lewis, Philip E. 1985. 'The Measure of Translation Effects.' In *Difference in Translation*, edited by Joseph F. Graham. 31–62. Ithaca: Cornell University Press.

Li, Xiaochang, 2009. 'Collaborative (Transnational) Audienceships: ViiKii.net.' *Canary Trap.Net: Dis/Junctures of Digital Media, Globalization and Consumer Culture*, 4 June. <http://canarytrap.net/2009/06/collaborative-transational-audienceships-viikiinet/> (last accessed 13 March 2012).

Liang, Lawrence. 2005. 'Porous Legalities and Avenues of Participation.' *Sarai Reader* 5: 6–17. <http://archive.sarai.net/files/original/8d57bfa1bcb57c80a7af903363c07282.pdf> (last accessed 30 June 2016).

————. 2009. 'Meet John Doe's Order: Piracy, Temporality and the Question of Asia.' *Indian Journal of Intellectual Property Law* 9. <http://www.commonlii.org/in/journals/INJlIPLaw/2009/9.html> (last accessed 30 June 2016).

————. 2010. 'Beyond Representation? The Figure of the Pirate.' In *Access to Knowledge in the Age of Intellectual Property*, edited by Gaëlle Krikorian and Amy Kapczynski. 353–76. Cambridge, MA, and London: MIT Press.

Liepa, Torey. 2008. 'Figures of Silent Speech: Silent Film Dialogue and the American Vernacular, 1909–1916.' PhD Thesis. Cinema Studies, New York University, New York.

Lo Kwai-Chung. 2005. *Chinese Face/Off: The Transnational Popular Culture of Hong Kong*. Hong Kong: Hong Kong University Press.

Lobato, Ramon. 2008. 'The Six Faces of Piracy: Global Media Distribution from Below.' In *The Business of Entertainment (Vol. 1): Movies*, edited by R. C. Sickels. 15–36. Westport: Greenwood Publishing Group.

Lu Danjun. 2009. 'Loss of Meaning in Dubbing.' In *Dubbing and Subtitling in a World Context*, edited by Gilbert C. F. Fong and Kenneth K. L. Au. 161–5. Hong Kong: Chinese University Press.

Lu, Sheldon. 2007. 'Dialect and Modernity in 21st Century Sinophone Cinema.' *Jump Cut: A Review of Contemporary Media* 49: 1–17. <www.ejumpcut.org/archive/jc49.2007/Lu/text.html> (last accessed 28 June 2016).

Lukács, Gabriella. 2010. *Scripted Affects, Branded Selves: Television, Subjectivity, and Capitalism in 1990s Japan*. Durham, NC, and London: Duke University Press.

Luczaj, Kamil, Magdalena Holy-Luczaj and Kaorlina Cwiek-Rogalska. 2014. 'Fansubbers: The Case of the Czech Republic.' *Journal of Comparative Research in Anthropology and Sociology* 5 (2): 175–98.

Luyken, Georg-Michael, Thomas Herbst, Jo Langham-Brown, Helen Reid and Herman Spinhof. 1991. *Overcoming Language Barriers in Television: Dubbing and Subtitling for the European Audience, Media Monographs*. Manchester: The European Institute for the Media.

MacDonald, Christopher. 2003. 'Unethical Fansubbers (Australia Edition)

[Editorial].' Anime News Network, 8 May. <http://www.animenewsnetwork. com.au/editorial/2003-06-08/2> (last accessed 30 June 2016).

MacDonald, Scott. 1994. *A Critical Cinema 4: Interviews with Independent Filmmakers*. Berkeley and Los Angeles: University of California Press.

Mailhac, Jean-Pierre. 2000. 'Subtitling and Dubbing, for Better or Worse? The English Video Versions of *Gazon Maudit*.' In *On Translating French Literature and Film II*, edited by Myriam Salama-Carr. 129–54. Amsterdam and Atlanta: Rodopi.

Mamula, Tiijana, and Lisa Patti. 2016. *The Multilingual Screen: New Reflections on Cinema and Linguistic Difference*. London: Bloosmbury.

Mangiron, Carmen. 2012. 'The Localisation of Japanese Video Games: Striking the Right Balance.' *Journal of Internationalisation and Localisation* 2: 1–20.

Mäntylä, Teemu. 2010. 'Piracy or Productivity: Unlawful Practices in Anime Fansubbing.' MA Thesis. Department of Media Technology, Aalto University.

Marks, Laura. 2000. *The Skin of the Film: Intercultural Cinema, Embodiment and the Senses*. Durham, NC: Duke University Press.

Massidda, Serenella. 2015. *Audiovisual Translation in the Digital Age: The Italian Fansubbing Phenomenon*. Basingstoke: Palgrave Macmillan.

Mattar, Yasser. 2008. 'Perceptions and (Re)presentations of Familiarity and Foreignness: The Cultural Politics of Translation in the Subtitling of Japanese Animation by Fans.' *Leisure/Loisir* 32 (2): 353–78.

McClarty, Rebecca. 2014. 'In Support of Creative Subtitling: Contemporary Context and Theoretical Framework.' *Perspectives: Studies in Translatology* 22 (4): 592–606.

McDonough Dolmaya, Julie. 2012. 'Analyzing the Crowdsourcing Model and Its Impact on Public Perceptions of Translation.' *The Translator* 18 (2): 167–91.

McIntosh, Joanna. 2015. MPAA Letter to USTR re Notorious Markets, 5 October. <http://www.mpaa.org/wp-content/uploads/2015/10/MPAA_ Notorious_Markets_2015-Final1.pdf> (last accessed 30 June 2016).

Meers, Philippe. 2004. ' "It's the Language of Film!": Young Film Audiences on Hollywood and Europe.' In *Hollywood Abroad*, edited by Richard Maltby and Melvyn Stokes. 158–75. London: British Film Institute.

Mehta, Monika. 2009. 'Reframing Film Censorship.' *The Velvet Light Trap* 63: 66–9.

Mera, Miguel. 1999. 'Read My Lips: Re-Evaluating Subtitling and Dubbing in Europe.' *Links & Letters* 6: 73–85.

Mereu Keating, Carla. 2016. ' "The Italian Color": Race, Crime Iconography and Dubbing Conventions in the Italian-language Versions of *Scarface* (1932).' *Altre Modernità: Riviste di studi letterari e culturali / Other Modernities* <http:// riviste.unimi.it/index.php/AMonline/article/view/6851> (last accessed 26 June 2016).

Michelson, Annette. 1998. 'Gnosis and Iconoclasm: A Case Study of Cinephilia.' *October* 83: 3–18.

Mika, Bartosz. 2015. 'The Polish Amateur Fansubbing Community as an

Example of Online Collaboration Project.' *Miscellanea Anthropologica et Sociologica* 16 (2): 143–68.

Mikul, Chris. 2015. *Access on Demand: Captioning and Audio Description on Video on Demand Services.* Sydney: Media Access Australia.

Miller, Toby. 2010. 'National Cinema Abroad: The New International Division of Cultural Labour, from Production to Viewing.' In *World Cinemas, Transnational Perspectives*, edited by Natasa Durovicová and Kathleen Newmann. 137–59. New York: Routledge.

Montgomery, Colleen. 2008. 'Lost in Translation: Subtitling Banlieue Subculture.' *Cinephile* 4: 8–12.

Monti, Silvia. 2016. 'Reconstructing, Reinterpreting and Renarrating Code-Switching in the Italian Dubbed Version of British and American Multilingual Films.' *Altre Modernità: Riviste di studi letterari e culturali / Other Modernities*, 68–91. <http://riviste.unimi.it/index.php/AMonline/article/view/6849> (last accessed 26 June 2016).

Moon, Jiwon. 2008. 'Welcome to ViiKii.' *The ViiKii Story* (blog), 25 June. <http://viikii-en.blogspot.com.au/2008/06/welcome-to-viikii.html> (last accessed 28 June 2016).

Moriarty, Justin. 2015. 'Fansubs: Do They Really Help Or Hurt the Industry?', Honey's Anime, 18 August <http://blog.honeyfeed.fm/editorial-tuesday-fansubs-do-they-really-help-or-hurt-the-industry/> (last accessed 26 October 2016).

Morris, Meaghan. 2004. 'Transnational Imagination in Action Cinema: Hong Kong and the Making of a Global Popular Culture.' *Inter-Asia Cultural Studies* 5 (2): 181–99.

Mowitt, John. 2005. *Re-Takes: Postcoloniality and Foreign Film Languages.* Minneapolis and London: University of Minnesota Press.

Munday, Jeremy. 2001. *Introducing Translation Studies: Theories and Applications.* London and New York: Routledge.

Myers, Lora. 1973. 'The Art of Dubbing.' *Filmmakers Newsletter* 6 (68): 56–8.

Naficy, Hamid. 2006. 'Dubbing, Doubling, and Duplicity.' *Pages Magazine* 4: 113–17. <http://www.pagesmagazine.net/2006/article.php?ma_id=7830 018> (last accessed 28 June 2016).

Nagib, Lúcia, Chris Perriam and Rajinder Dudrah (eds). 2012. *Theorizing World Cinema.* London and New York: I. B. Taurus.

Napier, Susan. 2001. 'Peek-a-Boo Pikachu: Exporting an Asian Subculture.' *Harvard Asia Pacific Review* 5 (2): 13–17. <http://web.mit.edu/lipoff/www/hapr/fall01_health/pikachu.pdf> (last accessed 30 June 2016).

Newitz, Annalee. 1994. 'Anime Otaku: Japanese Animation Fans Outside Japan.' *Bad Subjects* 13. http://english-www.hss.cmu.edu/BS/default.html.

Nord, Christiane, Masood Hoshsaligheh and Saeed Ameri. 2015. 'Socio-Cultural and Technical Issues in Non-Expert Dubbing: A Case Study.' *International Journal of Society, Culture and Language* 3. <http://www.

ijscl.net/issue_1980_2315_Volume+3%2C+Issue+2%2C+Summer++a nd+Autumn+2015%2C+Page+1-130.html> (last accessed 7 November 2015).

Norman, Louis. 1974. 'Rossellini's Case Histories for Moral Education.' *Film Quarterly* 27 (4): 11–16.

Nornes, Abé Mark. 1999. 'For an Abusive Subtitling.' *Film Quarterly* 52 (3): 17–34.

———. 2007. *Cinema Babel: Translating Global Cinema*. Minneapolis and London: University of Minnesota Press.

Nowell-Smith, Geoffrey. 1968. 'Italy Sotto Voce.' *Sight and Sound* 37 (3): 145–7.

O'Hagan, Minako. 2008. 'Fan Translation Networks: An Accidental Translator Training Environment?' In *Translator and Interpreter Training: Issues, Methods and Debates*, edited by John Kearns. 158–83. London: Continuum.

———. 2009. 'Evolution of User-Generated Translation: Fansubs, Translation Hacking and Crowdsourcing.' *The Journal of Internationalization and Localization* 1 (1): 94–21.

———. 2011. 'Community Translation: Translation as a Social Activity and Its Possible Consequences in the Advent of Web 2.0 and Beyond.' *Linguistica Antverpiensia* 10: 1–10.

———. 2016. 'Massively Open Translation: Unpacking the Relationship Between Technology and Translation in the 21st Century.' *International Journal of Communication* 10: 929–46.

O'Neill, Sionann and Regan McMahon. 2011. 'For Subtitler Sionann O'Neill, It's about Idiom.' *San Francisco Chronicle*, 5 April. <http://www.sfgate. com/entertainment/article/For-subtitler-Sionann-O-Neill-it-s-about-idiom-2376493.php> (last accessed 30 June 2016).

O'Sullivan, Carol. 2008. 'Multilingualism at the Multiplex.' *Linguistica Antverpiensia* 6: 81–95.

———. 2011. *Translating Popular Film*. New York: Palgrave Macmillan.

O'Sullivan, Carol, and Caterina Jeffcote (eds). 2013. 'Special Issue on Translating Multimodalities.' *Journal of Specialised Translation* 20. <http://www.jostrans. org/issue20/issue20_toc.php> (last accessed 30 June 2016).

Olohan, Maeve. 2012. 'Volunteer Translation and Altruism in the Context of a Nineteenth-Century Scientific Journal.' *The Translator* 18 (2): 193–215.

Omega, Jan. 2015. 'Viki: Online Streaming Site that Features Crowdsourced Subtitles Hits an Epic Milestone with 1 Billion Words.' *Inquisitor*, 13 October. <http://www.inquisitr.com/2492797/viki-online-streaming-site-that-fea tures-crowdsourced-subtitles-hits-an-epic-milestone-with-1-billion-words/> (last accessed 27 June 2016).

Ong, Burton. 2007. 'Separating Bona Fide Fans from Freeloaders.' *The Straits Times*, 27 August. <http://news.asiaone.com/News/The% 2BStraits%2BTimes/Story/Separating%2Bbona%2Bfide%2Bfans%2Bfrom %2Bfreeloaders.html> (last accessed 26 October 2016).

Ortabasi, Melek. 2007. 'Indexing the Past: Visual Language and Translatability in Kon Satoshi's *Millennium Actress*.' *Perspectives: Studies in Translatology* 14 (4): 278–91.

Pajala, Mari. 2014. 'East and West on the Finnish Screen: Early Transnational Television in Finland.' *View: Journal of European History and Culture* 3 (5): 88–99. <http://journal.euscreen.eu/index.php/view/article/view/83/117> (last accessed 28 June 2016).

Pang, Laikwan. 2004. 'Mediating the Ethics of Technology: Hollywood snd Movie Piracy.' *Culture, Theory & Critique* 45 (1): 19–32.

———. 2005. 'Copying *Kill Bill*.' *Social Text* 23 (2.83): 133–53. doi: 10.1215/01642472-23-2_83-133.

Parini, Illaria. 2014. '"I'm going to f***** kill you!" Verbal Censorship in Dubbed Mafia Movies.' In *Enforcing and Eluding Censorship: British and Anglo-Italian Perspectives*, edited by Guiliana Iannaccaro and Giovanni Iamatino. 144–66. Newcastle-upon-Tyne: Cambridge Scholars Publishing.

Patel, Sahil. 2015. 'How Rakuten's Viki Plans to Grow Its Global Streaming Service.' *Digiday*, 22 December. <http://digiday.com/publishers/video-streaming-service-viki-wants-grow-subscriptions/> (last accessed 27 June 2016).

Patten, Fred. 2004. *Watching Anime, Reading Manga: 25 Years of Essays and Reviews*. Berkeley: Stone Bridge Press.

Paul, Joanna. 2008. 'Homer and Cinema: Translation and Adaptation in *Le Mépris*.' In *Translation and the Classic: Identity as Change in the History of Culture*, edited by Alekandra Lianeri and Vanda Zajko. 148–65. Oxford: Oxford University Press.

Pauletto, Sandra. 2012. 'The Sound Design of Cinematic Voices.' *The New Soundtrack* 2 (2): 127–42.

Pauluzzi, Fausto F. 1983. 'Subtitles vs. Dubbing: The *New York Times* Polemic, 1960–66.' In *Holding the Vision: Essays on Film*, edited by Douglas Radcliff-Umstead. 131–7. Kent, OH: International Film Society, Kent State University.

Pedersen, Jan. 2011. *Subtitling Norms for Television: An Exploration Focusing on Extralinguistic Cultural References*. Amsterdam and Philadelphia: John Benjamins.

Pérez-González, Luis. 2006. 'Fansubbing Anime: Insights into the "Butterfly Effect" of Globalisation on Audiovisual Translation.' *Perspectives: Studies in Translatology* 14 (4): 260–77.

———. 2007. 'Intervention in New Amateur Subtitling Cultures: A Multimodal Account.' *Linguistica Antverpiensia* 6: 67–80.

———. 2010. '"Ad-hocracies" of Translation Activism in the Blogosphere: A Genealogical Case Study.' In *Text and Context: Essays on Translation and Interpreting in Honour of Ian Mason*, edited by Mona Baker, Maeve Olohan and Maria Calzada Pérez. 259–87. Manchester: St Jerome.

———. 2014. 'Multimodality in Translation and Interpreting Studies: Theoretical and Methodological Perspectives.' In *A Companion to Translation*

Studies, edited by Sandra Bermann and Catherine Porter. 119–30. Oxford: John Wiley and Sons.

Pérez-González, Luis, and Sebnem Susam-Sarajeva)eds). 2012. Special Issue on Non-Professionals Translating and Interpreting. *The Translator* 18 (2): 149–65.

Perrino, Saverio. 2009. 'User-Generated Translation: The Future of Translation in a Web 2.0 Environment.' *The Journal of Specialised Translation* 12: 55–78. <http://www.jostrans.org/issue12/art_perrino.php> (last accessed 28 June 2016).

Pinsker, Beth. 2005. 'Lost and Gained in Translation.' *Boston Globe*, 23 January. <http://archive.boston.com/ae/movies/articles/2005/01/23/in_the_tough_jobof_marketing_foreign_films_sometimes_not_telling_all_is_the_best_policy/> (last accessed 28 June 2016).

Pointon, Susan. 1997. 'Transcultural Orgasm as Apocalypse: *Urotsukidoji: The Legend of the Overfiend.*' *Wide Angle* 19 (3): 41–63.

Porzucki, Nina. 2014. 'Meet the Folks Behind the Subtitles on Your Favorite Movies and Streaming TV Shows.' *Public Radio International*, 24 November. <http://www.pri.org/stories/2014-11-24/meet-folks-behind-subtitles-your-favorite-movies-and-streaming-tv-shows> (last accessed 28 June 2016).

Pujol, Didac. 2006. 'The Translation and Dubbing of "Fuck" into Catalan: The Case *From Dusk till Dawn.*' *Journal of Specialised Translation* 6 (July): 121–33, <http://www.jostrans.org/issue06/art_pujol.php> (last accessed 15 June 2016).

Pym, Anthony. 1995. 'Doubts about Deconstruction as a General Theory of Translation.' *TradTerm* 2: 11–18. <http://usuaris.tinet.cat/apym/on-line/research_methods/decon.html> (last accessed 28 June 2016).

Quaresima, Leonardo. 2006. 'Mehrsprachenversion/Dubbing?' In *Babylon in FilmEuropa: Mehrsprachen-Versionen der 1930er Jahre*, edited by Jan Distelmeyer. 19–38. Munich: Text + Kritik.

Raine, Michael. 2015. 'From Hybridity to Dispersion: Film Subtitling as an Adaptive Practice'. In *Media and Translation: An Interdisciplinary Approach*, edited by Dror Abend-David. New York: Bloomsbury, 151–72.

Ramael, Aline. 2001. 'Some Thoughts on the Study of Multimodal and Multimedia Translation.' In *(Multi) Media Translation*, edited by Yves Gambier and Henrik Gottlieb. 13–22. Amsterdam: John Benjamins.

———. 2012. 'Audio Description with Audio Subtitling for Dutch Multilingual Films: Manipulating Textual Cohesion on Different Levels.' *Meta: Transtors' Journal* 57 (2): 385–407.

Ramière, Nathalie. 2010. 'Are You "Lost in Translation" (When Watching a Foreign Film)? Towards an Alternative Approach to Judging Audiovisual Translation.' *Australian Journal of French Studies* 47 (1): 100–15.

Ranzato, Irene. 2016. *Translating Culture Specific References on Television: The Case of Dubbing*. London: Routledge.

Ray, Rebecca, and Nataly Kelly. 2011. *Crowdsourced Translation: Best Practices for Implementation*. Lowell, MA: Common Sense Advisory.

Rayner, Keith. 1998. 'Eye Movements in Reading and Information Processing: 20 Years of Research.' *Psychological Bulletin* 124 (3): 372–422.

Rée, Jonathan. 1994. 'Return of the Translator.' *Radical Philosophy* 67: 40–2.

Rembert-Lang, LaToya D. 2010. 'Reinforcing the Tower of Babel: The Impact of Copyright Law on Fansubbing.' *Intellectual Property Brief* 2 (2): 21–33.

Rich, B. Ruby. 2004. 'To Read or Not to Read: Subtitles, Trailers, and Monolingualism.' In *Subtitles: On the Foreignness of Film*, edited by Atom Egoyan and Ian Balfour. 153–69. Cambridge, MA, and London: MIT Press.

Robinson, Douglas. 1997. *What Is Translation? Centrifugal Theories, Critical Interventions*. Kent, OH: Kent State University Press.

Rose, Barbara 1971. 'Where to Learn How to Look at Movies: New York's New Anthology Film Archives.' *Vogue*, 1 November: 70.

Rosenbaum, Jonathan. 1997. 'Dubbed and Dubber.' *Chicago Reader*, 21 February. <http://www.chicagoreader.com/chicago/dubbed-and-dubber/Content?oid=892741> (last accessed 28 June 2016).

Rosenberg, Grant. 2007. 'Rethinking the Art of Subtitles.' *Time*, 15 May. <http://content.time.com/time/arts/article/0,8599,1621155,00.html> (last accessed 30 June 2016).

Ross, Steve. 2001. 'A Flop in the East.' *The Irish Times*, 17 February: 65.

Rossholm, Anna Sofia. 2005. 'Towards an Aesthetics of Subtitling.' *Cinemascope* 1. http://www.cinema-scope.net.

———. 2006. *Reproducing Languages, Translating Bodies: Approaches to Speech, Translation and Culture*. Stockholm: Almqvist & Wiksell International.

Rowe, Thomas L. 1960. 'The English Dubbing Text.' *Babel* 6 (3): 116–20.

Ruh, Brian. 2010. 'Transforming U.S. Anime in the 1980s: Localization and Longevity.' In *Mechamedia 5: Fanthropologies*, 31–49. Minneapolis: University of Minnesota Press.

Rundle, Chris. 2008. 'The *Subtitle Project*. A Vocational Education Initiative.' *The Interpreter and Translator Trainer* 2 (1): 93–114.

Russell, Jon. 2013. 'Global Video Site Viki Is Bringing Social Back, as It Reintroduces Improved Real-Time Commenting System.' *The Next Web*, 9 May. <http://thenextweb.com/media/2013/05/09/global-video-site-viki-is-bringing-back-social-rolls-out-improved-real-time-commenting-system/#gref> (last accessed 27 June 2016).

Sallis, John. 2002. *On Translation, Studies in Continental Thought*. Bloomington: Indiana University Press.

Sanborn, Keith. 1991. 'La dialectique peut-elle casser des briques / Can Dialectics Break Bricks?' In *San Francisco Cinematheque 1990 Program Notes*, edited by Kurt Easterwood. 93–6. San Francisco: San Francisco Cinematheque.

———. 2010. 'Vienet Subtitles.' E-mail correspondence with author, 30 September.

Sanderson, John D. 2010. 'The Other You. Translating the Hispanic for the

Spanish Screen.' In *Polyglot Cinema: Migration and Transcultural Narration in France, Italy, Portugal and Spain*, edited by Verena Berger and Miya Komori. 49–71. Vienna and Berlin: LIT Verlag.

Sandrelli, Annalisa. 2016. 'The Dubbing of Gay-Themed TV Series in Italy: Corpus-Based Evidence of Manipulation and Censorship.' *Altre Modernità: Riviste di studi letterari e culturali / Other Modernities*, 124–43. <http://riviste. unimi.it/index.php/AMonline/article/view/6852> (last accessed 26 June 2016).

Sargent, Benjamin B. 2012. 'The Growing Market of Global Information Consumers.' *MultiLingual*, October/November: 49–50.

Schamus, James. 2000. 'HOLIDAY FILMS; The Polyglot Task of Writing the Global Film.' *New York Times*, 5 November. <http://www.nytimes. com/2000/11/05/movies/holiday-films-the-polyglot-task-of-writing-the-global-film.html?pagewanted=all> (last accessed 28 June 2016).

Scheuer, Philip K. 1960. 'To Dub Is to Flub: Critic Crowther's Argument Raises Storm of Disapproval.' *Los Angeles Times*, 26 September.

Schodt, Frederik L. 1983. *Manga! Manga!: The World of Japanese Comics*. Tokyo: Kodansha International.

Scholes, Wayne. 2014. 'Piracy's Ripple Effect on the Global Economy.' *Diplomatic Courier*, 14 January. <http://www.diplomaticourier.com/2014/01/14/piracy-s-ripple-effect-on-the-global-economy/> (last accessed 26 June 2016).

Schules, Douglas. 2014. 'How to Do Things with Fan Subs: Media Engagement as Subcultural Captial in Anime Fan Subbing.' *Transformative Works and Culture* 17 (September). <http://journal.transformativeworks.org/index. php/twc/article/view/512/461> (last accessed 28 June 2016).

Seagrave, Kerry. 2004. *Foreign Films in America: A History*. Jefferson and London: McFarland & Co.

Secară, Alina. 2011. 'R U Ready 4 New Subtitles? Investigating the Potential of Social Translation Practices and Creative Spellings.' *Linguistica Antverpiensia New Series* 10: 153–71.

Seguin, Karl. 2013. 'Scaling Viki.' <https://github.com/karlseguin/scaling-viki> (last accessed 27 June 2016).

Shetty, Amit. 2016. 'VAST 4.0 Arrives, Championing the Technology behind the Growth of Digital Video Advertising.' Interactive Advertising Bureau, 21 January. <http://www.iab.com/news/vast-4-0-arrives-championing-the-technology-behind-the-growth-of-digital-video-advertising> (last accessed 28 June 2016).

Shohat, Ella, and Robert Stam. 1985. 'The Cinema after Babel: Language, Difference, Power.' *Screen* 26 (3–4): 35–58.

———. 1996. 'From the Imperial Family to the Transnational Imaginary: Media Spectatorship in the Age of Globalization.' In *Global/Local*, edited by Rob Wilson and Wimal Dissanayake. 145–70. Durham, NC, and London: Duke University Press.

Sinha, Amresh. 2004. 'The Use and Abuse of Subtitles.' In *Subtitles: On the Foreignness of Film*, edited by Atom Egoyan and Ian Balfour. 171–92. Cambridge, MA, and London: MIT Press.

Sisto, Antonella C. 2010. 'The Sonic Object of Italian Cinema: from the Ideology of Dubbing to the Audio–Visual Images of a Cinema of Poetry.' PhD Thesis. Italian Studies, Brown University, Providence, Rhode Island.

Sitney, P. Adams. 1975. *The Essential Cinema: Essays on Films in the Collection of Anthology Film Archives*. New York: Film Culture Non-Profit Inc.

Sitney, Sky. 2005. 'The Search for the Invisible Cinema.' *Grey Room* 19: 102–13.

Sliwowski, Matt. n.d. '*Shagai, Soviet!* (Stride, Soviet!) 1926.' Translated transcript of film intertitles. Held in the collection of the Anthology Film Archives, New York.

Small, Irene. 2008. 'One Thing after Another: How We Spend Time in Hélio Oiticica's Quasi-Cinemas.' *Spectator* 28 (2): 73–89.

Smith, James K. A. 2005. *Jacques Derrida: Live Theory*. New York: Continuum.

Smith, Paul Julian. 2012. 'Transnational Cinemas: The Cases of Mexico, Argentina and Brazil.' In *Theorizing World Cinema*, edited by Lúcia Nagib, Chris Perriam and Rajindra Dudrah. 63–75.

Sokoli, Stavroula. 2011. 'Subtitling Norms in Greece and Spain. A Comparative Descriptive Study on Film Subtitle Omission and Distribution.' PhD Thesis. Barcelona: Universitat Autònoma de Barcelona.

Spivak, Gayatri Chakravorty. 1976 [1967]. Preface to *Of Grammatology*, by Jacques Derrida, ix–lxxxviii. Translated by Gayatri Chakravorty Spivak. Baltimore: Johns Hopkins University Press.

Stam, Robert, Robert Burgoyne and Sandy Flitterman-Lewis (eds). 1992. *New Vocabularies in Film Semiotics: Structuralism, Post-Structuralism and Beyond*. London and New York: Routledge.

Stephenson, Chloë. 2007. 'Seeing Red: Soviet Films in Fascist Italy.' In *Modes of Censorship and Translation: National Contexts and Diverse Media*, edited by Francesca Billiani. 235–56. Manchester and Kinderhook, NY: St Jerome.

Stone, Evan, and Gia Manry. 2011. 'Interview: Evan Stone.' *Anime News Network*, 10 May. <http://4nn.cx/61738> (last accessed 30 June 2016).

'Strategic Agenda for the Multilingual Digital Single Market: Technologies for Overcoming Language Barriers towards a Truly Integrated European Online Market, Version 0.5.' 2015. Cracker and LT Observatory. <http://www.meta-net.eu/projects/cracker/multimedia/mdsm-sria-draft.pdf> (last accessed 26 October 2016).

Straub, Jean-Marie, and Danièle Huillet. 1985. 'Direct Sound: An Interview with Jean-Marie Straub and Danièle Huillet.' Translated by Bill Kavaler. In *Film Sound: Theory and Practice*, edited by Elisabeth Weis and John Belton. 150–3. New York: Colombia University Press.

Strömbäck, Per. 2015. 'Dubbing the Way to Digital Single Market.' *Netopia: Forum for the Digital Society*, 14 December. <http://www.netopia.eu/dub bing-the-way-to-digital-single-market/> (last accessed 28 June 2016).

Sundaram, Ravi. 2001. 'Recycling Modernity: Pirate Electronic Cultures in India.' *Sarai Reader* 1: 93–9. <http://archive.sarai.net/files/original/d2c8b7bfa11a02d3747771892d9aee09.pdf> (last accessed 30 June 2016).

Sussman, Elisabeth (ed.). 1989. *On the Passage of a Few People Through a Rather Brief Moment in Time: The Situationist International 1957–1972.* Boston Institute of Contemporary Art. Cambridge, MA: MIT Press.

Svelch, Juroslav. 2013. 'The Delicate Art of Criticizing a Saviour: "Silent Gratitude" and the Limits of Participation in the Evaluation of Fan Translation.' *Convergence: The International Journal of Research into New Media Technologies* 19 (3): 303–10.

Takanay, Asli, and Sirin Baykan. 2009. 'Who Is the Censor? Anonymous Translations and Translators as "Gatekeepers".' Paper presented at the 3rd IATIS conference Mediation and Conflict: Translation and Culture in a Global Context, 10 July. Monash University, Melbourne.

Tauro, Janet Hope Camilo. 2002. 'Anime Transform Landscape of Philippine TV.' *Living in the Philippines* Web Magazine. http://livinginthephilippines.com/Culture-And-Arts/telenovela.html (last accessed 21 June 2013).

Taylor, Christopher. 2003. 'Multimodal Transcription in the Analysis, Translation and Subtitling of Italian Films.' *The Translator* 9 (2): 191–205.

Tegel, Simeon. 2000. 'Hollywood Gets Last Word in Mexican Dubs Dispute.' *Variety*, 13–19 March: 16.

Thompson, Howard. 1970. 'Silence Says a Lot for Film Archives.' *New York Times*, 4 December: 55.

Tolentino, Rolando. 2006. 'Piracy and Its Regulation: The Filipino's Historical Response to Globalization.' Asian Edition Conference Proceedings. <http://www.asian-edition.org/Piracy%20and%20Its%20Regulation2.pdf> (last accessed 28 June 2016).

Toury, Gideon. 1981. 'Translated Literature: System, Norm, Performance. Toward a TT-Oriented Approach to Literary Translation.' *Poetics Today* 2 (4): 9–27.

Trinh T. Minh-Ha. 1991. *When the Moon Waxes Red: Representation, Gender and Cultural Politics.* New York and London: Routledge.

————. 1992. *Framer Framed.* New York and London: Routledge.

Tushnet, Rebecca. 2007. 'Copyright Law, Fan Practices, and the Rights of the Author.' In *Fandom: Identities & Communities in a Mediated World*, edited by Jonathan Gray, Cornel Sandvoss and C. Lee Harrington. 60–71. New York: New York University Press.

Tveit, Jan-Emil. 2008. 'Dubbing versus Subtitling: Old Battleground Revisited.' In *Audiovisual Translation: Language Transfer on Screen*, edited by Jorge Díaz Cintas and Gunilla Anderman. 85–96. London: Palgrave Macmillan.

Tymoczko, Maria. 2005. 'Trajectories of Research in Translation Studies.' *Meta: Translators' Journal* 50 (4): 1082–97.

————. 2009. 'Why Translators Should Want to Internationalize Translation Studies.' *The Translator* 15 (2): 401–21.

UNESCO Institute for Statistics. 2012. 'Linguistic Diversity of Feature Films.' UIS Fact Sheet 17. Montreal: UNESCO. <http://www.uis.unesco.org/FactSheets/Documents/fs17-2012-linguistic-diversity-film-en5.pdf> (last accessed 28 June 2016).

United Nations, Department of Economic and Social Affairs, Population Division. 2015. *World Population Prospects: 2015 Revision, Key Findings and Advance Tables*. Working Paper ESA/P/WP.241. <https//esa.un.org/unpd/wpp/publications/files/key_findings_wpp_2015.pdf> (last accessed 29 June 2016).

Upbin, Bruce. 2010. 'Viki Unlocks the Other 85% of Television.' *Forbes: Tradigital Blog*, 8 December. <http://blogs.forbes.com/bruceupbin/2010/12/08/viki-unlocks-the-other-85-of-television> (last accessed 30 June 2016).

Uroskie, Andrew V. 2011. 'Beyond the Black Box: The Lettrist Cinema of Disjunction.' *October* 135: 21–48.

Vandaele, Jeroen. 2007. 'Take Three: The National-Catholic Versions of Billy Wilder's Broadway Adaptations.' In F. Billiani (ed.), *Modes of Censorship and Translation: National Contexts and Diverse Media*. 279–310. Manchester and Kinderhook, NY: St Jerome.

Vanhée, Olivier. 2006. 'The Production of a "Manga Culture" in France: A Sociological Analysis of a Successful Intercultural Reception.' Paper presented at Asia Culture Forum, October. <http://www.studymode.com/essays/The-Production-Of-a-'Manga-Culture'-1015090.html> (last accessed 28 June 2016).

Vellar, Agnese. 2011. '"Lost" (and Found) in Transculturation. The Italian Networked Collectivisim of US TV Series and Fansubbing Performances.' In *Broadband Society and Generational Changes*, edited by Fausto Colombo and Leopoldina Fortunati. 187–99. Oxford: Peter Lang.

Venuti, Lawrence. 1995. *The Translator's Invisibility: A History of Translation*. London: Routledge.

Viénet, René. 2006 [1967]. 'The Situationists and the New Forms of Action against Politics and Art.' Translated by Ken Knabb. In *Situationist International Anthology*, edited by Ken Knabb. 273–7. Berkeley: Bureau of Public Secrets.

Viki. 2011a. 'ViKi's Offical Policy on QC (Qualified Contributors) – Updated.' *ViKi*, 9 February. <http://www.viki.com/channels/4-viki-help/posts/5403-viki-s-official-policy-on-qc-qualified-contributors-updated> (last accessed 10 September 2011).

———. 2011b. 'ViKi New Policy.' *ViKi*, 18 March. <http://www.viki.com/channels/4-viki-help/posts/6192-viki-new-policy-ver-mar-20> (last accessed 10 September 2011).

———. 2011c. 'Abuser Policy.' *ViKi*, 15 July. <http://www.viki.com/channels/4-viki-help/posts/8864-abuser-policy-july-15> (last accessed 10 September 2011).

———. 2011d. 'Features to Come in July/August.' *ViKi*, 26 June. <http://

www.viki.com/channels/4–viikii–help/posts/8367-features-to-come-in-july-august-ver-jul-26> (last accessed 10 September 2011).

'Viki a Small Wonder.' 2012. *Reverse Thieves: An Anime and Manga Blog and Podcast*, 16 July. <https://reversethieves.com/2012/07/16/viki-a-small-wonder/> (last accessed 27 June 2016).

'ViKi Announces $4.3M in Series A Funding and Launches Out of Beta.' 2010. *PR Newswire*, 8 December. <http://www.prnewswire.com/news-releases/viki-announces-43m-in-series-a-funding-and-launches-out-of-beta-111525579.html> (last accessed 10 September 2011).

'Viki Changes and Viki Pass.' 2013. *Viki Discussions* thread, October. <https://discussions.viki.com/t/viki-changes-and-viki-pass/501/3> (last accessed 28 June 2016).

Vincendeau, Ginette. 1988. 'Hollywood Babel.' *Screen* 29 (2): 24–39.

———. 2011. 'The Frenchness of French Cinema: The Language of National Identity, from the Regional to the Trans-national.' In *Studies in French Cinema: UK Perspectives 1985–2010*, edited by Will Higbee and Sarah Leahy. 337–52. Bristol and Chicago: Intellect.

Vöge, Hans. 1977. 'The Translation of Films: Sub-Titling Versus Dubbing.' *Babel* 23 (3): 120–5.

Von Sychowski, Patrick. 2014. 'China Cinema Future – Barrage 2: Return of the Tucao.' *Celluloid Junkie*, 12 August. <https://celluloidjunkie.com/2014/08/12/china-cinema-future-barrage-2-return-tucao/> (last accessed 27 June 2016).

Wagstyl, Stefan. 2006. '"What did you expect me to look like? Tom Cruise?,"' *Financial Times*, 19 December. www.ft.com/intl/cms/s/1/a1dff32e-8c57-11db-9684-0000779e2340.html#axzz2M53rAHfj.

Wahl, Chris. 2007. '"Paprika in the Blood": On UFA's Early Sound Films Produced in/about/for/with Hungary.' *Spectator* 27 (2): 11–20.

———. 2016. *Multiple Language Versions Made in Babelsberg: UFA's International Strategy, 1929–1939*. Amsterdam and London: Amsterdam University Press.

Wajda, Andrzej. 1997. 'Two Types of Censorship.' In *Film and Censorship: The Index Reader*, edited by Ruth Petrie. 107–9. London and Washington, DC: Cassell.

Wang, Shujen. 2003. 'Recontextualizing Copyright: Piracy, Hollywood, the State, and Globalization.' *Cinema Journal* 43 (1): 25–43.

Wark, McKenzie. 2009. 'Détournement: An Abuser's Guide.' *Angelaki* 14 (1): 145–53.

———. 2013. *The Spectacle of Disintegration: Situationist Passages out of the Twentieth Century*. London and New York: Verso.

Washeck, Angela. 2014. 'A Push for Closed Captioning in the Digital Age.' *MediaShift*, 5 May. <http://mediashift.org/2014/05/a-push-for-closed-captioning-in-the-digital-age/> (last accessed 14 June, 2016).

Watt, Michael. 2000. 'Dubbing and the Manipulation of the Cinematic

Experience.' *Bright Lights Film Journal* 29, 1 July. <http://brightlightsfilm.com/29/dubbing1.php#.UcgugBaBLs0> (last accessed 30 June 2016).

Wee, Willis. 2014. 'Razmig Hovaghimian: From Failed Pizza Maker to Founder of Viki.' *TechInAsia*, 21 April. <http://www.techinasia.com/profile/willis-wee> (last accessed 7 June 2016).

Wehn, Karin. 2001. 'About Remakes, Dubbing & Morphing: Some Comments on Visual Transformation Processes and their Relevance for Translation Theory.' In *(Multi) Media Translation: Concepts, Practices, and Research*, edited by Henrik Gottlieb and Yves Gambier. 65–72. Amsterdam and Philadelphia: John Benjamins.

Weinberg, Herman. 1948. 'I Title Foreign Films.' *Theatre Arts*, April/May: 51.

———. 1985. 'Herman Weinberg on Subtitling: Interview by Rick Rofihe.' *Field of Vision* 13: 10.

Weis, Elisabeth. 1995. 'Sync Tanks: The Art and Technique of Postproduction Sound.' *Cineaste* 21 (1–2): 56–61.

Welsh, Sean. 2011. 'Movie Rip-Offs: A User's Guide – Détournement and Dub Parodies.' *The Physical Impossibility of Rad in the Mind of Someone Bogus* (blog), 22 May. <http://physicalimpossibility.wordpress.com/2011/05/22/movie-rip-offs-a-users-guide-detournement-and-dub-parodies/> (last accessed 30 June 2016).

White, Courtney. 2010. 'Transliterated Vampires: Subtitling and Globalization in Timur Bekmambetov's *Night Watch* "Trilogy".' *Spectator* 30 (1): 11–18.

Whitman-Linsen, Candace. 1992. *Through the Dubbing Glass: The Synchronization of American Motion Pictures into German, French and Spanish, Anglo-Saxon Language and Literature*. Frankfurt am Main: Peter Lang.

Williams, R. John. 2009. 'Global English Ideography and the Dissolve Translation in Hollywood Film.' *Cultural Critique* 72 (1): 89–136. <https://muse.jhu.edu/article/269331/pdf> (last accessed 23 October 2016).

Wollen, Peter. 1975. 'The Two Avant-Gardes.' *Studio International* 190: 171–5.

Wongseree, Thandao. 2016. 'Creativity in Thai Fansubbing: A Creative Translation Practice as Perceived by Fan Audiences of the Korean Variety Show *Running Man*.' *Centre for Translation and Intercultural Studies Occasional Papers* 7: 60–86.

Woods, Michelle. 2011. 'Love and Other Subtitles: Comedic and Abusive Subtitling in *Annie Hall* and *Wayne's World*.' In *Translating Emotion: Studies in Transformation and Renewal Between Languages*, edited by Michael Clarke and Kathleen Shields. London: Peter Lang.

'YouTube Translation Tools Aim to Globalize Content.' 2015. *The Economic Times*, 19 November. <http://economictimes.indiatimes.com/tech/internet/youtube-translation-tools-aim-to-globalize-content/articleshow/49850791.cms> (last accessed 28 June 2016).

Zabalbeascoa, Patrick. 1997. 'Dubbing and the Nonverbal Dimension of Translation.' In *Nonverbal Communication and Translation: New Perspectives and Challenges in Literature, Interpretation and the Media*, edited by Fernandos Poyatos. 328–42. Amsterdam and Philadelphia: John Benjamins.

———— 2016. 'Censoring Lolita's Sense of Humour: When Translation Affects the Audience's Interpretation.' *Perspectives: Studies in Translatology* 24 (1): 93–114.

Zabalbeascoa, Patrick, Natàlia Izard and Laura Santamaria. 2001. 'Disentangling Audiovisual Translation into Catalan from the Spanish Media Mesh.' In *(Multi) Media Translation. Concepts, Practices, and Research*, edited by Yves Gambier and Henrik Gottlieb. 101–11. Amsterdam and Philadelphia: John Benjamins.

Zabalbeascoa, Patrick, and Montse Corrius. 2012. 'How Spanish in an American Film is Rendered in Translation: Dubbing *Butch Cassidy and the Sundance Kid* in Spain.' *Perspectives: Studies in Translatology* 22 (2): 1–16.

Zabalbeasco, Patrick and Elena Voellmer. 2014. 'How Multilingual Can a Dubbed Film Be? Language Combinations and National Traditions as Determining Factors.' *Linguistica Antverpiensia New Series* 13: 232–50.

Zhang, Xiachun. 2012. 'Censorship and Digital Games Localisation in China.' *Meta: Translators' Journal* 57 (2): 338–50.

Index

Note: bold indicates illustrations